It's Like a Miracle

Richard E. Soltero DVM
&
Connie M. Stoffels Ed.D.

&
Contributing Author

Michael R. Soltero DVM

Arctic Tern Publishing

Published by Arctic Tern Publishing

"Let your mind take wings."

Authors:
Richard Soltero, Doctor of Veterinary Medicine
&
Connie Stoffels, Doctor of Education

ISBN 978-0-9802013-0-7

Printed in the United States of America

PUBLISHER'S NOTE.

Neither the publisher nor the author is engaged in rendering professional advice or services to the individual reader. The ideas, procedures, and suggestions contained in this book are not intended as a substitute for consulting with your physician. All matters regarding your health require medical supervision. Neither the authors nor the publisher shall be liable or responsible for any loss of damage allegedly arising from any information or suggestion in this book.

This book is intended to reach readers about a healthy diet for dogs and cats as used by Dr. Soltero in his veterinary practice, and to serve as a guide for them in seeking treatment for their pets. However, this book is not intended as a substitute for proper veterinary care. Readers whose pets may be experiencing medical problems or symptoms should consult a veterinarian.

Cover by Zach Smith
Assisted by Stephanie Johnston

Arctic Tern photo by Dave Hall

TABLE OF CONTENTS

"Keep in mind, that you are the most important player on your medical team."

"You can achieve any goal if you put all your effort into it, but never forget what you might be doing to your health along the way."

"Doctors prescribe what they have been taught because they really don't have time to get smarter."

"Enjoying life reduces stress and is a major contributor to your overall good health."

Contents

Contents

Contents

DEDICATION

By Rick Soltero

I am sitting here trying to decide who inspired me the most to write this book. At first I think to myself, *How can I choose because there are so many who have touched my life.* I think about all the people I love like my grandparents, my dad, my mother, my wife, my children, the Westmans, as well as my dear friends, just to mention a few.

A warm feeling comes over me and I realize that even though my life has been blessed by so many, there is only one choice: **The animals all around us.** Some may wonder if I've lost my mind, but those of you who have known the unconditional love of a pet understand fully. I'm sorry for anyone who hasn't been fortunate to know this all encompassing love, but it's never too late.

Think back to your own experiences, be they: illness, financial distress, divorce, death, depression, devastating loneliness, or simply the highs and lows of life. Who was always there for you? Who never left your side? Who loved you the way you were? Who cheered you up? Who gave back love when you showed none? Who was always happy to see you no matter what? Who worshipped you? Who even licked your hand when you struck him/her? Who might have even given his/her very life for you? **It was your loving, totally devoted pet!**

I have personally experienced this overwhelming love. I have watched such relationships unfold before my eyes at my veterinary clinic. I've been there, and believe me; I know the devastation people go through when they lose such a close companion.

I've been the one to help ease the pain these magnificent creatures have felt, a multitude of times. I have always known that if there was no other choice and I had to put an animal to sleep, it was better sooner than later because prolonging their agony was only going to leave more bad memories for the owner. I would rather leave them with the good memories of a healthy pet.

I always worry about the owners and how they will be able to deal with the loss. I'm very well aware that sometimes this pet is the only good thing in that person's life and how devastating their loss is going to be. I want to help these gentle creatures live happier and healthier lives. I want to ease their pain when the time is right.

So, without hesitation, I dedicate this book to the animals of the world who are God like. Like Him, they are full of love and so forgiving. I hope that their lives will be made better by the words on the following pages. They come from my heart and my soul.

I would like to thank my wife, Karn, for helping me throughout this process. She is a good listener and my most loving friend. I would like to thank my children: Jodi, Mike, John, and Lia.

I would especially like to thank Connie Stoffels, for approaching me, because this book would never have been written otherwise. She listened to countless hours of my tapes to get the story just right. She took the stories that I wrote and put them in such a form that the book took on a life of its own. She has agonized and spent a lot of her time making this whole thing happen. It has been a pleasure working with her. Thanks Connie!

DEDICATION
By Connie Stoffels

I would like to dedicate this book to Cherokee, my Doberman, who died of bone cancer at just barely eight years of age. She was my wonderful companion and friend for all of her years. She taught me a lot about life. With her devotion and love, I managed to survive some very difficult times.

Together we became a companion animal team and we had the privilege of visiting home care facilities for the elderly in the Phoenix area. Cherokee was a natural care giver from the first day. She never backed away from any patient or anything I asked of her. Even the smell of blood or urine did not stop her.

I have especially fond memories of her on the Alzheimer Ward. I had actually taught her not to lick, but the nurse asked me if she would lick the patients who wanted the loving feeling of her soft tongue. The moment I asked that of her, she didn't hesitate. She seemed to sense what each person needed and never passed anyone by.

When the cancer struck, I was devastated, but when she began chewing on her leg, I knew I had to have the courage to let her go. I didn't want her to be in pain. I realized that there was no cure and no hope; I did what I had to do and put her to sleep.

My husband, Dieter, built her a wonderful casket and we placed her inside it on her sponge bed, with her favorite stuffed animal beside her. We buried her and I built a garden around her resting place. Right now as I type this dedication to her, I am looking out of my second story window and I can see her garden. I know she appreciates the work I've put into this book.

After her death, I wrote another book, *The Red Door*, which is a young adult novel. During the research for that book, the pet food recalls started hitting the news. It was the potential melamine contamination that had obviously led to serious illness in pets and even death.

When Menu Foods started recalling their products, other pet food producers soon followed, and well over a hundred different products were taken off the shelves. My husband and I were shocked. Knowing what I know now about nutrition, I probably could have extended Cherokee's life, if I had fed her only healthy people food and raw meat.

It was Cherokee's impact on my life that caused me to contact Rick Soltero to ask him if he would be interested in co-authoring a book with me. It seemed to me that we were both fighting a battle and had a lot to say. We decided that we would make the book about his own struggle with a serious liver condition as well as the Early Death Syndrome we both were watching in pets.

It has been a pleasure working with him. Rick had an abundance of stories to tell both about his life and his work as a veterinarian. They inspired me throughout this process. His devotion to his work with animals and his personal integrity will speak to you as you read this book.

I also want to acknowledge my husband, Dieter, who has spent countless hours listening to me as I worked on this book. He did a lot of research and was an outstanding proof reader as well. He didn't mind when I got so tied up with my writing that other things didn't get done around our home.

I hope this book will take on the same meaning for you as it has for us.

Cherokee 1996-2004

INTRODUCTION

What would you do if this were the last day of your life?

- Would you watch TV?

- Would you get upset with anyone, especially your spouse or your children?

- Would you go to church?

- If you were me, would you opt for liver surgery and put your son's life in jeopardy?

- Would you sleep the day away?

- Would you tell the people you see that you love them and wish them God's blessings?

- Would you hug someone?

- Would you be in a hurry?

- Would you be impatient?

- Would you concentrate on how sick you are?
- Would you think about the bad things that have happened in your life, or would you think about the good things?

This list could go on and on but please think for a moment about what you would really do? I was diagnosed with Primary Sclerosing Cholangitis (PSC), explained by Dr. Birgit G. Terjung, MD, "....a chronic liver disease of unknown cause. Most researchers suspect PSC to be an autoimmune disorder. PSC is a disease that progresses silently, but relentlessly, for many years and frequently leads to liver cirrhosis. The problem is that PSC does not respond to immunosuppressive therapy and therefore does not halt the course of the disease. For end stage liver cirrhosis, liver transplantation remains the only long-term effective treatment."[1]

I was faced with the very real possibility that this could be my last day. Upon hearing that it was an incurable disease, my whole focus changed and I have spent a lot of time thinking. C.E. Pelc wrote another article which explains

[1] Birgit G. Terjung, MD, "Diagnosis and Treatment of Primary Sclerosing Cholangitis (PSC)." (http://rr.healthology.com/focus_article.asp?f=liver_disease &c=liver_psc_article). (8/15/2003).

more about this disease in which he states: "A patient with PSC is maybe 1,000 or 1,500 times more likely to have bile duct cancer than if they didn't have PSC." [2]

I now know what I'd do and I'm doing it! I've pretty much been up the whole night because I didn't want to waste a minute. I've spent four hours writing because I want people to know what I think. I want my kids to know how much I love them.

I want to leave them with a sense of *family,* and the realization that they had a father who was worth calling a father. I want my very heart and soul to be part of them so they can feel what I feel, see what I see, and do what I do, just like my father did for me. He knew how to live and he knew how to die and he didn't have to say a word. All I had to do was watch.

My day will be filled with love and caring. The animals and the people I'm around will be benefactors, but not as big a benefactor as me. I will be the one who grows the most. It's like shining the sun into a mirror which is reflected back at you creating twice the warmth.

As you shine your love through a magnifying glass, it intensifies one hundred fold. It becomes so hot that it will burn you. It forever

[2] C.E. Pelc, "Primary Sclerosing Cholangitis: An Overview" (www.hepatitisag.com) (October – December 2003).

brands your soul. From that day forth you can never be the same. With each day that you live as your last, you become stronger and stronger. The reflections of love and caring continually change you. It's almost more than you can stand.

I can't believe that I have so much joy in my life. By being a husband, a father and a veterinarian, I am blessed with so many people who are praying for me and holding good thoughts for me. Am I not the luckiest person in the world? By living today as though it were my last, it *becomes* the best day of my life!

I haven't always lived my life like this. The reason I wrote this book was to share my story with you. It is about how I grew up, made good and bad choices and ultimately how I found my way to the truth, and about what really matters.

For the past thirty years, my life has been dedicated to animals. At my veterinary clinic, I have always taken pride in doing my very best to keep them healthy. But through the years I have come to realize that maybe I didn't know everything I needed to know.

It seems we often unknowingly float along with our own perceptions which are far from the stark truth. I thought I was doing a good job with the pills I was prescribing and shots I was giving. After all, that's what they taught me in veterinary school, and they were the experts.

I recommended dry pet food to the animal lovers of the world, because at the time, I thought it was the best thing for them. That too had been drummed into my head and I had never questioned it either.

It wasn't until my own health started to falter did I embark on a path to find answers. When I was diagnosed with PSC, my journey to save my own life began to interconnect with the lives of my animal patients in unexpected ways.

I didn't just wake up one morning and say, "I know what's wrong." Rather, it came on slowly through the years, hidden by the many habits and the boxed in thinking to which we all fall victim.

It became clear that for some reason, animals were not living to fifteen or even eighteen years of age anymore. As a matter of fact, they were dying younger and younger. Today, animals are not dying of old age or kidney failure. Instead, they are dying from cancer or some immune mediated problem.

As I researched my files, I began to see a pattern. I used to diagnose cancer once or twice a month, now it is often two or three times a day! Some days I don't diagnose any, but on an average, cancer pops up at least once every single day. I felt there had to be a reason for this drastic change. My observations led me to believe that it looks like there is a distinct correlation between pet food and cancer, especially dry pet food. Case after case, which you will read about in later chapters of this book, will reveal the major changes in animals' health when taken off pet food and placed on *healthy* people food.

As my liver condition worsened and I continued to see despair in the eyes of the owners of my animal patients, my awareness heightened. My focus changed. I became desperate to find answers for myself and for them. I began to read any and everything I could get my hands on, searching for answers to why my world was shattering around me.

Knowing now what I have learned, I'm not surprised that good health for humans and for animals is one and the same. We as humans are responsible to supply healthy food and exercise for our pets. In return their unconditional love gives us a much more positive attitude, thereby reducing our stress.

Animals naturally live each day as if it were their last because they are always upbeat and positive. They love you, kiss you, walk with you and in general just like to be with you. We have to be hit with some catastrophic illness to wake us up. So the bond between animals and humans provides both with the opportunities for a healthy life. Remember:

*Live today as if it were your last
*Think for yourself

*Eat healthy food
*Have a positive
*Reduce stress and don't forget to
  Exercise

I'm sure if you live each day as if it were your last, that you will actually live longer. It is as simple as that. When I started living as if this were my last day, putting my faith in God, and paying attention to these six areas, my health started improving. I am much better today.

I'm not totally well, but I'm a hundred miles down the road, and I feel essentially normal. One procedure that has helped me is an ERCP (endoscopic retrograde cholangio pancreotography). " An ERCP is used to diagnose and treat conditions of the bile ducts....combines the use of ultra sound and an endoscope..."[3] Dr. Harrison, who has been performing my ERCPs said that with my disease, people get progressively worse and the ERCPs have to be performed closer and closer together.

I felt really good when he told me that I was the first patient he has ever seen where the ERCPs are continually getting further and further apart. This is one indication that I am getting better. I have gone from three weeks, to three

---

[3] National Digestive Diseases A-Z List of Topics and Titles: ERCP. (http://digestive. Niddk.nih.gov/ddiseases/pubs/ercp/index.htm (NIH Publication, No. 05-4336). November 2004.

months and now six months since my last ERCP. I am hoping to make it a year or even more before the next one.

There are other signs as well that show I am improving. My itching used to be a ten on a scale of one to ten, but now it is a one or two and I often don't even notice it. My enzyme alkaline phosphatase test (for liver function) ran between 900 and 1000 and it has held steady at 1000 for some time now, instead of getting worse as predicted. My ALT (a liver integrity test which tests if cells are breaking down and causing more liver damage) has dropped from 600 or 700 down to only 150. This is a significant!

Final proof is the fact that I was not able to work before, and now I am able to carry a full day's load and then sit up and write at night. Basically, I am not getting worse, and in fact according to my blood work and symptoms, I am improving. In this book I will share with you what I've been doing to improve my own health and that of my patients.

As you read, I PROMISE you that these six areas will truly make or break your own health and that of your pets'. If you are willing to make the changes needed in your life and to follow this path, you and your pets will improve so much that you too will say, just as so many of my clients have already said:

It's Like a Miracle!

Chapter 1

Shocking news

"You need a liver transplant." The doctor's words burn into my brain. My thoughts whirl like a tornado circling all around me: *This can't be happening – my wife – my kids – my work. I have so much I still want to accomplish, so much more living to do......*

I didn't know it then, but a new phase in my journey of life had begun. I thought I had faced hardships such as: long years of studying to graduate from veterinary school, thirty years of practicing medicine, as well as raising a family. But now I was fighting for my life, and my whole perception shifted.

On the way home, there is silence in the car. I glance at my wife, Karn, but say nothing. Her blond hair and blue eyes have always attracted me to her, not to mention her fit 5'6"

(125 pound) frame. But now my mind is elsewhere and I think to myself: *What will happen to her if I die?* Tears well up in my eyes, but I try to hide them, to be brave for both of us.

My thoughts turn inward: *What's going to happen to me? I've always worked out, lifted weights, and worked hard. What will this do to me physically and emotionally?* I become deadly aware of the weight I've lost, and more than that, my lost stamina. *This can't be fun for Karn to live with. God, what's happening to me?*

I want to share with you how all of this began. I know there are many others out there in the world that have experienced something similar to what I am going through. Unfortunately many more of you will face a life altering experience with your health in the future. Maybe my story will help.

As I started getting seriously ill, the symptoms came on so gradually that I overlooked or simply dismissed them. I imagine that's the way with many illnesses. I think we often are in denial when our health changes. I guess I thought it would just go away because I'd always been healthy.

At first I was uncomfortable after eating. I thought I had a simple digestive problem and maybe I had just eaten too much. As my discomfort continued to get worse, I knew I had a bigger problem. A routine blood test revealed that my liver count was elevated for no obvious reason. I was referred to my first liver specialist.

As I sat in the doctor's waiting room, the walls started closing in on me. The room suddenly appeared very small. The time seemed to stretch forever. I vowed that I would never keep one of my clients waiting. Finally, the door opens and in walks the doctor. We shake hands more out of standard protocol than anything else.

"Hi, nice to meet you," I try to sound normal.

Without any fanfare he answers, "I'm sorry," he glances at his chart, "uh...Rick, I can't find any obvious reason for your elevated liver enzymes."

I answered, "Something has to be causing this. I mean I've always been healthy. I've never had any serious medical problems. You have to know the answer, you're a liver specialist." I said in a voice louder than I intended, but it was the way I was feeling.

My plea was answered with a shrug of his shoulders, "I don't know." He answered in his best authoritative voice as if that would make me stop asking questions.

I was left to stew about what was happening to me. Being a veterinarian, I knew how important blood results were in finding a correct diagnosis. Facts never lie. Yet, the answer in my case seemed to be elusive.

Once again, I tried to ignore my condition, but it grew to chronic colitis and irritable bowel syndrome. Every time I had a nice meal, I'd pay for it all night long. I would just hurt. In addition, I was starting to become more fatigued and restless. My weight continued to steadily drop.

My symptoms couldn't be ignored any longer, so I made an appointment with another liver specialist. He decided to do an ERCP (Endoscopic Retrograde Cholangiopancreatography). This is a procedure where a doctor takes a scope and runs it through your mouth, down your esophagus, into your stomach, your duodenum, and up your bile ducts. At that point, your constricting bile ducts are stretched, using a balloon type instrument.

I had a bad feeling going into this procedure because everyone was so busy and in such a rush. I expected them to fail, and they did. After the procedure, while I was in recovery, the doctor went out to talk with Karn. He told her that he didn't really know what I had, because he couldn't find the opening to the common bile duct. He explained that it could be my gall-bladder or Chronic Sclerosing Cholangitis, but he couldn't tell for sure, because he couldn't complete the procedure. When she told me, I wasn't surprised.

Karn didn't have a clue what that meant. Her nerves were running on edge, so she called Carol, who had been working at the clinic for twenty-five years and had become a wonderful friend.

"Carol, things are not good," Karn said hanging onto the phone as if it were a safety cord.

"Do you want me to come down there?" Carol quickly asked.

"No, that's okay."

Karn later explained to me that she told her no because she knew if someone showed up, that she would just cry even more. You know how that goes. If you're having a major problem in your life, the minute everyone knows about it and tries to comfort you, you break down. But if no one knows you are emotionally upset, you can at least try to cover it up or hide it.

When I came out of recovery that day, it was the first time ever that anyone, especially Karn, had ever pushed me in a wheelchair. We had both figured, that one day during our lifetime, one of us would be pushing the other out of a hospital, but we had figured it would happen in our eighties, not in our fifties.

For the first time in my life, I'm not sure of what is happening to me. I don't have any answers for myself and I still haven't figured out why my animal patients are having so much trouble. All this stress coming down on me is just adding to my declining health.

The doctor decided that maybe it was my gallbladder and scheduled another surgery to remove it. At the same time, he planned on doing another ERCP and liver biopsy. I agreed to the procedure because I was so uncomfortable after every meal, that I didn't know what to do anymore. I figured that I could live without my gallbladder and maybe, just maybe, it would fix my problem and I would be normal again.

But when all was said and done, my condition only grew worse. It hadn't been my gall bladder after all. Perplexed, I sought help. Never in my wildest dreams did I ever think that I might need a liver transplant. I had spent my entire life trying to be healthy and I just didn't understand how all of this could be happening to me.

As my liver conditioned continued to worsen, I agreed to see another liver specialist. He suspected PSC (Primary Sclerosing Cholangitis) of the large bile ducts. My wife and I were stunned but didn't really grasp the full meaning of this disease.

A client from my clinic recommended another liver specialist at the Mayo Clinic in Rochester, Minnesota. Believing in more than one opinion, I made an appointment in May of 2003. While I was going through three days worth of tests, Karn spent her time in the hospital library. She came back with a six page brochure.

"Rick, they don't know the cause for PSC. But worse than that, they don't know of a treatment." Karn clears her throat and continues, "It eventually affects not only the bile ducts, but the liver itself." From the expression on her face, I can tell that she is worried, and so am I.

Our path leads us back to Scottsdale, and in 2004, a doctor performs another ERCP. Stents are put into the ducts to drain the bile out of the liver. It's temporary, but helps. The only problem is that I can feel the stents that are left in for four weeks at a time and then removed to prevent infection.

As if that isn't enough to deal with, we receive a bill for $60,000 from the hospital, only to find out that our insurance company doesn't have a contract with them. You would think we would have been informed about something of this magnitude before surgery. The doctor did finally manage to get that reduced to $40,000, but that's still a huge hunk of change in my book, and should never have happened.

As I begin to feel worse again I am forced to go to a hospital that my insurance company has a contract with. But when the ERCP is performed there, it makes little difference, except that my itching and fatigue are a *little* better.

After seeing four doctors about my worsening condition, I remember walking into Mayo Hospital on yet another referral. I couldn't believe my eyes, the sign on the door read: LIVER TRANSPLANT DEPARTMENT. Suddenly, I realized that they were going to try and take my liver! All I could think about was that they were out of their minds. I didn't need a liver trans-plant!

At that point, I spent most of my waking hours trying to deny the inevitable. Doctor after doctor came up with the same diagnosis. I was stunned, but finally forced to accept that they couldn't all be wrong. They actually have you thinking that you're going to get a liver transplant, but you won't get one.

They all agreed that I had a slow progressive liver disease (Primary Sclerosing Cholangitis) of the large bile ducts, and that there was no known cure. They said that my bile ducts would continue to gradually close up, leaving bile and bacteria behind, which would end up causing infection and sclerosis of the liver.

Some of the doctors said that I had a 70% risk of having bile duct cancer, while others were convinced that my risk was 100%. I was told that my days were numbered and ultimately that I would die from bile duct cancer. Apparently this type of cancer is so malignant that it is hopeless to try any treatment because of its ability to spread so rapidly to other parts of the body.

I didn't want to die so I went into a panic mode. The thought that I already had cancer made me willing to do any and everything. It gave the doctors the control they wanted. It made me willing to sacrifice either one of my sons or anybody else who was willing to give me part of his/her liver. I became extremely selfish because I was so scared.

My downward spiral progressed to the point that I had gone through five hospitals and twelve doctors. I was in a total panic mode and I screamed: "Save me please! Do something! I don't want to die!" But I was yelling to the wind! I kept getting much worse and so uncomfortable from the bile duct blockage that I wanted to die – or at least that's what I felt like at the time.

I went through several episodes of abdominal pain, severe chills and profound weakness. During these episodes I would focus on dying. If that wasn't bad enough, between these episodes I would itch day and night. It became especially difficult to sleep at night because the symptoms would intensify to the point that it was literally impossible to get comfortable.

I tried every kind of anti-itch cream or lotion available to stop or even slow down the incessant itching. Then I would pray that I could fall asleep. I learned that if I played Spider Solitaire on the computer, it would take my mind off the itching. If I played long enough, I would become so exhausted that I would pass out and get a little sleep.

It took me four months to win the first solitaire game. Then I learned how to win daily and sometimes I could win four times in one day. I needed the distraction that badly. My life had become a *nightmare.*

On one of my visits to a new liver specialist, it was clear that he hadn't even looked at my history. An assistant had collected the data about my condition, but the doctor had obviously never even been briefed. It was very disconcerting because I could tell he was just getting through his day. He didn't care about me.

I was very irritable now because of the toxic level of my liver. I frantically asked question after question. This specialist was not used to such scrutiny by someone who was medically savvy. He much preferred patients who thought he was always right and that he always knew everything there was to know. Since I came on strong and demanded answers, he referred me for a psychological examination.

I'm here to say: don't ever stop asking questions. Doctors don't know everything there is to know. And by the way, I came out of the psychological exam just fine. I wasn't the one refusing to look for the truth or afraid to admit that I didn't know everything. Basically he was part of the liver transplant team and he just wanted to move onto the next patient.

In 2005 I had become desperate enough to consider a liver transplant from either of my sons. However, they were both turned down, one because of high levels of copper in his blood and the other because of an abnormal blood vessel. I was devastated and had pretty much given up all hope of surviving.

I became very ill the day after I got home from the Colorado University Hospital. I felt so bad that I truly wanted to die. I had chills so fierce that I felt frozen. I wouldn't even move because it hurt too much. Karn put two heating pads on me and piled the blankets on. It didn't matter what she did, nothing could warm my tormented body. I took Cipro (an antibiotic) and hoped the pain would pass. The chills were usually related to secondary bacterial infection in a clogged bile duct.

Karn called the doctor at Mayo to see what to do. They wanted to send an ambulance to pick me up, but I refused because I knew that if they tried to move me, I'd get colder and that the pain would become even more excruciating and totally unbearable.

That was pretty much the bottom for me. I decided that I needed to go through another

ERCP. I felt like my only chance was with Mayo and Dr. Harrison. I put all my hope on this one man because he had been the only one who had been able to help me. After each of his ERCP procedures I had felt a lot better.

So I went through the ERCP, stopped working, and Karn and I went to Del Mar, California, located right on the Pacific Ocean. We had spent time there before to find peace. I had decided that I wasn't going to end up with a liver transplant. I would never get a MELD score (Model for End-stage Liver Disease) high enough to warrant a cadaver liver and both my sons had been turned down as donors.

When I got ill, I weighed 186 pounds. I have since dropped to 157 pounds, all the while focusing on the cancer I **knew** I had. I was convinced I was dying. At that point, I realized that my own health, as well as the health of my patients, was literally hanging in the balance.

It became perfectly clear that I was at the pivotal point on which everything in my future and theirs would depend. I had to stop panicking and sitting on the side lines. It was time for me to take charge and find answers.

Keep in mind, that you are the most important player on your medical team.

Chapter 2

My younger years

I need to back up and tell you about my life and how I got to the dilemma with my liver because I was born just another ordinary person, like everyone else. I want you to understand that it is what we do to ourselves over a span of many years that can harm our bodies. At the time, we don't even think about it.

My love for animals started when I was a young boy. If a baby bird fell out of its nest, I was there to scoop it up.

"Rick, what in the world do you think you're doing? Everyone knows you can't save those baby birds." My neighbor often laughed.

I just bit my bottom lip and became even more determined to help the little creatures hunkering helplessly in the palm of my hand. I used to get such a kick when their little heads bobbed wildly as their orange mouths opened wide just begging for food. I would grind up worms and put small amounts in their mouths in the hopes that it would satisfy their hunger.

As night approached, I would grab my sleeping bag and head outside. I knew it was critical for them to stay warm. I would crawl inside my bag, lie on my back and place the new charge between my legs to give it warmth from my body.

"You're gonna be all right." I whispered in the dark and I believed just that. It felt so good thinking I could save their lives.

Sometimes this approach worked and I managed to save my little friends. But one night when I tried my best to save three Redwing Blackbirds, who had taken a tumble, I did as I always had. I snuggled down in my sleeping bag to wait out the morning. Needless to say, I was young and I fell asleep. When I awoke, to my horror, I had rolled over onto the helpless birds. They were all dead. I will never forget the agony I felt when I realized what had happened.

Looking back now, I probably didn't do a great job of saving many birds. As a kid, I had good intentions, but not such a good track record. I wanted to save them because I loved watching them, having them sit on my shoulder, eat out of my hand, or just go about their own business while I watched from afar. Something about them was just really special and fascinating to me.

That desire went with me all the way through veterinary school, and I even took continuing educational courses about birds. I learned how to anesthetize and feed them, with better results than when I was a young boy.

Karn shared my enthusiasm for the wonderful little fellows too. I even spent around $20,000 just for incubators and other materials to satisfy my drive to help them. We loved to start with eggs, hatch them and raise the birds. We have had so much fun with them, but at times it was a bit frustrating for Karn. She would work so-o-o hard, give them so much love, and then they would bite her. That's when we just looked at each other and laughed. These birds have truly enriched our lives.

The affection for birds started back when I was a young boy and has grown throughout my life and remains strong today. I just have this kind of thing for birds. I've fixed hawks, owls, and other large birds, but I never had the opportunity to help an eagle. Maybe that will come too.

Going back to my boyhood, one time while I was visiting my grandmother, another incident happened with a bird.

"Rick would you like to go to the zoo?" she asked.

"You bet I would."

We strolled around, stopping to watch an orangutan swinging in the trees. I chattered to him, and as if he understood me, he curled his top lip up – sort of like I've seen horses do. Then he made some funny noises back. The game continued until my grandmother decided she had heard enough monkey talk and moved on with me in tow.

My attention fell on something beside the path and I stopped to see what it was. A tiny bird lay helpless and partially hidden between the blades of grass, half baked from the sun. In my mind, there was literally no other choice but to snatch it from the grips of death and take it home. So, I carefully placed it in my pocket and continued following after my grandmother.

When we arrived back home, my grandmother gave me a puzzled look and said, "Rick, what do you have?"

"Oh, just a little bird I found." I smiled as I cupped the fragile body between my hands.

"You can't keep that. We're going right back to the zoo and you will take that back. Do you understand me?" My grandmother put her hands on her hips and marched me back to the car.

I didn't reply. I had no choice but to do as I was told, but I was very mad at her at that moment. I knew I was taking this little bird back to its death and I knew for sure that I could have saved it. Out of respect, which my parents had instilled in me, I didn't say anything to my grandmother, but to this day, I'm still mad at her for not letting me nurse that little bird back to health.

I was lucky to grow up in a family of dedicated people – people not afraid to work hard and to set high goals for themselves. They taught me that what a child witnesses is a far greater motivator than what he is told. And I had some excellent role models.

My grandfather came from Puerto Rico as an immigrant and worked as a teacher for awhile. Then he took a job as a customs agent at the border, so that he could earn enough money to go to the University of Chicago Medical School. While at the U of C, he met my grandmother who was a nurse. They fell madly in love and were married.

It wasn't necessarily such a good time to get married, because they didn't have much money. But love is blind, so they did it anyway. I know for a fact that they lived off of corn flakes for several months, because his dream was to become a medical doctor and while he was struggling through school, they couldn't afford anything else.

Ironically, that probably helped him live to a ripe old age of ninety-four because he didn't consume hormone laden meats. The interesting part was that because he grew up poor, he couldn't afford much meat of any kind. His favorite meal was actually white rice and vegetables and that put him in good stead later on. He never really developed an appetite for our modern day diet.

My grandparents were very religious. That was a day when people relied on prayer, tender loving care, and healthy food to stay well. It must have worked for them because he graduated from medical school and they settled in Lewistown, Montana, where he began his practice. They raised a loving family of two boys and two girls. It was a true love affair that continues for all of us in the family and God remains our main focal point even today.

I visited Lewistown when I was on the high school football team. Even though that was fifteen years after my grandfather had moved to Billings, every time I mentioned his name, people's faces would light up. They not only remembered him, but would expound about his love and caring and tell how he would get in his horse drawn buggy and go live with these people until they got well.

You know that's all he had in those days, but it seemed to be just what was needed. Maybe doctors today, who only know how to give shots or pills, could take a lesson from him. I know I have. I was delighted when one of my clients in Scottsdale told me how my grandfather had delivered her. It's truly a small world and I loved listening to her praise him.

He never worried about money and didn't even bill the people until later, often long after they had recovered from their illnesses. Some paid their debts to him in money and others bartered with fruits, and vegetables or whatever they had. Some never paid at all.

The true character of my grandfather was displayed when one night, as my father tells it, he built a bonfire and one by one he tossed unpaid bills into the flames. As he burned them, he said, "Well, there goes my retirement." His deep devotion to the people he served overrode the need to be compensated. He wasn't going to milk his beloved patients, many of whom had little or nothing to start with.

You have to remember – he would stay with his patients at their homes for as long as was needed. They felt the warmth of his devotion. I guess somehow deep inside he knew his future would be secure because of his relationship with God. He trusted God to take care of him until the end of his life on earth.

My father was cut from the same cloth. I have so many wonderful memories of him as a young boy and as a man. It is difficult for me to explain to you what he meant to me without getting choked up. But I guess that isn't all bad, it just shows how much I love him. All I have to do is *think* about his hands – those gentle, guiding, healing hands, and I am filled with emotion.

When it came to his children, he would always lay a gentle hand on our head and/or shoulder with that reassuring touch. I have very fond memories of how wonderful his hands were. I especially liked to go to the hospital with him because all the nurses adored my father as a doctor. I was so proud of him, and because of that, he became my guiding force.

Sadly, prostate cancer took him at a young seventy-four years of age. I now believe that his diet, filled with hormone laden meat, especially beef and pork, shortened his life, unlike my grandfather who couldn't afford such luxuries.

As a young boy I loved going with my father. On one of our trips, my dad saw a buck deer. He proceeded to get out of the car to take a picture of him. What he didn't know was that this particular animal had been raised by people, so he had no fear. As my dad was walking along the car with the camera, the buck attacked him. Thank goodness the car door was still open as the buck charged, and my dad was pushed back into the car. I kid you not, he literally had him by both horns, managed to put a foot on the buck's forehead, and shoved him back enough to slam the door shut and drive off.

You can imagine how I felt sitting there next to my dad, who I was sure could do anything in the world. He was my idol. He worked hard to provide for his family, studied furiously, and became a medical doctor with the same compassion as his father before him. I don't ever remember anyone questioning my father's diagnosis or treatments, and I never did either. Now I feel we live in a day and age, when we need to be proactive about our health. We need to question doctors. We need to read about our illnesses and become a part of the solution.

Sometime later in my life I remember when I lost a dog under anesthesia. It was so unbelievably devastating. It was like I had lost a family member and I was very depressed about it. I was agonizing about the death of an animal when I began to fathom what my father must have been going through if such a thing happened to one of his patients. This made me love him even more.

That day, I just broke down – hysterically crying. I knew I had to call him and fought hard to stay composed. When I heard his voice, I managed to say, "Dad today is the first day of my life that I finally realized what you went through as a doctor."

My dad didn't say much, but I know he must have felt the closeness between the two of us. This bond is so strong, that to this day whenever I start thinking about him, I choke up. I feel his presence all around me. Every single second of the day, he's a part of me and it just feels good. It's kind of like having his hands (those wonderful hands) or arms around me all the time and realizing how lucky I am.

In case you don't believe that mistakes haunt doctors to their dying day, I'll pass on a situation my dad had told me about. While treating a sixteen year old boy, he gave him a shot of penicillin and the boy had an anaphylactic reaction. My dad then gave him what he had to counteract the reaction and rushed him to the hospital, the boy died on the way. Penicillin was relatively new at that time. I don't know all that happened, but I do know that my dad talked about this sad experience just a few hours before he died.

I spent my younger years helping birds and loving animals. My dad never interfered or made fun of me. He sort of let me find my own way, within his boundaries, of course. One of the main things he did, however, which changed the course of my life forever, was to introduce me to a special family, the Westmans, who lived in southeastern Montana on a homestead.

You know how you have sketchy things that you remember from your youth. I think I was around six the first time I met the Westman family because I have a picture of two of my brothers, one of my sisters and me posing on the back of a horse. We were lined up according to height: Ray, Karen, me and Greg. When I look at that photo today, it takes me right back to those wonderful years and I think my love for horses probably started on that ranch, too. They had a tame antelope that lived inside the house as well as out. As a child, just to see that was so neat. I loved it.

The Westman family moved west and homesteaded on a 2,500 acre ranch. It was located in Decker, Montana, about two and a half hours outside of Billings. I remember that they were dirt poor, but that didn't bother me even when I had to use the outdoor toilet. To me, they were high above anyone else I knew. Through them, I could spend more time outside with nature and be close to the animals I loved.

When I was old enough to drive, I would borrow my dad's truck and hit the road for their ranch – every single weekend if possible. Being a rancher was my dream. It was the very life blood that drove me to spend all of my free time there.

I was going through growing pains that every teenage boy goes through, as he finds his way to manhood. I might have gotten into trouble if it hadn't been for this family. I bet my dad knew that too.

From the day I started going there by myself, I was too busy to be pulled into problem situations in which others my age got involved. I would beg to do anything around the ranch. I would chop wood, herd cattle, clean stalls. You name it. I would do it. My dream of being a real cowboy, maybe even a roper, grew bigger and more vivid with each visit.

The Westmans couldn't really afford to pay me any wages, but I remember one time, they took me into town and bought me my first cowboy hat for stacking their hay. I can't even describe the way I felt as I positioned it on my head and my reflection stared back at me from the mirror. Wow! It was great!

During the summer months, I worked at the O.W. Ranch which was owned by Kendrick Cattle Company out of Sheridan, Wyoming. They paid me a whopping $5.00 a day. I became a professional hay stacker. I would still help out the Westmans when they needed me because the two ranches were next to each other.

One day, while I was helping build a house on the property, I almost lost my hand. We were pulling logs with a cable and I got my hand caught in the metal chains, but someone was watching over me and I was spared my limb.

Maybe my future had already been set by someone of higher authority.

I loved this family so much that I even took food from my mom's freezer to give to them. If she knew, she never said a word. Maybe it was her way of supporting my love for others. Maybe she watched quietly from the background as I developed into a young man with a big dream.

Grandma Westman was a heavy set woman. She was plagued with diabetes and glaucoma which limited her ability to get around. But that never stopped her from doing for others. She was always in the kitchen fixing something or other for someone else.

One time I sat across the table and listened to her as she told tales of when her children were little. She was crying so hard that I even had a lump in my throat. She explained that she didn't even have enough money to buy them shoes. Well, come to find out, she was peeling onions instead of potatoes. She served what she thought was potato salad. Not one of us told her it was more like onion salad. We ate it with a smile plastered on our faces just because we loved her so much.

One of my major goals at that time was to own my very first horse. It took two or three summers to get there. I had finally saved up enough money to buy a mare with a colt. Her name was Lady and the baby's name was Count Down.

I had enough money left to buy a saddle from a friend of my dad's who was a veterinarian. He was inspecting cattle at the Billings stockyards the day I pulled up in the truck. I was so eager, that in my excitement, I barely shut the door after I jumped out.

I found him at the pens and I can remember how much I envied him because he was working with all those cattle. I'll never forget how muscular he was and how the veins just popped out of his arms. I reached in my pocket for the money, but it wasn't there. I instantly panicked because I wanted that saddle so bad. I had worked so hard to come up with the $250.00.

In my frenzy, I reached into every single pocket. I could feel myself getting lightheaded and I broke out in a sweat. I wheeled around and went running back to the truck. Halfway there, I spotted the money lying on the ground. I could not believe that I could be that lucky. I grabbed it and dashed back to give it to him before anything else could happen. I will always remember that day because it was that important to me.

I would spend hours watching the brown and white faces of the Hereford Cattle and was drawn to every birth on the ranch. I loved to assist pulling a calf. When others would gag from the ordeal, I exalted in it and would race to be there. I never read much back then, but I did savor books like: *Black Beauty* and *My Friend Flicka*. I was drawn to any kind of book along those lines. I especially enjoyed James Herriot: *All Creatures Great and Small*.

Straddling the arena fence one day, I eyed a rope all coiled up and ready for a cowboy to pick up. I glanced out of the corner of my eye without turning my head to see if anyone was watching. I picked it up. I could just picture myself roping a calf as I swung it over my head. It was during branding season, so there were a bunch of calves in the corral.

I twirled the rope and let it fly. Much to my surprise it went around a calf's neck just like I'd witnessed real cowboys doing. But then, there was a problem. She panicked, started bawling, and pulling back on the rope which choked her down. Then it was me who panicked. I quickly dallied the rope around the fence post, because I didn't want to lose it.

She pulled so hard that she fell on the ground gasping for air. I raced to her side and struggled to get the rope off her neck because it was cutting off her oxygen supply. Finally I succeeded. She recovered and bellowed at me as she ran back to the other calves. At that point I coiled the rope up and put it back on the fence post and was so relieved to see that no one had witnessed this episode.

I knew then that I could be a cowboy. I had my horse, my saddle, and the "know how" to rope a calf. My dream was fueled with each new experience on that ranch. I could literally taste my future. In my mind I would own a 30,000 acre ranch. Of course I didn't take into mind that it took a whole thirty acres, in those days, to support one cow. But nothing else mattered to me except moving toward my dream.

I even approached my dad and asked him if he would help me buy a ranch, but he said no, that he couldn't. I then thought and thought about how I could manage this on my own. I knew that I could be a rancher and truly believed with all my heart that it was my fate.

I began to talk to myself one day, "Rick, there are two ways to get a ranch: one – inherit one, which isn't going happen, and two – marry one." Well, I guess that thought might have worked, but at my age, it didn't seem the way to approach it, so I was back to square one.

Sitting at the tip top of a haystack, at eighteen years of age, I met with the harsh realization that I couldn't afford to buy a ranch. My dream was beginning to fade rapidly and I was devastated. Then in the middle of my self-pity-party, I sat up: "Rick, if you can't own a ranch, then you can become a veterinarian and still get to be around these animals!"

From that day forward, my dream changed. I now knew what I had to do and I became obsessed with my new direction. No one thought I would make it because up until then my grades in school hadn't been the best, so I can understand where they were coming from, but nothing anybody could say was going to hold me back. No matter what their comments were, they couldn't faze me. Nothing could touch my new dream, my destiny.

After making the decision to become a veterinarian (and to everyone's amazement) I went from a 1.3 GPA to a 4.0. I skipped down the road because it felt s-o-o-o good. I knew then that nothing was ever going to deter me. I literally started studying the minute I got up and the only time I wasn't studying was when I was eating – or sleeping. With this new burst of energy and filled with my own belief about what I could do with my future, I never looked back. I dreamed it – and I lived my dream! And I'm still living it today.

I am convinced that if you want something bad enough, you can achieve it. Nothing is too far a stretch if you try with everything you have. The only thing I did was stop short of my full dream which was to be a rancher.

My second choice was to become a large animal veterinarian, but even that dream withered because I was mixed in with several fellow students who had grown up on ranches. I was afraid that their twenty years of experience would only point out what I lacked. Their background clearly showed by the way they handled the animals, and I just knew that they were way ahead of me when it came to caring for them.

There was another reason too as to why I didn't pursue large animals, maybe even more important to me. When performing surgery on large animals, they are usually given a local anesthetic which makes it hard to be precise with the surgery because they are able to move around.

A good example is trying to do a C-section on a cow or a goat. They resist being tied to the surgery table, and in straining, their intestinal tract is forced out. This isn't a nice picture and it isn't much fun because I like to be precise.

On the other hand, if you need to do surgery on a dog or cat, you can anaesthetize them and do really what you want. I'm kind of a perfectionist and I much prefer anaesthetizing my patients so I can do exactly what is needed. It bothered me a lot that I couldn't do the same when operating on large animals. To this day, the thing I'm best at is surgery. I love it and am glad I can do it my way with small animals.

Between my junior and senior years, I spent all my time reading through surgery books, attending continuing education courses, and practicing the surgeries that I had read about. I lived in a time when most of these surgeries weren't being done in a routine practice. But luckily I didn't know that, otherwise I might not have learned them.

I can remember when one of my class-mates said, "Well, you don't need to know that." And it kind of shocked me. I was fortunate at that time that I had not worked for a veterinarian because I might have developed the same attitude. Since I didn't know what I needed to know, I tried to learn everything.

By the time I graduated, I knew all these surgeries. It seemed like I saw everything that you could see, all in that first year. I was also fortunate because I had moved back to Billings, my home town. My dad was a much respected physician and knew everybody. So, when I would run into a case that I couldn't fix, I would call the local (human) specialist and they would come over and help me do the surgery.

One time the open heart surgery team from the hospital came over to the animal hospital and repaired a patient's ductus arteriosis (a blood vessel that bypasses the blood from the right side of the heart to the left side that goes to the lungs in fetal circulation. It is supposed to close when the fetus is born, but if it doesn't, s/he dies of right sided heart failure). This team also removed an artery that was impinging on the esophagus of another puppy, which was making it difficult for the puppy to swallow his food. Both surgeries were very successful.

It didn't matter what the problem was, every specialist I called came and helped. I learned a ton, which has put me in good stead for surgery ever since. I always used the latest, best anesthesia and leading equipment available.

Performing surgeries, I may have ultimately affected my own health profoundly for two reasons. One, I was under enormous stress because I worked day and night, essentially seven days a week because I was the "young" vet. There were many days when I might have gotten four hours of sleep a night. I would go home, lie down for an hour and come back to work. My head got to hurting pretty bad and I was tired. It was the type of job where there was so much stress because you had to perform, and there is no doubt that it affected my overall health.

The second reason my health suffered had to do with the use of gas anesthetics which were really making a move and were replacing injectable anesthetics. When gas machines came out, they actually vented into the room where you were doing surgery.

The first gas anesthetic was Metaphane which was slower acting, and then they progressed to a faster gas anesthetic called Halothane. At the time they seemed like medical marvels, but remember that I was in that environment doing surgeries from morning to night. And these machines were venting into the very room where I spent all my time.

In retrospect, I should have known better than to expose myself to these things back then. But as a young veterinarian I wanted to succeed, and I simply used what was state of the art: such as gas anesthetic, radiations, as well as various disinfect solutions, etc. Well, after a year in Montana, I was thoroughly exhausted.

I went on a vacation to Arizona to visit my in-laws. I lived in the swimming pool. I couldn't believe how relaxing it was and I loved every minute of it. Then out of the blue, a veterinarian from Scottsdale for whom I had handled a case in Montana, offered me a job. I decided since I had grown up in Montana and pretty well knew about everything there, I needed a change of scenery. I took the job and looked forward to my new life treating animals in Arizona.

You can achieve any goal if you put all your effort into it, but never forget what you might be doing to your health along the way.

Chapter 3

My beginning years as a veterinarian

I am truly happy as I come to work at my own small animal practice. All my studying has paid off and I've made it. I think: *You know, Rick, you're a lucky guy….getting to live your dream. Not many people are that blessed.* I smile as I think of my past and the smile doesn't fade, but rather it grows as I make my way from room to room to administer to my patients.

"Hi, how's Ginger today?" I stoop to pet the twelve year old Cocker Spaniel.

"Dr. Soltero, she's not doing so well. She's had diarrhea for three days now and she isn't eating much. I'm beginning to get worried."

"Well, let's see what's going on." I begin to check the dog all over, take her temperature, listen to her heart, look at her teeth and all the while her owner is standing nervously by waiting for me to help her beloved pet.

"I don't see anything drastic, but let me check her blood work and if that doesn't show anything, it's more than likely her diet." I add.

"I mostly feed her table scraps like everybody else. I mean as a little girl I remember my mother scraping all our plates after dinner and giving me the dish to take out for the dogs. What else is there to feed a dog?" A puzzled look comes over her face.

You need to realize that this was the day and age when most of my clients didn't really feed much dry dog food. It had been on the market for a few years, but the habit was strong at that time not to waste money or food, so feeding table scraps was the norm.

"I'll call you with the results on the blood work, and if everything is okay, we'll go on the assumption that it is diet. You know, the newest thing on the market now is dried pet food. I've been reading about nutrition and the literature is clear that every individual animal has different needs at different times in their lives. Would you believe that many different kinds of dried food have been researched and fit specific needs such as: HD= Heart Diet, ID= Intestinal Diet, KD= Kidney Diet, PD= Pediatric Diet, SD= Stone/bladder Diet? Now we can zero in on what your dog needs." I smile truly believing this

information is correct and that I will help her dog.
Little did I know about the long term effect.

She looks at me with renewed hope in her
eyes as she strokes Ginger.

"Stop her food for twenty-four hours and
restrict her water for about twelve hours."

"What? Oh that will be hard not to feed
her anything for twenty-four hours." She wrings
her hands.

"I know it sounds harsh, but believe me it's
not. She will thank you for helping her."

She shakes her head, "Okay, if you say so."

"Her teeth actually look pretty good, but
her diarrhea could be caused by the bones she's
been chewing on, so you might want to stop that
too for now."

"Give her liquid Pepto-Bismol two or three
times a day and that will probably take care of the
problem. Stop feeding table scraps and go buy
some dried dog food. Then slowly start with a
small amount of food. Since she is having
trouble with diarrhea, I would recommend the ID
(intestinal diet) for now."

"Thank you." She says as she leads her
dog out of the room.

"Call me back if that doesn't work or if she
gets worse." I say as I turn toward the next room
– "And don't forget – no more table scraps."
Now, as I look back I sure wished I had known
better.

My day had been moving along pretty much normal, when Carol came walking down the hall carrying a small white cat, and I knew I was in trouble. Everyone in the office loves cats and we were always finding homes for strays. Karn loved them too and the word must have gotten out because people were always bringing us litter after litter. One week we actually found twenty-three kittens a home. That was our record I think.

The girls would always come up with the cutest names for them. One example was a cat that had an injury to his eye, which had actually popped out of the socket, and was just hanging there by a few muscles and the optic nerve. I couldn't save the eye because it had already dried up, so I had no choice but to remove it. It was a simple procedure and the girls named him Popeye. We had no trouble finding him a home.

So here comes Carol with the white male cat about six months old and she was calling him Snowball, like so many white cats. I suppose if it only had three legs it would have been called Tripod. But, I could tell right away that this cat was in deep trouble and that it was going to take a long time to fix.

Carol explains, "Someone found him injured alongside the road."

Upon inspection, I answered, "He's got two broken legs and a dislocated hip. He's not a pretty sight." I was used to getting cats that had been hit by cars because people knew I would fix them. But Snowball was in deep trouble and I was buried with work. I knew I would have to bone plate two of his legs and the plates alone would cost over $100. Each plate needed at least six screws at a cost of six dollars each which added up to the grand total of $172.00.

I might have been able to afford the hardware, but it was going to take me at least three to four hours to fix him and that was the minimum. So the financial loss in time would be approximately $1,500. I don't mean to sound calloused, but those were the facts and I am not exaggerating. I knew it would take three different surgeries to fix him because he was in such bad shape.

I felt for this cat, but also didn't know if I should put him through so much. Besides fixing the two broken bones, I'd have to do an exision arthoplasty of his right hip. So when you add the pain, cost, and time away from the rest of my patients, his fate was pretty much sealed.

I knew it wasn't going to be easy because he was a beautiful white tom cat and he had not stopped purring since Carol had brought him to me. I think he was so happy that someone had found him that he couldn't quit purring a thank you. At any rate, it was just too much and I dreaded facing Karn and Carol, but I had a busy schedule and bills to pay.

I made my mind up and thought to myself that this was one time I wasn't going to let them sway me. I took x-rays to be sure of my diagnosis and after everyone saw how broken up his little body was, they seemed to know that putting him to sleep was the only answer. We all privately asked ourselves if it was even fair to Snowball to do the surgery.

I drew up 3cc's of Euthanol and had Marilyn hold Snowball on his side. It was always easier to give the shot in the inside of the rear leg. There is a vein there that is easy to hit and no nerve running along side it.

Marilyn and I both braced ourselves as I put the needle into the vein. I could see blood coming into the needle so I knew I was there. We apologized to Snowball, who was still purring up a storm. He couldn't have been happier because he had found someone who cared about him.

The scene reminded me of the movie, Old Yeller where the golden lab died. I didn't want to drag it out for him or us, so I put my thumb on the plunger of the syringe. I was pretty upset at the time, but I had to do what was reasonable. He continued to purr like nothing I'd ever heard before. I knew that sound was going to haunt me, but what other reasonable action could I take?

I started to stroke him and he purred louder and louder. He wasn't making this very easy. I took a deep breath and started to push the plunger…..but couldn't. I jerked the needle out in-stead and said to Marilyn, "I can't do this! It would be easier to fix him and I don't care what it costs."

I cancelled all my appointments and surgeries for the rest of day and concentrated on fixing that purring mess. Boy, what God does to see what we're made of. Actually, Karn probably had as much to do with it as God, because I would have hated to face her if I had put Snowball to sleep.

I spent the rest of the day fixing him. At least I didn't have to listen to him purr. All three of his surgeries went very well and he was walking within a week; maybe not walking real well, but at least walking, and of course purring. I couldn't believe this guy. He could get anything he wanted just by purring.

He recovered over a period of six to eight weeks and was totally normal by his first birthday. We were lucky to find him a home after the first month, but I think it was his purring that did the trick. A couple, Ann and Jim, came to the clinic for a yearly checkup on their own cat. When I happened to mention this gorgeous white cat that wouldn't stop purring; they went back to look at him and fell in love instantly.

That's usually how it goes. It's either love at first sight or it doesn't go at all. I'm sure you can relate to that because it seems to be a human frailty.

Funny, that we had been calling him Snowball, but we didn't mention that to Ann or Jim because it is always better for the new owners to name their new love. The funny thing was that on the return visit, they introduced him as: Snowball. Surprise!

A few months later they came again and he was still purring up a storm. He just seemed to love life. We could all take a lesson from him. Well, this time he was here to get neutered (a lot of people refer to this procedure as getting tutored). All I know is he came in that day with Snowballs and he left with No Balls. I guess I had the last say after all.

By the time I finished my surgeries, I was bushed and ready to call it a day. I was also famished and grabbed a quick bite to eat at a fast food restaurant. The double cheese burger and fries tasted mighty good and I washed it all down with a 32 oz. soft drink.

When I got home it was getting dark, but I still grabbed my sweats and headed for the fitness center. Doing the kind of work I do in my practice, I realize that exercise is critical. Like everything else in my life, I don't back off when I pursue something. I'm literally finding myself working out seven days a week – two to three hours in the early morning before work and another two - three hours after work.

"Hey, Rick, how's it going?" George calls as he lifts the barbell.

"Never felt better." I respond as I add another five pound weight to my machine.

The conversation turns quiet as we push our bodies harder and harder until the sweat trickles down and soaks our tee-shirts. It feels good and I feel better since I know this is going to keep me in good shape.

George sits up and wraps a towel around his shoulders. "Are you taking that protein powder everyone is talking about?"

"Of course, it really helps build muscle and it's good for your body. I've been taking it for quite some time. As a matter of fact, I take it several times a day. If it's good for you, then more must be better. How about you?"

"Yeah, me too. Not gonna let you leave me in the dust." He pops my leg with his towel.

"I'm taking vitamins three times a day as well. With my practice, I don't always eat right, so I want to be sure I'm getting all the minerals and trace elements I need."

George stops and turns back, "Do you think we can get too many vitamins?"

"Naw, they say if you get more than your body needs that they'll just be washed out by your kidneys anyway. So I figure it's better to be safe than sorry. Besides they're not expensive."

As I drive home, I'm feeling pretty good. The work-out relaxed my muscles and the adrenalin gave me a wave of energy. I was still thinking about Snowball and it felt good inside to know I had saved him. Then I laughed out loud just thinking about how the girls always named the cats.

It came to mind about another kitten that had been brought into the clinic because it needed a home. Thank God there was nothing wrong with him. After a day in the cage, whenever any-one would open it, he would jump for them and go immediately for their throat area and throw both his legs around their neck and hang on for dear life. It was easy to name him because he always looked like he was hugging someone.

So he was blessed with the name Hugger and he's been a lover ever since. I know be-cause my mother-in-law couldn't resist him. Who could?

First on my schedule the next morning is a little Boston Bulldog who is fifteen years old. I read his chart before entering the room and I shrug my shoulders. I guess not every case can be as good as Snowball's.

"Morning, Mrs. Taylor." I kneel beside the box holding Buffy, who is lying on his side and just staring into space. He doesn't move or show any sign as I check him out.

"When I got up this morning, he was just lying there on the floor." She sniffs and fights back the tears. "I tried to get him to get up, but he didn't respond. Before that he had started throwing up and finally stopped eating all together."

"It's possible it could be a problem with his kidneys so we need to do a blood test which we can do here at the clinic, and I'll have the results in about fifteen minutes."

Mrs. Taylor agrees, so I draw the blood and do the test. The BUN was 265.

"I know this is hard for you, but the blood test confirms that Buffy's kidneys are no longer doing their job. You know he is *fifteen*, but I know how much he means to you. Living with you, there's no doubt he's had a wonderful life."

The tears start falling harder and harder. I feel deeply for this lady because I know how this hurts. "He's a great dog. I can remember him when you first came to me. He was around ten then and doing well." I gently stroke Buffy's head as I continue, "I know how awful this is for you. He's been a member of your family for a long time. But I'm telling you that you are doing him the biggest service you could do now. We have no choice, but to stop his suffering." I swallow hard, "If it were you lying there, you would want someone to help you. We can't do that for humans, but we can help this gentle soul."

"But I just can't tell you to put him to sleep. I can't!" She doesn't even try to hold back the tears and she sits on the floor next to her beloved friend. "He's always been here for me especially when I was so sick. He never left my side. He's the love of my life. He probably saved my life when I went through my divorce. If he hadn't been there I don't know what I would have done. I can't imagine life without him."

"You don't have to decide, his system has already shut down and he's already decided for us. He's going to die, it's now just a matter of how. I will just give him something slowly that will put him at ease and then gently he will just go to sleep." I pat her shoulder. "If you would like, you can have some time here alone with him first and then when the time comes, you can hold him as he passes on. We have to love him enough now to let him go peacefully."

She nods her head and I quietly leave the room and close the door. I instruct everyone to just let her be until she comes out. Everyone on my staff understands because they all love animals or they wouldn't be working here.

"Carol, let me know when she's ready. I don't want to hurry her, but when she's ready, I don't want her to have to wait at all." I turn to go into the next room.

Carol answers, "Sure," and she adds, "I just want to let you know that this next client is very upset. I spoke with her while she was waiting just trying to ease her pain. She told me she was a gymnast and even though she was really quiet, she did let me know that you are her last hope for her dog."

I pick up the folder and read what my assistant has written down: Ten year old Beagle diagnosed with a liver tumor.

"Good morning." I study the young face and see what Carol was telling me.

After a few seconds of silence she speaks in a soft voice, but her eyes stare at the floor. "I've gone to a number of vets and they all tell me that he has a tumor on his liver and that it is all over for him." She chokes on the last few words.

"Well, we need to x-ray him and then we'll talk about the diagnosis." I can see that she is reaching out for help. I take the dog into the x-ray room, hoping inside that I wouldn't find what had already been diagnosed, but there it is before my eyes. There is no denying the big liver tumor. I can tell how much she loves this dog and my steps are slow as I walk back down the hall and into the room where she is waiting.

"I'm sorry but they were right, the tumor is very clear. I can feel the pain and instinctively realize that she is low on money. I say, "I'll tell you what – for $250.00, I'll go in there and if I can cut it out I will, but if I can't, I want to put him to sleep while I have him under already." The price was well under what this type of surgery would normally cost, but I knew I had to help her.

She gets really quiet and I think it is probably because as a gymnast she has had someone lording over her every move her entire life. Carol cracks the door and from the look on her face, I can tell that Mrs. Taylor is ready to put Buffy to sleep. In this kind of practice, there is a lot of non-verbal communication that goes on.

I turn back toward the gymnast, "I'll let you think about that for a few minutes while I see another patient. I'll be right back." I quietly close the door behind me.

"Carol, see if you can find out what's wrong. She won't talk to me. I'll put Buffy out of his misery and then be right back."

I open the door quietly and give an encouraging nod. "Would you like to stay, or you can wait in the other room? Whatever is easiest for you."

"Oh, I have to stay and be with him. I can't leave him now." She swallows hard.

"I agree. He knows you're here with him and that will make this much easier for him. You are doing the only humane thing you can do and it's important to me that you can see that there's nothing else we can do. He's not likely to make it until morning and this way he doesn't have to suffer."

I stroke his head one last time and as she talks to him, I inject the medicine that I know will ease him from this world. I think to myself: *This is a blessing for him. I know I'm doing the right thing.*

She feels him relax. "Does it work that fast?"

"Yes, Mrs. Taylor, he is gone and before I even finished giving him the whole shot." I help her up and ask, "Do you want him cremated?"

"Yes, please." She says in a squeaky voice even she doesn't recognize, but I can tell that she is relieved that it went well.

"I'll call you when the ashes are ready. But now, know you did the right thing and remember he lived a good life and a long life. I wish I had the words to help you now. I am so sorry you had to go through this. He was a wonderful friend, and he thanks you for letting him go." I give her a reassuring smile. "Is there anything I can do to help you?"

She shakes her head and walks off.

I return to the room where I had left the gymnast, but she is nowhere to be found. I walk back out into the hallway, "Carol, where did she go?"

Carol shakes her head, "She didn't have the money."

I was overwhelmed with the love I clearly saw in this girls eyes and quickly add, "Carol, call her back and tell her not to give her dog the last supper....and tell her to bring him back in the morning. As long as she will allow me to put him to sleep if I can't fix him, I'll fix him for nothing."

The next morning I began the surgery and found a grapefruit sized tumor attached to the liver. It was attached to one lobe. Surgery to the liver is really tricky because of its soft consistency. I had not done liver surgery at that time, but I knew I had to try. I expected it to bleed excessively. So in order to limit the bleeding, I used a needle with an attached thread to cut through the tissue about ½ inch at a time. Then I tied it off, which also tied off the blood vessels.

To my delight, it bled very little and the surgery lasted less than an hour. It came out beautifully. As I walked over to the waiting room, I was overjoyed to get to tell her that her dog was going to be fine. The look on her face was worth any amount of money. That dog lived to be fourteen. She's adored me ever since and it feels good to be that important to someone. God has given me such a wonderful gift to help others.

At the end of the day, I relived every moment of the surgery, especially the high I got when she lifted her eyes to look into mine. She had a smile across her entire face. I knew at that moment – why I had become a vet.

I left the clinic but didn't have time to stop for food, so instead popped a frozen pizza in my oven while I relaxed in front of the television. I was thankful that I didn't have mounds of home-work or studying like I used to have before I graduated. I was proud that I had worked hard for all those years and that now I had the information (or so I thought) needed to successfully administer to the animals under my care. It felt good. Later, I knew I'd be working out like crazy once again. It was a major part of my life.

For years this pattern continued, and I gave the shots and prescribed the medications that I had learned about in school. It all seemed so simple, but I had no idea what I would be facing over the next few years or how ill prepared I really was.

Doctors prescribe what they have been taught because they rarely have time to get smarter.

Chapter 4

Life shouldn't be all work and no play

The car pulls up and stops at 52nd St. in Paradise Valley. The lady rolls down her window and yells, "You've got to be kidding me!"

"Nope, I love every minute of it!" I yell back.

I guess I was a sight in my shorts and cowboy hat, jogging down the street with my horse, running behind me. I just smiled and continued along the path with my hat pulled down low and Judy, my eighteen year old mare beside me. What people think hasn't fazed me since I began my journey into veterinary school. I know what I'm doing and I want Judy to be safe for my children to ride. She needs her exercise just like we do. Besides, I'm having a blast running with her.

This has become a daily routine even though the guy that I used to jog with has dropped out of the scene. I don't think he enjoyed running with a horse because we stood out too much. But that doesn't bother me. Judy and I both enjoy our outings, except she drags her feet, which ends up squaring the front of her toes off. Unfortunately I have to quit jogging with her.

About the same time, I encountered Solid Set, a broken down race horse at Turf Paradise. I learned about him through a client. He told me that Solid Set was just in a stall and that nobody wanted him. I was sure that I could heal him or I at least wanted to try. I asked the owner what he wanted for him and he told me $500.00. I later learned that he probably would have just given him to me.

Another client of mine had some acreage on which he let me create a race track. He was kind enough to let me use his tractor to do the work. I was determined to heal this horse and get him back on the track. I knew I could do it. I've always loved horses and I've always wanted to be able to fix them. I even bought him a heart monitor so I could tell how much I was stressing his heart as I began jogging with him. I had a dream of taking him back to the race track.

Solid Set and I jogged around that race track every single day which helped him get better and better. As time passed he got to feeling so good that he started bucking and kicking. One day he managed to kick me with his hind leg. I thought he was just feeling good and took that as a good sign. But the second time he kicked me, I got upset. And the third time he kicked me I yelled, "Screw you!" I walked him back to the barn and decided it was time to go to the track.

I obtained a stall at Turf Paradise next to Danny Hunsaker, who was one of the better trainers at Turf. He watched as I pushed Solid Set harder and harder. He knew I was overdoing it, but didn't know me well enough to say anything.

Solid Set bowed his tendon again. It really got me down because I had tried so hard to help him. Danny sensed how dejected I felt when he came over to my barn one day. He offered to work with Solid Set. That's when my close friendship with Danny began. We started training together and he also started jogging with me at five a.m. every morning. We became inseparable friends. I just loved working with the horses. Danny and I even ended up going to Alaska on a wonderful fishing trip which included catching our limit of King Salmon. We became friends for life.

After Danny and I got close, he felt comfortable telling me what he thought. One day he said to me, "Rick, you just pushed him too hard."

"I know, but he was coming along really well."

"I think I can help you with him, but we're going have to go easy, and it's going to take time." Danny said.

I shrugged my shoulders, but the drive to get this horse on the track held me on course. "Okay, we'll work slowly."

While Danny diligently worked with Solid Set, we attended race after race. One day Danny explained to me that if you own a horse at the track, you can claim another horse that is entered in a 'claiming race.' He told me that this practice keeps people from cheating and putting in more experienced horses to gain a winning record. Since my limit was $2,500.00, we looked for a $2,500.00 claiming race from which to pick a horse.

You make your claim at the time of the race. When the gate opens for the race, the horse is yours. If s/he gets hurt during the race, s/he is still yours, so it can be risky.

That is when seven year old Colonel Shannon showed up. I put a bid in to claim him. Since there were some other people interested, we all drew numbers to see who would get the horse.

The numbers were on little balls which were dropped into a jar. Lucky for me, they drew my number.

We worked with him and he was a delight. For his first race, he placed second. I was ecstatic. Then he won his next three races. I can't explain the excitement my body was going through. I just loved horses and I loved to watch them run. At this point I was bragging that I was the 'Race Horse Baron' of Paradise Valley.

Turf Paradise closed for the summer so Danny and I took Solid Set to Santa Fe, New Mexico. We won enough races to buy as many as thirteen race horses and we won twenty-six races in one year. Anyone who knows the racing business knows that winning that many races is an impossible task. Since I was a veterinarian, some thought we were doping the horses, but the ones who knew me well, knew I would never do that. I simply loved the great creatures too much to hurt them. It all boiled down to good honest training and Danny's know how.

We were always so hot that our horses were the favorites in most of their races. With as few horses as he had, Danny just missed being the lead trainer for the meet. Our barn was picked #1 for being the best cared for.

But Solid Set was still my love and when he healed, we decided to run him. I didn't want to take a chance on losing him, so we entered him in a $5,000.00 starter 'allowance' race which was a hard race to win, especially for a horse that hadn't run a race in a year. Normally a horse needs a couple of races to build up his stamina to the point of winning, especially if he's going to run a mile. Nobody would give him a chance.

I was so excited and could hardly believe we got him back to the track. Solid Set was even more excited and he was loving every minute of it. He was a winner before and soon hoped to be one again. He looked magnificent.

I was deeply involved with horse racing and I sat in the stands holding my breath. This was a one mile race and I knew it would be difficult for Solid Set, but I just wanted him to do his best. I was trying not to expect too much as he entered the gate and I could see the anticipation in his eyes. He loved to run. My heart was pumping fast and furious and my stomach was literally eating me up. As he broke from the gate, he fell back. I was not surprised because he usually came off the pace, but it still concerned me.

Then on the back side of the track, he moved up to fifth place and then turned the corner and was heading for home. All this time he was passing horses. I jumped to my feet yelling and screaming as I watched him pull out in front further and further. I couldn't believe my eyes and tears of joy streamed down my face as he crossed the finish line at least ten lengths ahead of the pack. I couldn't believe what I had just seen. It was and still is the greatest race I've ever been a part of and no doubt one of the most exciting days of my life. I will remember it to my dying day. I owe Danny for that race and I will be eternally grateful. Thanks Danny!

Solid Set came back to the winner's circle and he was s-o-o-o proud. Believe me, horses know when they've won. He has won several horse races since that day, but none that big. Everybody had given up on Solid Set. They figured he was finished. Nobody wanted him but me and WE did it!!!!!!!!

I had a routine when my horses would run. As my horse would pull up to the front, I would literally be jumping up and down and yelling "Ride him, ride him!" I can't tell you how excited I would get. One day when I was in that routine, my horse was the favorite and not going to pay much if people bet on him, but that didn't matter to me. When the race started, a young lady in the stands looked at Danny and said, "What's his problem?"

Danny looked at her and simply said, "It's his horse."

Boy was that a good feeling to know that it was my horse. My life was going great and my practice was too. The excitement of the race track just added to it. I invited my mom and dad to go with me on several occasions. On opening day at Turf Paradise, Solid Set and another of my horses, Chief Red Feather, were both running.

It was a magical day because both horses won and I was so happy that my dad and mom got to share the excitement. I could never do enough to thank them for being my parents. I ushered them down to the winner's circle and let them feel the exhilaration of the moment. To think that I could create that much excitement in their lives filled me with joy. They shot a video in the winner's circle and throughout the filming, I was pointing at the camera telling my dad to look up so that later he could see himself on the video with the horse. It was such great fun. I was able to do the same for his brother, Uncle Tuk (Don), on another race day.

Later on St. Patrick's Day, I planned a big party at Turf Paradise since my family roots included a lot of Irish Blood. As always, I made sure my mom and dad could come. I invited all of the people important to me which included relatives and friends. I rented The Directors Suite because I wanted them to know how much I loved them. The room was at the top of the track, which was appropriate because I was on top of the world. It couldn't have been nicer.

The finish line was directly below us. The track was beautiful with lush grass growing here and there around water ponds which were decorated with fountains. There were ducks swimming on the ponds and birds were flying over-head. It couldn't have been a better setting. I made sure we were going to have a wonderful smorgasbord of food topped off with prime rib.

Danny and I sat there reading the racing form, determined to make the best bet for every-one. By the end of the day, we had won the feature race and the green horse blanket with the name St. Patrick's Day Race on it. Everyone with us got their picture in the winners' circle and $1,000. It couldn't have been a better day. My mom and dad couldn't have been happier.

Later, I was lucky enough to be able to take them to the Suns' games at a time when the Suns were on a winning streak and going for the title. I had clients with seats on the floor and I was able to get my parents up real close to the action. They were devoted fans and at that time my mom adored Charles Barkley.

I'll never forget the night mom and dad were sitting so close they could reach out and touch the players. Karn and I were in other seats up a little ways in the stands. When they introduced the players prior to the start of the game, we both gasped when the spotlight landed on my mom, standing in the middle of the players and reaching for Charles Barkley in an attempt to get his autograph. As we laughed our heads off, out came the Gorilla, the team's mascot. He went over and gently ushered my mom back to her seat. She never did get the autograph, but fell in love with the gorilla.

While I'm on the subject of my parents, I want to tell you about another fantastic time I got to spend with them. Most of the time, parents take their kids to Disney Land, but Karn and I got to take my parents there and to Sea World. We saw everything and did everything. They loved being the kids and us the parents for a change.

Karn and I stood in line for at least forty minutes to buy a half a chicken for each of us for lunch. Sea World is a fantastic place to go, but food costs a fortune. When I saw a tantalizing dessert, I had to buy some for my mom since I knew she had a sweet tooth. When we walked up with the food and she spotted the dessert, her eyes lit up. Before I knew it, she was tossing the one-half chicken up in the air for the sea gulls, which caught it in "mid-flight." Then she happily ate her dessert and I loved the look of a little girl on her face.

My dad couldn't believe what he had just witnessed and said, "Marion, what the hell are you doing?" But she knew what she was doing. She was getting right to the dessert just like all the other kids would do.

Enjoying life reduces stress and is a major contributor to your overall good health.

Chapter 5

Meeting my wife

Most things that happen in our lives don't enter in a dramatic fashion. They kind of slowly creep up on us and we're often totally unaware. It was like that when I met Karn.

I've always loved sports and in high school, played football, basketball and wrestling, which was my favorite. I remember a match where I was wrestling a guy who had never been beaten. As a matter of fact, he had beaten me before. And when I got to the state meet and found out he was my opponent, I was more than nervous.

I was a wreck by the time my turn came around. My mom and dad were in the stands and mom was being her usual vocal self. It was always easy to hear her. When my match started, I could tell things were different this time. I either had more confidence or he had less, but at any rate, I was ready.

I was doing really well, when all of a sudden he flipped me onto my back. I wasn't about to let him pin me, so I arched my back more and more. He pushed harder and harder. I was arching my back one way and he was pushing me the opposite way, when I suddenly jerked the same way he was pushing and I was able to flip him onto his back.

Mom's voice bellowed above it all, "Pin him. Pin him!" I won.

I wasn't always good at the different sports activities, but I did really enjoy them. So it was just natural for me to continue with my workouts after I graduated from veterinary school.

I'm at the La Camarilla Tennis and Fitness Center this morning for at least two to three hours just like always. It doesn't matter that I was here last night for the same amount of time. It's the same everyday with me. Karn is doing aerobics just behind me, but I really am not paying any attention to her. My mind is on getting rid of the tension in my life.

I am so engrossed in my workout that I seize any opportunity to give back rubs to anyone at the gym. I find that it really helps build my forearms. You're probably not going to believe me, but this wasn't about making passes at the girls.

Peddling her exercise bike, Karn starts talking to the lady next to her, "What's up with that guy?" She points at me.

"You mean Rick, the one with the nice butt'?" Gail answers.

"Yeah, he does have a nice body, but he's so noisy. I mean at five in the morning I'm half asleep and his booming voice never stops. It's enough to give a person a headache."

"Oh I can put up with that….." Gail grins.

"And another thing that turns me off is the way he's always giving all the girls back massages." Karn frowns.

Gail stops her peddling, "Karn, his hands do magic and his back rubs are to die for – you should have him give you one. I bet he could help that calf muscle of yours that's giving you trouble."

Karn reaches down and rubs her leg, "Well, maybe it's worth a try."

When Karn approaches me, she is limping slightly.

"Rick – is it?" She says in a cool tone.

"Yeah, Rick Soltero."

"My name is Karn and I've noticed that you seem to give a lot of back rubs."

"I like to help when I can. Would you like one?"

"No, not a back rub, but I do have a really sore calf muscle. Do you think you could help me with that?"

"Sure thing here let me see what I can do."

I rub her calf for just a short while and she says in a warmer tone, "That's nice."

I am happy to have been able to help her, but nothing much comes from that first meeting. Looking for a relationship is the furthest thing from my mind and I can tell that she's not looking either.

For a time, she continues to do aerobics and works out on the exercise bikes back behind me. I notice that she is getting skinnier and skinnier and then just out of the blue, she starts lifting weights. As I watch, I see that she's doing it all wrong. So I walk over to show her how and we start talking.

Now she catches my attention. I think to myself: *Nice Lady. I like her personality. I like the way she talks and she is so darn sweet.* Of course my thoughts don't stop there as my eyes take in her whole body. My mind talks to me: *She looks like she's been sculptured....like her body is chiseled and made perfect with every detail down to her fingers and toes. She is so refined and pretty and she has great legs as well.*

I always wondered what she thought about me in those early days. Just a few years ago, after dating for four years and being married for fourteen years, she finally told me. She said when she first saw me that see didn't like me at all. She said I was way too loud and always whooping and hollering and she also didn't take to my habit of rubbing so many girls' backs. Of course, she was quick to add that she wasn't jealous, just didn't like it.

Finally she gave me the truth that from the beginning she loved my height and skin tone. I think she described my stomach as a six-pack. Of course, I thought it was at least an eight pack. I was all muscle. Then she laughed as she told me she saw a picture of me at a costume party where I went as a Chip & Dale dancer. I guess I was a little brass in those days, but we had fun.

Well, one thing led to another and we started dating. I knew I wanted this woman as my wife. Just as always, I set my goal and went after it. She didn't stand a chance. I would stop at A.J.'s Fine Grocery Store after work and pick up the best stuff I could find and invite her over for dinner. I tried to be Quizo the Romantic. Actually, as it turned out, I was good at it. I always had fresh flowers, romantic background music, and I never served dinner without lighted candles.

One such night I had picked up groceries for a nice salad, cocktail shrimp, horse radish and filet steaks. I always had fresh cut flowers and I left no stone unturned. The background music set the mood and the table looked great, not to mention the food. I could tell when she walked in the door that she was overwhelmed and I knew then that I would win her over.

Well, it wasn't all that easy but it sure was a fun journey. Over the next year, we grew closer and closer until finally I decided to ask her to be my wife.

"Karn, you're the best thing that's ever happened to me and I want you to be my wife." I watched carefully for her reaction.

It didn't take long and she replied, "Rick, I love you too, but I'm not about to marry someone I've only known for one year. We'll have to go another year and then we'll see."

I wasn't real happy with that response, but heck what's one more year? We were having the time of our lives anyway. I continued to ask every once in a while until after two more years, I quit asking.

We spent all our time together and she even came to work at my practice. One of our favorite places to spend time was Del Mar. We would walk up and down the beach for hours. We would walk all the way from Del Mar to La Jolla and then on to Mission Beach and back. It wasn't unusual for us to walk twelve to fifteen miles and once we even walked twenty-three. If we got tired, we would just catch the bus back to Del Mar.

Four years after we met, our relationship had grown in leaps and bounds. She had become my best friend. I think that's the way real love happens. It is something you experience together and that grows the more you talk. To this day, she is the nicest, kindest person I know, and eventually, she agreed to marry me. Finally! We still work out and walk all the time. We look at the time we share as the best part of our day

We had forty acres in Williams in those days and after work on most Saturdays, we would head there. We would often listen to Laura Schlessinger on the radio and we both liked the way she tried to help people. She had a great heart. We would get so interested in her that we were still listening to her when we crawled into bed at night and would fall asleep with the radio on. Laura was so sensitive and caring that she held our attention. I related to that feeling and have tried to keep it a part of my life. Karn's always been that way.

Often we would pack a lunch, take two large garbage bags and cut holes for our head and arms so we could slip them on to stay dry just in case it rained. Then off we'd go on our ATVs, headed deep into the woods. We were both at home there. It wasn't out of the ordinary to come upon three hundred elk or so just out in the middle of nowhere.

Many of the elk, deer, rabbits and birds would come visit us too. They would show up for dinner at night because we always kept plenty of alfalfa hay and bird seeds for them. Karn and I were happiest when we could enjoy all the creatures around us.

When we went into the woods, we would find a nice spot and spread a blanket on the ground. We'd have our lunch, lay back on the soft cover, and let the wind whispering through the pines lull us to sleep. The stress just melted away and if there is a heaven on this earth, we found it there together.

At night we especially loved to go out on the porch and watch the stars. We were at 6,500 feet above sea level so they were really clear. We would spend the night trying to see how many shooting stars we could spot. It was all so magical. We were blessed. We knew it and we know it today.

The bond between us grew stronger and stronger. I'd never known a woman who loved the things I loved and who was so easy to be with. She was truly my soul mate. We always knew what the other one was thinking. She knew me and I knew her. It was kind of scary because we would always mail each other cards. One day we each received a card from the other and when we opened them – they were the same cards.

If it rained, we would stretch a cheap blue canvas over some branches and crawl under it and giggle like children. Then when evening was upon us, we'd pull on our garbage bags and hop back on our ATVs and head for home. We were side by side on our ATVs and when we reached home, we would jump in the shower and the dirt mixed with the water would turn to mud.

I have never been sorry that I married Karn because she has proven over the years to be even more loving and giving. I've never seen anyone with the patience she has. Everyone I know from children to adults loves to talk with her. She makes them feel that they are the most important person in the world because she really listens and cares.

My father loved her the most. While he was suffering for four years from his cancer, she took care of all of his business such as paying bills and handling insurance questions. His burden was so heavy from the disease, but she managed to give him some joy those last years.

My dad loved golf and Karn had never played a day in her life, but she learned all about it so she could spend hours upon hours listening and discussing the game with him. The thought of golf brought pleasure to a man who had lost just about everything else.

On the day he died, he held her hand for hours and I mean hours and she gave him comfort and helped ease him from this world. I will always be grateful to her for the love she showed him.

She is especially in love with her three cats and falls asleep brushing and stroking them. I've heard people say that when they died, they'd like to come back as her cat. Now you already know how I love animals, but I think the bond is even deeper between Karn and the animal world.

I'll tell you a funny story: one day a little girl brought in a brown paper bag with an injured bird in it. The day was exceptionally busy and I was totally up to my eyeballs in work. Well, I could see Karn coming down the hall with that paper bag in her hand and she looked at me with those tender loving eyes of hers and I knew I was going to do whatever it took to fix this bird.

Remember the movie with Tom Cruise as Jerry McGuire, when Renee Zellweger said, "*You had me at hello*"? Well I was tired and even a little irritated, but with Karn, nothing bad lasts very long. She started with the story about how a little girl brought in this bird and that is as far as I let her get when I said, "What do you want me to do about it?" Obviously I already knew what she wanted, so I took the bag from her hand.

I didn't know how badly it was injured so I started walking down the hall to the examination room so I could check it out. Between you and me, I loved being Karn's white knight in shining armor. But I didn't need to be at this moment because as I turned around the bag began to shake. It kept shaking so I decided to go down the hall and out the back door.

I opened the bag and much to my surprise, the bird up and flew away. I was relieved. I thought to myself that there really is a God. I turned around and walked back inside and down the hall and handed Karn the empty paper bag and said, "Fixed! I turned around with a smug look and just walked away.

Just before I turned, I noticed here eyes light up and she literally skipped down the hall to the front desk where the girl was anxiously waiting and I could hear her say, "See, Dr. Soltero really is a miracle worker!"

Well, I have to say that Karn is the miracle. I don't know what I would have done without her when I was diagnosed with my liver disease. When I was told I needed a transplant, she immediately stepped up and said she would donate part of hers. She didn't even have to think about it, she knew what she wanted to do without hesitation. The only thing that stopped her was her size and the fact that they would not accept her as a donor.

Even though she couldn't donate her liver, she has walked every inch of the way with me and carried far too much of the load. She has handled the paperwork and appointments and still had the energy to sit up and listen to me long into the night on many, many occasions.

She has withstood my cranky and sometimes downright lousy attitude and never ending problems, both physically and emotionally. She wouldn't let me give up when I was at my lowest moments in time just begging to die and escape the pain. She remains today my strongest supporter, my soul mate, my love.

I want you to know that her devotion, loving attitude and persistence have provided the strongest armor against my liver disease. And I want to publicly thank her for all she has done and continues to do for me. I am truly the luckiest man in the world because I have Karn as my wife.

Love contributes so much to our overall well being.

Chapter 6

Pets are not living as long

I stand beside her as she strokes the head of her Doberman, Cherokee. My heart aches as it has so many times before, but there is no alternative. "I'm so sorry, Connie, but it's *cancer*."

"Dr. Soltero, she's only seven and a half and I saw what happened. A squirrel ran by our screen door and Cherokee smacked into the door as she chased after it. Then she began to limp. I think she's just sprained her leg or something."

"I wish that were the case, but I'm afraid she's right at that age. I'll still take x-rays, but I've seen this so many times that I know I'm sure of the diagnosis."

All I can do is watch the tears fall and be witness to the human animal bond before me

now. I know what she is going through. I know
it's too late for this dog and that all I can do now
is to keep her comfortable for her remaining days.
The fact that Cherokee is a therapy dog, who
brought joy to elderly people, makes it all the
harder.

"Why don't you sit down and we'll get the
x-rays. I'll be back in just a little bit." I take the
leash and lead the big gentle dog to the room for
her x-rays, but in my heart I already know the
outcome.

Connie is trying hard to keep her compo-
sure, but the tears fall as I show her the proof.
She asks, "What about amputation?"

"Honestly, I won't do it. I did amputate
the leg of Cherokee's father, just a few years back
and he died anyway within a few months. If it
was another breed of dog, I might consider it, but
with a Doberman, once cancer rears it ugly head,
it will appear in other areas. I refuse to put her
through the surgery and pain only to die a month
or so after that. And I refuse to do it to you as
well. You don't need a large bill or all the hurt of
prolonging her death."

"I trust you – you've always been upfront
with me, but – but how long does she have? Will
she be in pain?" Connie manages to choke out.

"It's hard to say….maybe three to six
months give or take. And yes it does hurt, but it's
not excruciating and we'll put her on 20 mg of

prednisone a day and that will help until the pain becomes too much."

"I don't want her to suffer, but I don't want to end her life too soon either. How will I know when it's time?" She sobs.

"Oh, you'll know. You know her so well that you will know. I'm so sorry. She's a great dog and much too young."

It was only a couple of months later, when Carol received the call from Connie, saying that it was time. She and her husband, Dieter, drove down from Strawberry, which is about 1 ½ hours from the clinic. He came in while Connie sat on the tailgate of their truck, cradling Cherokee in her lap. I got the medication and walked out to the truck so it would be easier for everyone.

Cherokee sensed something and immediately ran to the front of the truck bed and Connie had to pull her back to the tailgate so I could inject the drug. Dieter held her head, while Connie talked to her and stroked her. She died quickly and quietly, but I knew the devastation for Connie and Dieter would last a long time.

They chose to take her home and bury her on their own property. They told me that Dieter had already made a nice wooden casket for her and that she would be placed on her soft sponge bed with her favorite toy beside her. Connie has since built a lovely garden, including a trellis over her resting place.

Cherokee was the reason Connie Stoffels came to me one day with a note asking if I wanted to co-author this book with her. Her love for her own pet and the agony she felt losing her at such a young age, moved Connie to want to help others find ways of keeping their dogs healthier. This is one of the main goals of this book.

Cherokee died on August 24, 2004, just a few days past her eighth birthday. She was the catalyst that got Connie and I together. Following is a letter Connie wrote to me just after Cherokee's death. I thought you might like to see the strong love that she not only had for her companion, but also the love that has guided her throughout the writing of this book.

The card read: "An act of kindness is long remembered." And the following letter, on the next page, was inside.

August 27, 2004
Dear Dr. Soltero,

We wanted to write and thank you for your kindness and assistance in helping us release our Doberman, Cherokee, from the pain of cancer. It was the most difficult thing we have ever done, but you brought us great comfort because you cared.

It was impossible to talk that day, because of the emotions, but you knew exactly what to say and do to help us. We know that it was also painful for you and that you have to do this many times over for others as well. You need to know that your sincerity and devotion to animals is felt by all. Your skills as a doctor are outstanding, but you, as a person, bring so much more to this world which is often so harsh.

We also want to thank you for being so frank, honest, and upfront with us from the beginning. At first it was a shock to find out she had a tumor, but you could have made a lot of money from us and put Cherokee through the pain of amputation and still she would have died in just a short time. Thank you for sparing all of us.

Sincerely,
Dieter and Connie Stoffels

My day didn't stop there, and as I went back inside, a couple came running through the door screaming for help. I hurried to their side and could see the man holding a wet lifeless cat.

I immediately grabbed the cat and looked for any sign of life, but there was no breathing, no heart beat, and the cat was blue. I looked at the couple, "I'm sorry, there's no hope."

I turned and started walking down the hall holding the cat by his chest and then it happened. I felt a heart beat just one time. And I mean it was only one time, but it was enough to throw me into action. I ran to surgery where the oxygen was and called for Marilyn at the same time.

While I was pumping the cat's chest, Marilyn grabbed a mask and hooked it up to the oxygen and started breathing for the cat. As Marilyn controlled the breathing, I became the stimulator for heart action.

The heart would beat a couple of times and then quit again. It would beat more and more, but it always stopped for a brief time. Meanwhile, Marilyn hooked Snowball (yet another Snowball) up to the heart monitor so we could see what the electrical conduction of the heart was doing.

The EKG looked normal but there would be only a dozen in a row and then they would stop altogether. This went on for well over an hour. The string of EKG's kept getting longer and longer, but they would always stop.

After an hour, we were all pretty exhausted and about ready to quit, when all of a sudden the heart took off and no longer stopped. Snowball's color improved but he still wasn't breathing, but at least now we knew he had a chance.

I no longer had to do cardiac massage, but we did need to keep breathing for him. If you thought we were exhausted, you should have seen Mr. and Mrs. Benson because they stayed and witnessed this whole thing.

Since his breathing wouldn't kick in, I decided to try a respiratory stimulant. I gave him a very small amount because I didn't want to throw him into a seizure by overdoing it. Initially it didn't seem to work, but after about a minute it kicked in. He took one big gigantic gasp and then nothing. I didn't know if he was starting or stopping.

After a short time, he took a couple of gasps and his breathing started almost the same way his heart had done. We weren't out of the woods yet, but we had come a long way. There are a lot of animals you can get started only to have them quit. I felt like that was the most likely scenario here because we had worked so hard and long just to get to this point. I had been through enough to know not to get my hopes up too high, but at least I had some hope.

The breathing started to smooth out a little, but was still pretty rough for at least another thirty minutes. But it continued to get better. We were now already into this procedure for over two hours. Finally we had a steady heart beat and the breathing had now smoothed out, but Snowball was still unconscious. We'd saved his heart and lungs, but now we needed to save his brain.

I had already given him solu-delta-cortef intravenously, for shock. I hoped it would also help his brain. At this point all we could do was play the waiting game. I knew if he was brain damaged, that he would arch his head over his back, so I watched to see if we had lost the final battle.

Snowball wasn't arching yet and I was keeping my fingers crossed. We put the cat in a cage so he could be observed for the next few hours. Everything had happened so quickly, that I didn't even know what had happened to him in the first place. So I turned to Bill and said, "What happened?"

Before Bill could speak up, Mrs. Benson said, "I was cleaning the dishes at the kitchen sink, when I happened to look out the window. I saw my black cat, Midnight, pawing at the pool skimmer cover and he wouldn't quit. He just kept pawing away. I thought that was pretty strange behavior so I went out to see what was going on. I pulled Midnight off the skimmer cover, pulled the cover off and looked inside. My poor Snowball was floating face down in the water going around and around."

"I heard her screaming, so I ran to where she was." Bill added. "I pulled the cat out and we ran for the car and headed for your clinic. I didn't think he'd make it to be honest with you. I'm still not sure. What do you think?"

"Don't know. We'll have to just wait and see. I'm worried about brain damage, but at least he is responding now." I answered. "I'll have Carol give you a call as soon as we know something."

The Bensons thanked me for trying so hard and said they would be waiting by the phone. Meanwhile I went back to seeing patients. I think it was about two hours later when I heard some rustling from his cage as I passed by the door. I hoped that he wasn't arching his head back and was almost afraid to look.

As I came up to the cage, I stopped and said, "Thank you God!" He was awake and walking around. At that moment I knew he was going to be okay. He was able to go home an hour later, thanks to his buddy, Midnight.

By the end of my day, I was pretty tired from all the emotion weighing down on me throughout the whole day. But after diagnosing cancer first thing in the morning, I at least felt good about the cat that saved another cat's life and when I got home I told Karn the good story first. But my joy was short lived as my mind went back to all the cancer I was diagnosing.

"Karn, you know something's not right. When I began my practice, dogs were living to old age. Many made it to fifteen or sixteen and then they were dying of kidney failure, but lately, I'm diagnosing cancer almost everyday. I wonder why? There has to be a reason. But I can't put my finger on the cause."

"Honey, you'll find the answer. I'm sure of it." Karn pats my hand.

As I go through the next several months, my mind is beginning to look for patterns that will explain why I am diagnosing so much cancer and valley fever. These thoughts are continually running through my mind as I tend to one pet after the other.

"Dr. Soltero, she's been bleeding from the mouth, but I don't know why.

"We've got to find out the cause. I'll have to sedate her just a little so we can get a good look." I respond.

The lady explains, "I was waiting for my older daughter to get home because I couldn't lift her to bring her in and she kept bleeding."

I turn to the concerned owner,

"You can stay or leave whatever you're comfortable with…."

"I'd like to stay."

"Okay, now we're going find out what's going on. I'll be able to tell you in thirty seconds. We'll find it." I continue to probe and then I see it. "It's a big gigantic bloody tumor." I pause. "We started treating this a little while back, didn't we?"

"Yes, it's the one you cauterized, and at that time you told us it was a melanoma and that she had three to nine months probably." The lady put her arm around her young daughter who was sobbing.

"It's just a mess. I can see there's not much I can do but try to burn it, but obviously it didn't work before. It's an oral melanoma, there really isn't any hope, especially when it's this advanced. So you have to decide if you want to deal with it or let her go. Personally if it were me, I wouldn't want to live this way. You deserve better and so does your friend."

The mother talks to her little girl, "Honey, she's your dog. What do you want to do?" But obviously she is too young to understand so she runs out of the room. Later I found out that as she stood outside the clinic crying, another client walked up and asked her what was wrong. She replied, "They're killing my dog." When I was told, it really hurt even though I knew what had to be done, this child only knew her dog was going to die.

Inside, I continued to talk with her mother. "If you had the choice and you were like this, would you rather die too soon or too late? I know how hard this is and especially for a child. If you want, I can stop the bleeding, but I can promise you that it won't be a week, in truth just days before it will start back up. It wouldn't be what I would want for myself. See she's having trouble even getting up and she's not likely to stop bleeding. Your friend does not wish this mess for you."

I look into the mother's eyes almost pleading with her, "I'll tell you something even worse. If you are out having lunch some day and come back a few hours later there is going to be blood all over and she might very well be dead." I'm thinking to myself how some people just can't let go. I'm just hoping and praying for the dog's sake, that she will.

"You're right," the mother looks lovingly at her friend. "Let's do it here. That would be better and I know it's the right thing to do. I'd like to call my husband because I know he'd like to be here too."

"No problem there's a phone you can use right here on the wall." I point the way.

In a short time, her husband walks through the door holding his little daughter's hand. The mother breaks the silence by saying, "We've lost a couple other dogs and this is going to be our last dog." She strokes her daughter's hair as she cries.

I hear that statement a lot because some people just can't stand the pain of losing their pet, and I know they are hurting. I answer softly, "Time heals and I bet there's another animal out there looking for a good home like yours. You don't want to cheat yourself out of that much love down the road."

I quietly go about preparing the shot and inject it while the mother holds the dog's head on her lap and the little girl hides her face against her father's side. Their dog goes to sleep peacefully.

I hand them a box of Kleenex and say, "Take as much time as you want." I quietly leave the room and tell Carol to go over the cremation details when they are ready. Sometimes people are ready to discuss the remains while others need more time. Carol always knows how to handle this best. She always lets them know that we use a very reputable crematory and that their pet will be handled with respect. They can be sure that they will get their own pet's remains and not someone else's.

On the way home I am still thinking about the pattern that's beginning to emerge and that evening Karn and I talk well into the night.

"I put another dog down today with cancer. This one was melanoma and really ugly. I can't figure out why this seems to be happening more and more often. You know I don't remember the last time I had a dog with kidney failure." I pace around the room.

"Rick, you'll find the answers, but I'm getting worried about you. You seem to be so tired lately and you have a lot of indigestion as well. Is there something wrong?"

"You worry too much. I'm just trying to find the answer here. You know how I get when I start up a path." I say a bit irritated.

"Oh, I know that…." Karn walks into the kitchen to get some hot tea.

"Here, have a cup of this. It'll help you sleep." She says soothingly.

I ignore the cup steaming on the table, "You know they never mentioned anything like this when I was in school. I thought then that they had all the scientific answers, all researched and proven. I worked hard to learn all that stuff – but now I don't think I know all there is to know. Somehow we're really missing the boat."

Karn sits back on the couch and listens while she sips her tea.

"You know, I've never questioned any-thing I learned. I mean there was no reason. The bottom line is I'm tired and I don't have time to get smarter. It feels like such a dead end street."

Karn nods her head and I continue, "I don't think any doctor or vet has time to study much or learn about advanced medicine. I think we all fall back on the tried and true things. I figure things couldn't have changed that much since I started practicing medicine, but they have. Something has got to give."

She breaks her silence, "Honey, you're so tired tonight. Worrying like this won't help. Why don't you come to bed now and then tomorrow maybe you should start going through some files. You just might find a common thread that explains what is happening. I mean I'll help look if you need me to, but you have to get some sleep. You're looking a little pale to me."

I think inwardly: *I'm a lucky man. Karn has always looked out for me; thank you God for sending her to me.* I follow her to bed, but as she falls asleep, my insides hurt and my mind is still racing and I can't find any answers; maybe tomorrow. As I lay there, one line from a John Denver song comes to mind: "Tomorrow is just one of yesterday's dreams." I hope finding answers will not just be a dream.

An act of kindness is long remembered.

Chapter 7

Turning the corner

I drive silently in my car trying to figure out what is happening with my life. I think back to my childhood and those happy days on the Westman's ranch and my dream of being a rancher. I talk to myself: *I wonder if I took the wrong path? But I love what I'm doing. I have it all: Karn, my kids, my practice, but not my health; nor the health of my patients.*

I pull over and park on the hill overlooking the valley. I don't know if you've ever been in this kind of situation but it is shocking to say the least. I've always been a strong person and very determined. You know the kind of man who takes control of the reins and blazes a path. I've never been a follower. Maybe I've been a bit headstrong and determined, but I've done well. That is until now.

As I look down at my hands still resting on the steering wheel, I think of my dad's hands and how they felt around me. I lean on the steering wheel and cry. But, I can feel his presence all around me and I know I have to keep going and that somehow I will find the answers to my problems. My dad set that example for me long ago, but I guess I've forgotten. I know I can't give up and that I must keep fighting. My dad was always so close to God so I decide at that moment to pray for help and I've maintained that close relationship with God ever since. He has definitely led me out of the Valley of Darkness.

I make my way on to the clinic and my full schedule. *I have to get better. There are so many depending on me.* I realized then that the will to live has a lot to do with how you think. It has everything to do with healing yourself and/or staying healthy. I've seen what the will to live can accomplish many times in my practice. Animals don't seem to play the same mind games that we do.

I know at the time of my own liver diagnosis, I totally played the part of the victim. I just followed along the path the doctors were leading me, even to the point that my sons were tested to see if they could be my liver donor. It never occurred to me that I might be able to get well on my own.

But, as soon as I changed the way I was thinking, almost instantly I started to get better and I've been improving ever since. It was a major lesson learned for me. That got me to thinking about animals who, when in critical shape, don't know it. Many times when I was trying to fix an animal and in my human way of thinking, thought it was hopeless, my patient suddenly got better.

When I got to the clinic I talked to Carol before I started my rounds. "Would you please pull some of the files where we had to euthanize dogs because of cancer. I want to review them and I'm going to get some books on pet food and see if we can find some answers."

"Sure thing," Carol turns to answer the ringing phone on the front desk.

My first patient was a prime example of just that. *Wild at Heart*, [4] (a non-profit sanctuary) brought a Red Tail Hawk with a broken humerus (wing) to the clinic for me to fix. He had already been through a couple of other surgeries and it didn't look good for him. It was bad enough to have to deal with the scarring from one surgery, but two was too much. And to top that off, it had

---

[4] Sam and Bob Fox. **Wild at Heart.** 31840 N. 45th St. Cave Creek, Arizona, 85331. (480-595-5047) Donations are tax deductible.

been at least two months since he had broken his wing.

I x-rayed him and could clearly see that the bone was fragmented to the point that it wasn't likely that I could help. I knew that trying to fix old fractures was a daunting task, especially where they've had two previous surgeries.

Sam is the name of the sweet lady who runs *Wild at Heart.* She is so dedicated and works tirelessly to save birds. She deserves all the accolades we can give her. I hated to give her bad news, but called to let her know that I wasn't real excited about trying to fix this particular bird because he was in such bad shape.

She mentioned that maybe we should put him down because he had already been through so much. I told her that I would at least re-evaluate his condition and then make my decision.

When I opened the box, the hawk's head popped right out. He was bright and alert. There was no sign that he had ever been through anything. He just wanted to get on with life. It was easy to tell that this bird wanted to live. As I looked more closely into his eyes, I could see his determination. It's hard to explain, but I knew that this bird was going to make it one way or the other.

After seeing him, I really didn't have a choice. I had to try. The surgery was difficult, but I did get things together well enough to give him a chance to live. But, when he returned four weeks later, he was not healing well. As much as I wanted to give up, the look in that bird's eyes would not let me quit.

So, I took him back to surgery and readjusted the pieces of bones and applied an external fixation apparatus to hold his bone together. It worked pretty well because he was able to use the wing now. I felt good about the surgery and told Sam that I wanted to see him again in four weeks.

Once again, I was extremely disappointed when the follow-up x-rays revealed that he had not healed well enough. Sam and I were both ready to just give up because we had done everything possible for this hawk.

I opened the box and out came that vibrant bird. Even after all his surgeries, nothing had slowed him down. He was just as active as ever and bright eyed and bushy tailed. When his head popped out he seemed to say, "What's up Doc?"

I looked into those unbelievable eyes and somehow I just knew he'd make it. I once again anaesthetized him and this time I decided to go for broke. I knew it was my last try. I opened the wing up the total length of his bone. I found pieces of dead bone I hadn't seen in my prior surgeries.

I removed the dead pieces of bone and broke down as much of the scar tissue as I possibly could. Then I realigned the living bone fragments and put on another external fixation device.

The hawk did so well with the external fixation device that Sam didn't bring him back for six weeks. When I put his carrying box on the table and opened it, out popped his head with that same look. I was afraid to get my hopes up and wondered if I was reading too much into his spunky behavior.

I anaesthetized him and x-rayed him and to my amazement, the bone was actually healing. In fact, it had healed enough that I could take off the external fixation device.

Sam took him home, but it was still pretty iffy. I talked to her about two weeks later and was braced for bad news. I said, "How's our Red Tail Hawk doing?"

Sam answered, "You won't believe it but he's out in the flight pen flying all over the place."

All I could think was, "That's my boy!" Now I knew he'd come far enough that he would make it. Nobody thought he would make it back to the wild, but he did. Sam released him with a mate a couple of months later. She checks on him from time to time and he's doing fantastic.

I'd like to take the credit for fixing him but as far as I'm concerned he willed himself well. I was just the instrument. We can all take a lesson from him. There was no hope, yet there was. Your will to live can transcend a doctor's diagnosis: just like mine.

That got me thinking about how important attitude really is. Through all my illness I now realized that my attitude had been really negative. If this hawk's attitude had been like that, I probably wouldn't have tried again. I began to see a light at the end of the tunnel, or at least a tiny glow which would lead me.

When I got home that night I could hardly wait to tell Karn about my day.

"Honey, you won't believe what happened today."

Karn looked at me in disbelief, but before she could say a word, I rambled on.

"I stopped at our old place – you know the one we like where we can see the lights of Phoenix at night. Well, I sat there thinking about everything that's happened and about my dad. I thought about what he might do if he were in my shoes right now. I know he wouldn't give up or wait for the end to come. He'd fight with everything he had." She grinned with that knowing side that I love so much about her.

"Then, a Red Tailed Hawk saved his own life. You know how?" I asked.

"No, tell me." She responded.

"He had a good attitude and somehow he told me he wanted to live."

Karn gives me that look like yeah – right.

"Really, it was his attitude that saved his life. Karn, don't you see, my attitude has been terrible and that has contributed to my not getting better."

I was on a roll and Karn knew she couldn't get a word in edgewise when I started so she positioned herself on the couch and pulled one leg up under her. She knew she was in for a long night, but her attention told me she didn't mind.

"I am not going to get a liver transplant. I am going to heal my own liver. You know I'm actually glad my sons were turned down as donors because the more I think about it, I've had sixty good years and I don't want to cause anything to prevent them from having their sixty or more. I can't believe I really ever considered them as donors. It just shows how scared I was."

Karn's eyes widened but she remained silent.

"I'm going to start reading everything I can get my hands on. I'm going to find the answers to my liver problems. I'm going to educate myself. Who else knows the symptoms and the pain as well as I do? Who has lived with it day in and day out? Who else is as interested?"

Karn smiled, "Well, if anyone can do it, Rick, you can. You are the most relentless man I've ever known when you get moving on something. I know you can do it and you know I'll help all I can."

We talked long into the night and the room took on the warm glow of hope. I moved over to the couch and put my arms around the woman who had never flinched and whom I knew I could depend on to help me as I embarked on my journey to find answers.

"You know what else?" I said as I held her close.

"What?"

"I'm going to find out why my patients are dying younger and younger and why I am seeing more cancer and other health problems." I set my jaw firmly.

She turned her face toward mine and whispered in my ear, "They're lucky to have you and so am I."

Sleep came more easily that night. I think it was because I had turned the corner and I had a different outlook. I had the will to live and it felt good.

Attitude is a critical part of your overall health.

Chapter 8

Beginning to think and read

My hunger for truth and knowledge urged me on and I began reading more and more. I was now down to 157 pounds and, even though taking all the supplements I could find, I was not feeling healthy. I not only had the stress of my own failing health, I had stress at work too. I sat in our living room, in the blanket of darkness and felt like my life was doomed.

Why is this happening to me? Why are my patients dying younger and younger? Why can't I find any answers? Why aren't the supplements helping either of us? Is there a connection to what I eat and my liver problem? Is there a connection between dog and cat food and their growing problems?

I rested my head in my hands trying to push away a mounting headache of fear and overwhelming questions. The inky blackness seemed to be closing in and pressing against me from all directions.

Just as the morning sun slowly started seeping into the room and shooting tiny rays of light here and there, I started thinking about Del Mar. My tortured mind eased a bit as I relived walking up and down the beach with Karn and a smile replaced the tight lips that had pulled my face downward.

"Good morning." Karn walked up behind the couch and put her arms around my neck.

"Morning," I answered, but I felt pretty deflated. "Honey, you know what? I'm not going to last long at the rate I'm going."

She held me tighter and I could hear her sniffing softly, but she remained silent. I know she was at the end of her rope too.

"I don't know what the answer is, but I want to spend what time I have left in a happier mode for both of us. None of the supplements I've tried have helped, so I think I'm going to stop all of them. And I know the stress is killing me off. I want to spend more time with you."

She gentled kissed my ear, "Me too."

"I can't just stop work because we still have kids in school, but I can slow down. What do you think about my only working every other week?"

"Really?" she perked up.

"I'm dead serious. How about we go to Del Mar and spend a week and think about it. We need to just get away and get a new perspective."

Karn jumped up and headed for the bedroom. I could hear her voice trailing behind her, "I'm already packing."

I think the decision to get away, just the two of us, for a full week was the pivotal point in my search for answers. We literally spent our time strolling up and down the beach. Sometimes we talked for hours on end and at times we just held hands and silently prayed for help.

I stopped the supplements and began watching everything I was eating. I became focused on healthy food, reduced my stress by exercising, and it dawned on me that I needed an attitude adjustment. When we came home after that week, I felt a thousand times better.

I worked another week and made the definite decision that I would only work every other week. I knew I would still work hard looking for the answers for my patients and that I would continue to do the surgery I loved, but I also knew that without my health, all of these activities would come to an end anyway. Healing my liver and feeling better had to be my number one goal.

I continued to read and consciously began eating a much better diet. I cut down on my fatty meat and began eating more fruits and vegetables and even salad. I had never been a salad eater before, but I noticed I felt better when I didn't eat as much meat. At that time I wasn't exactly sure why. One thing I did know was that I felt a lot better.

The week in Del Mar had really helped in many ways. I felt better and therefore I must have had a better attitude. I noticed Karn and those around me were smiling more and that felt good. I guess I had been pretty difficult to deal with. For the first time since this whole nightmare began, I had hope.

It was early morning before the clinic opened and I was at my desk reading through some articles I had gathered when Carol walked in.

"I've pulled a number of files where dogs have gotten cancer like you asked. I read through them and looked for any common denominator. There wasn't any particular breed affected and most of them had fairly normal records. They got their vaccinations as required and teeth cleaning etc. I did notice many of them had skin problems and that you referred a number of them to the allergy specialist. You have little notes about overweight or dandruff and so on. But I didn't see anything else that would throw up red flags."

I stare at the ceiling for a moment and then slowly a thought comes to me. "Carol, what were all of these dogs being fed?"

She thumbs back through the first couple of folders, "Hmm, let's see. Oh yeah, here it is: dry dog food. And this one: dry and canned dog food, this one dry food, this one doesn't say, and this one again dry dog food."

"I know we need to keep researching this, but you know we are what we eat and so are our pets. Maybe this dog food holds the key to some of the problems. I know my eating habits have changed and I am feeling better."

"I can tell and I am so happy about that." Carol smiles

"I remember when I started this practice; most of my clients fed their pets from the table. Pet food companies had already starting making some food, but I didn't jump on that band wagon until my medical journals and research began to recommend pet food over table food. They said that it contained exactly what the animals needed and was better for them. So I started recommending it. Now I just don't know. I do know I'm not going to take anyone else's word for it this time. I'm going to zero in on what my patients are eating and see if I can find any correlation myself."

"One thing is for sure, your problem and the pets' problems didn't happen overnight.

Things have evolved over a long span of time and it may take us a little while to unravel it all. But just tell me what you want me to do and I'll help." Carol turned toward the ringing phone.

My mind raced back and forth between my liver problem and the cancer problem in my patients. I kept thinking that diet had to have something to do with both conditions. It just made sense to me. I guess I never thought much about my liver and I bet most of you haven't either. That is as long as it is functioning normally. Why would we? But now I see that everything we put into our mouth has to be filtered through our liver. Why didn't I think of that before?

I began to talk to my clients about their pets' health. I started listening more carefully to their comments. I began to stop recommending supplements since they hadn't helped me. Carol kept combing through the files when she could and we began to wonder more and more about what my patients were eating.

Karn and I started going to the bookstore on a regular basis and I literally devoured books on nutrition, exercise and pet food. My search began to lead me to subjects like: hormones, Stilbesterol, rendering plants, cancer, liver diseases, positive thinking, nutrition and so many more.

I found an interesting article about hormones. Leticia M. Diaz, in her article: *Hormone Replacement Therapy, or Just eat more meat: The technological hare vs. the regulatory tortoise,* stated: "We are a society advancing towards undetermined levels of technological sophistication. As we enter the new millennium, we bring a wealth of highly advanced biotechnology, allowing the synthesis of chemicals and hormones which are designed to kill or alter living organisms. Unfortunately, we as humans fall into the definition of 'living organisms.'" [5]

"Women continue to be prescribed hormones throughout their lives for birth control, regulating menses, and combating pre-menopausal and post-menopausal symptoms. Similarly, the Food and Drug Administration (FDA) continues to approve hormone use for livestock. Is there a correlation between the two, or is it a mere coincidence that women who eat meat and dairy products have more problems regulating their hormones and general health than women who eat a tofu dinner." [6]

---

[5] Leticia M. Diaz. *Hormone replacement therapy, or just eat more meat: the technological hare vs. the regulatory tortoise.* October 18, 2007.

[6] See generally Norine Dworkin, *22 Reasons to Go Vegetarian Right Now: Benefits of Vegetarian Diet. Vegetarian Times.* April 1, 1999. page 90.

"Livestock producers inject or feed hormones to their animals to increase weight and the efficiency of feed use." [7]

"But this efficiency does not come without risk. The issue to be evaluated is who bears this risk. Are women ingesting excess hormones through their food? If so, should the FDA continue to approve hormone use or should it follow Europe's lead in banning beef treated with hormones?" [8]

"Despite continued debate regarding the safety of the hormones, the FDA has determined that residue levels of the hormones found in food are safe and are below levels that pose health risks to humans. On the other hand, the European Union (EU) issued an extensive report concluding that at least one of the six growth hormones contained in U.S. beef exports causes cancer." [9]

"In 1999, an official EU scientific panel released a comprehensive report which confirmed that at least one of the six growth hormones contained in U.S. beef products, which are now

---

[7] ibid
[8] See Food & Drug Administration Center for Veterinary Medicine, *The Use of Hormones for Growth Promotion in Food Producing Animals.* (May 1996)
[9] See Food & Drug Administration Center for Veterinary Medicine, *The Use of Hormones for Growth Promotion in Food Producing Animals.* (May 1996)

banned in the EU, conclusively causes cancer." [10]
The EU panel further stated that all of the banned
hormones are thought to cause a variety of health
problems or diseases, including cancer, develop
mental problems, immunological breakdown,
brain disease, and others.

"These growth hormones are also known to
cause dangerous estrogenic effects that have been
calculated to be about 10,000 times higher than
some banned pesticides." [11]

"….the highest rates of breast cancer were
observed in North America, where hormone-
treated meat consumption is the highest in the
world…..natural does not mean safe…..the EU
ban is thus well grounded in science and policy
concerns about the health of Europeans, rather
than on economic or profiteering motives." [12]

"….although she asserted that hormones
are cleared from an animal prior to slaughter, she
conceded that the levels of the residues in the
meat are not monitored." [13]

"Due to the abundance of estrogen from
our environment, women may develop what is

---

[10] Ronnie Cummins & Ben Lilliston, *Beef Hormones, Irradiation, &
Mad Deer: American's Food Safety Crisis Continues,* Center for
Food Safety News # 19)formerly Food Bytes) June 4, 1999.
[11] Leticia M. Diaz, *Hormone Replacement Therapy, or Just Eat More
Meat: The Technological Hare vs. The Regulatory tortoise.* Oct. 18,
2007.
[12] ibid
[13] ibid

termed 'estrogen dominance,' a particularly difficult syndrome to treat." [14]

After I read the article, I realized the significance of hormones in human problems, but what about the beef ears that are injected with hormone pellets? If they are cut off before the meat goes for human consumption, then they are probably sent to rendering plants where they become pet food. If hormones can cause cancer in humans, then it can cause cancer in animals too.

My reading took me all over the place from diets and health issues for humans to dogs and cats. I read about attitudes, as well, like in the following books:

The Secret by Rhonda Byrne was one and it really made me think how negative thinking is so harmful. After reading it I knew that I needed to do a better job of guarding what I was thinking to give my body a chance to heal itself. It is the power of positive thinking and it really does work. It is actually a conscious effort that we must make for ourselves and in that is the magic.

Another book that caught my eye was *The Maker's Diet* by Jordan S. Rubin and I began to look more and more into healthy eating for not only people, but animals as well. More than anything else, these books made me think and ask

[14] Lee & Hopkins, supra note 5: see Sherrill Sellman, *Hormone Heresy, Estrogen's Deadly Truth*, part 1, <u>Nexus Mag.</u> June-July 1996.

uncomfortable questions both of myself and others. None of them had all the answers and I didn't even agree with everything in them, but doors were unlocked and cobwebs torn away in my mind, which had been stale much too long. The more I read, the more I wanted to read.

Everyday Greatness by Stephen R. Covey became one of my treasures. I found if I read a little in the morning, it put me in a more positive mode and set my day up for success. I never realized how much life had been living me instead of me living it. I began to practice positive thinking and it worked.

I have to mention my all time favorite author: James Herriot. I have loved his books all my life. Just a few months ago, one of his stories came to mind and helped me with a goat. I'd like to share this story with you.

I've always had a fascination for babies. My favorites were baby birds, as you already know, but I love all babies. Count down was my first baby colt and I spent hours playing with him and training him. I absolutely adored him.

Throughout my life, if I could deliver a baby I would go out of my way to be there. A few months ago, a client, Amy, called me because she had a pigmy goat that couldn't have her babies. I told her I couldn't go out to her place, but if she brought the goat to the clinic I would see what I could do.

It was kind of fun because my son, Mike, was home from veterinary school and I knew it would be a good learning experience for both of us. So when Amy arrived with the goat, I could see it was in a lot of trouble.

Goats usually have two babies, but at this point I couldn't tell exactly what was going on or how many she was carrying. All I could see was that there was a baby in her pelvic inlet that couldn't get out. There were two front feet presented, but the head was turned back.

That's where James Herriot's, *All Creatures Great and Small,* came to mind. I remembered several times in the book what he had done to fix such a problem. I've always devoured his work because from my youth I had dreamed of working with large animals. Obviously you know my story and the fact that it didn't happen, but at that time I could read his work and dream. Sometimes I think the dream is even better than the reality.

Well, I proceeded to take care of the goat's problem just the way James would have done. I pushed the baby back away from the pelvis so I could straighten its head out. Once I accomplished that, I proceeded to try to pull it out, but it was just too big.

Obviously this was not a good experience for the mother and she was very uncomfortable, so I decided to anaesthetize her. I hadn't anaesthetized a goat before, but I had done a baby horse, so thought it couldn't be that different.

Don't forget that I was trying to help a goat at a small animal clinic which was for cats and dogs. All I really had was gas anesthetic and all I could do was mask induce the goat. As I said, I had done it to a baby colt that had a laceration on his face and it went well, so I decided the goat would do well too.

She did so well that I was mad at myself for not doing it sooner because she didn't need to experience all the pain of my having to move her baby about inside her. She hung in there and dealt with the pain, but I only wished I had thought of anesthesia sooner.

Once she was anaesthetized, my son, Mike, and I were trying to decide on which side to open her up. I had never done a C-section on a farm animal before, but I knew it was different than a dog or cat because you have to open a goat's side instead of her ventral abdomen.

The best part was that I was actually living a dream. Some of my dream about working with different animals was coming true as I worked to help this goat. Since Mike had just taken an anatomy class, I turned to him and asked on which side the uterus was most accessible. Now, I don't remember which side he said, but whatever it was, we clipped her hair and did a surgical scrub.

I knew the baby goat presented at the inlet was dead because when I first checked, there was no movement. I had to get him out so I could see if there was another one inside, or it would die too. Most goats have twins so I was hoping there would be one live baby still in her.

I made my incision and located the uterus. I found the dead baby and removed it. It was obvious that it had been dead a long time. It didn't feel good to pull out a dead baby and it was a boy.

I searched around to see if there was another baby. When I searched a little further down the uterus, out popped the cutest nose you've ever seen and it was moving. I said to myself: Oh thank you God. Mama was going to have a live baby. Now that was more like it. It's hard to beat the feeling I had at that moment.

When we had the live baby out, we found it was a bouncing baby girl. Mike took care of the baby while I sewed up the mama. She did extremely well and was relieved to be out of pain, I'm sure.

Amy couldn't have been more grateful and she left with her mama goat and the new baby. I checked on her later to make sure everything was okay and she assured me that everything was just fine.

A few days later, I heard that the mama goat never took to the baby, but Amy did. Since

mama wouldn't nurse the baby, Amy went to the feed store and bought goat milk replacement and was having a wonderful time feeding the baby. I've been fortunate enough to know how much fun that is because I've raised two lambs and a baby deer the same way.

I've often thought if the mother hadn't gone through so much pain, she probably would have taken to her baby. I really don't know how long she was in labor before she arrived at my clinic. I do know it was quite a while because Amy had called all of the large animal veterinarians and couldn't find anybody to help her. I was her last ditch effort and thank goodness, because of James Herriot, I was able to help her.

It all turned out okay in the end because the mama goat was out in the barn enjoying her food and freedom and the baby was inside Amy's house, enjoying the amenities of living life inside. For all I know she is still inside, because it's pretty hard to kick one out once they've grown up inside with you.

My friends, the Westmans, raised a baby antelope the same way. She lived inside until she died and she lived to be a ripe old age and they loved her like one of their own children. I had the same experience with a baby deer, Thumper. I'm sure that Amy's baby goat thought it was human too. As long as they don't look in a mirror, they don't realize they are different.

All I know is that when it came to babies, I had a blast and I still do. What's there not to love about a baby? I get my biggest kick out of watching my wife Karn. She's a natural born mother. She gives so much attention and love. Her heart is as soft and loving as it gets. We all love you Karn. Thanks for caring so much.

Love and caring is a big part of staying healthy too. It bolsters the immune system and I think it's a critical part of wanting to live. I think, if you give up the will to live, you will soon die. If you have people around you that you love and care for, and they feel the same for you, why wouldn't you thrive? Most people by them-selves, with no one to love or to love them, seem to end up with some sort of illness.

They get so wrapped up in their misery that they can't find their way out. They do very little to improve their health. Outwardly and inwardly they fall apart. How is it that people who have lost a loving spouse, often die that same year? We hear these stories all the time.

We all need to love and be loved. That is why many old folks' homes have decided to let the elderly keep their pets with them. It has been proven that people live happier- healthier and longer lives when they have the love of their animals.

It was common, in the past, for an elderly person to be placed in a care home and the beloved pet taken from him or her. I can't think of a worse thing to do to someone and at a time when they have nothing else. To deprive them of this love and bond is unspeakable.

On the other hand, I get to witness just the opposite when people come into my clinic. They can be young or old, but they all have this unconditional devotion to their pet. I can see the happiness and love in their eyes. I've seen dogs who would not take their eyes off their owners, because they were so bonded to them.

There's so much mutual benefit that comes from this type of relationship. It bolsters the immune system of all involved. It bolsters mine too, just watching the joy. So if you have a friend who is lonely and unhappy and whose health is failing, you might want to think about getting him a friend. It may take a few weeks, but you'll see a change for the better.

What have you got to lose? They are miserable already, so what could possibly make that any worse? At least this way, there is a chance that things will get better when they have companionship.

I had a friend who lost his loving companion, Toby. He went into a terrible depression for at least a year, and nothing could cheer him up. At seventy-two years of age, after his loss, he felt like his life was over and started acting that way too. He told everyone that he never wanted another dog and that he just wanted to be left alone.

This behavior went on long enough and I finally couldn't stand it, so bought him a new puppy. When I gave it to him, I didn't care whether he was pleased with me or not. The results were unbelievable. I could literally see him come out of his self induced shell.

Within a few weeks, he was back to his happy self with plenty to live for. It felt so good to watch his transformation and all because of this new bundle of joy, Binji. This old man lived another twelve years and Binji helped make those good years for him.

Binji is now living with the gentleman's widow and I am sure helping her cope with her husband's death. There is no doubt that her life is now being enriched by this loving creature.

This will sound kind of funny, but animals go through bouts of depression when they lose someone too. It could be a life long friend or even a litter mate. Sometimes they get over it rather quickly, but some animals have a very difficult time. So it is also important to find them a new owner or friend to fill the void.

Many times, I've recommended that people get another pet for their dog or cat. The feedback has been really positive that the troubled animal pulled out of the depression it was in and returned to its active, happy self again. I think every living creature needs companionship.

You know my interest in race horses, and they fall into the same category when it comes to needs. Do you remember John Henry? He was one of the most famous race horses ever, but he didn't do well when he was by himself. At such times, he would be very unhappy and difficult to work with. It was clear to his trainer and owner that he needed companionship. They got him a goat and like many horses, he fell in love with it, and his attitude improved immensely.

You know, I don't think anything exists for long without love. It's been my wife's love that has allowed me to flourish. My work, my writing, and everything around me is so much better because of her. Everyone around her feels the same way. I am convinced that she has played a major part in my healing process.

For all creatures, if love's not present, what's the point in going on? How well you're doing internally, depends on love and that is reflected outwardly to others. If you think love is not important, then try to live without it and I think you'll get the point. **Love Matters.**

Listening is a part of love and everyone needs someone to listen to them. It may not solve their problem, but listening provides comfort and often helps the individual deal with their own problem or to at least think about it from a different angle.

A good example of how listening really works happened at the clinic. As I approached the front desk, I noticed one of my clients standing at the counter waiting to be helped by the receptionist.

I could tell that she was not very happy, so I decided to say something to see what the problem was. In my business I knew it could be just about anything such as: a sick pet, a bad day, someone got up on the wrong side of the bed, illness, etc. I didn't know what her particular problem was, but I knew there was something wrong.

So, I walked up with a smile on my face and said, "How are you today?"

She scrunched her face and answered, "Not very well."

"What's the problem, Sally?" I asked. Sally had been a client of mine for a long time so I felt comfortable delving into her life and I could tell she needed to talk to someone.

Often, people have an amazing confidence in their veterinarian and I've been told before that it was easier to talk to me than to their own doctor. I honestly believe it is because I do take time to listen. I haven't always taken the time, but my illness has taught me a lot and when I listen to others, it helps me too.

Every now and then, someone carries it too far because they begin to think I can fix anything. I got a call from one of my clients who wanted me to look at her cousin who had a long term illness. She just knew I could fix it and she said she'd be happy to pay me. She added that her cousin healed just like an animal.

I couldn't believe my ears, but realized that she was dead serious. I told her that I appreciated her confidence, but that she was taking it a little too far and that I was a veterinarian, not a human doctor so I couldn't help her cousin.

My thoughts turned back to Sally who explained that she was very concerned about her health. I really didn't have the time to spare right then, but knew it was important to her. And I have learned over the years that if you always wait until you have the time for something, it never gets done.

After we got into the examining room, she proceeded to tell me that she had reoccurring headaches for no good reason. She said that her doctor had decided to do an MRI and a CAT scan and had found a brain cyst.

By the way she was acting and talking, I could tell that it seemed almost like a death sentence to her. I began thinking of how people play into their diagnosis. She obviously felt that she was in a life and death situation and focusing on the worst scenario. I know I had done the same thing when my illness had been diagnosed.

I tried to console her, but also wanted to give her a different perspective on her problem. I began by saying, "Watch out how much you play into the diagnosis. A cyst is not a tumor. It may be something new or it just may be something that's been there for years. It may be growing or it may be stationary. Sally, until you have further information, I wouldn't allow it to drag you down."

I went on to tell her that there were lots of things that could cause headaches, like: personal relationships, jobs, your focus, and overall stress. "Sally, everyone's been there and maybe this isn't as bad as you're thinking. I like the saying: If you don't like the way you're feeling, change the way you're thinking."

As she looked at me, I could see the strain starting to go out of her face. I didn't know if it was a result of what I was saying or just the fact that someone had been willing to simply listen to her, but at this point, she sat down in a more relaxed position.

"Did the doctor say if he could drain the cyst?" I asked.

"Yes, he did say he could do that." As she answered, I think she began to think that maybe it wasn't so life threatening anymore. She became quiet for a short time and it appeared as though she was running different options through her mind.

I thought that if she could change her way of thinking, that she had a chance of getting well. I also noticed that there seemed to be more that was troubling her, but I didn't want to pry into her personal life so didn't ask. I figured she would tell me if she wanted me to know.

I don't know how much I helped her, but I did help her because she left the office much more relaxed and she had a smile on her face. Some of her burden must have been lifted. Maybe she just had a different point of view or now saw options that she hadn't considered before.

As I watched her walk out, the thought occurred to me that with the advances in medicine, a cyst could probably be taken care of, even if it had to be drained on a regular basis. She might have even been born with it. I hoped she would be able to keep a good attitude while dealing with her situation.

It was an interesting day because not only did Sally come in, but Terry followed and told me that she had a malignant breast tumor. I was surprised at the difference between the two ladies. Sally had been so depressed and yet Terry was so upbeat.

Terry had put her problem into the overall perception of life. She has a wonderful family and she was very close to God. She expressed that she had a close relationship with our Blessed Virgin Mother, Mary.

She was such a joy to talk to. She reviewed how they wanted to cut the lump out; put her on chemotherapy and have her undergo radiation therapy. She wanted to talk as much as Sally had, but it was in a totally different mode.

If you asked me which of the ladies was going to do the best, Sally with the brain cyst or Terry with a malignant breast tumor, I'd say Terry had the best chance because of her attitude. I've learned that has a lot to do with how successful a treatment can be.

Sally may not have a life threatening condition at all, but because of her perception and the way her body responds to it, it will become life threatening if she doesn't change her way of thinking.

The cyst will probably never kill her, but her attitude will. Your body obliges you in every way and if you continually tell it is dying, it will. In Sally's case, it might not have anything to do with the cyst, but her mind set might cause her body to develop a more life threatening condition. Often it is cancer or some other immune mediated problem.

Your immune system is very responsive and listens to your every vibration. If you eat, think and act like you're going to die, you probably will. People will themselves to death all the time. Look at the cases where someone has lost a long time spouse who dies and in a few short months the other dies as well. They give up their will to live and that kind of thinking is powerful.

Sally doesn't realize how she's playing into the diagnosis, but she is and it's slowly but surely taking her down. Terry, on the other hand is behaving in just the opposite way and she is the one who definitely has a life threatening cancer. But her focus is clearly on living and it is helping her. Terry is healthy and ready to go to war with her cancer. She is bound and determined not to let her breast cancer take her life.

I couldn't believe how upbeat she was when she came in. Her eyes bright and her smile warm. It was fun and comfortable to be around her. She gave me a lift when she explained how she'd looked into all her options and figured her best line of attack. She told me that she had listened to what her doctors had told her, but she had decided that she would be the one to decide how she wanted to treat her condition. She was in charge and had everything mapped out in her head and felt good about it.

The doctors had wanted to remove the lump, but she had decided that the whole breast had to go. She thought it was the best and most thorough course of action. She worked at a hospital where women were fitted with artificial breasts, following complete mastectomies. She could see how these women dealt with it.

Her knowledge in the area gave her courage and the understanding that her diagnosis wasn't a death sentence. She had worked with many other women who had been cured, so she had great hope. For her, it was a matter of the best way to deal with it.

She decided to have the total mastectomy and the reginal lymph node (the lymph node closest to the breast) removed as well. She had decided not to have any radiation therapy because she had seen how the radiation pellets had burned through the skin on many occasions. She had watched the pain these women had gone through.

She was still contemplating chemotherapy, but needed to look into the side affects further before making a final decision. She knew that the doctors hadn't found a huge, gross obnoxious tumor in her breast. They had only found a few cells.

Do you suppose the medical world over-reacts to cancer diagnoses? They seem to be more interested in protecting themselves. The doctors didn't create this situation, but they still have to work within the flawed system and it is essential for their own future in medicine, that they do everything possible not to get sued.

I bet the doctors found it refreshing when Terry took control over her own cancer treatment. They might have even been thinking that radiation, in her case, was overdoing it, but they still recommended it to her to be sure that they were doing everything possible. If it happened to come back, they would be in trouble. So it seems that doctors opt for overkill, not for the patient's sake, but for their own sake.

In Terry's case, the cancer was found very early on and the use of chemotherapy might have been questionable, but the use of radiation was even more questionable. I often wonder if in the future that they won't find that radiation is more detrimental than helpful. I especially have a problem with the pain they go through. To put someone through the pain of that sort of treatment, unless it is absolutely necessary, is a crime.

I watched my dad go through radiation treatment and I guarantee you that he would never do it again and it didn't save his life either. I believe patients need to be involved in the decisions that affect them so much, and I put my faith in Terry, herself. She will be the reason she survives this cancer.

I love the power of the spirit because it is the most healing trait that we have. If we feel like losers, we will be, but if we feel like winners, we are. Be careful what you think and focus on because that's what you're going to get.

I just read an article where doctors did everything to heal a cancer patient. They did surgery, chemotherapy, and radiation (twice), but the person died anyway. I know you've heard about cases too where people will their cancer away and did survive.

Kris Carr said it just right, "Cancer needed a makeover and I was just the gal to do it." [15] Her attitude and candid revelations, personal stories and useful resources are now inspiring and empowering women diagnosed with this disease.

I think it is more important how you live, not the length of your stay on this earth. I discovered that my own attitude either helped or hindered my own healing process. If I focused on my own plight, I became weak and would itch all the time, especially at night because I think I had more time then to think about it.

I try to keep busy by writing, helping people and animals. It gives me new direction and my strength improves and my itching actually stops. It has also become easy to listen, when I didn't before. I look forward to my work day and I enjoy it tremendously. I get so busy that I focus on my work and don't have time to even think about my illness.

---

[15] Kris Carr. <u>Crazy Sexy Cancer Tips.</u> Skirt, an imprint of the Globe Pequot Press. 2007.

Do you know how good it feels to fix a broken bone or fenestrate a disc so a dog or cat can walk again? I do. As I help them, I help myself as well. My life is full, no matter how long or short it is going to be.

I haven't reached Terry's level of determination yet, but I'm going to keep striving for just that. Maybe I can help others, like Sally, to get there as well. Life is whatever we perceive it to be. So guard your thoughts, be careful what you think because your mind is strong enough to give it to you.

Another good point to all of this talk about attitude is how a person with a positive outlook on life appears young and healthy. Just a smile can erase ten years. While people who are unhappy always look old and sickly.

If you want good things to happen, have good thoughts and remember you're only limited by your imagination.

Chapter 9

Things aren't always what they seem

I knew I was facing the biggest challenge in my life. I also knew I had gone to many doctors for help and only one had been able to do anything for me. I decided to continue getting ERCPs done by Dr. Harrison when needed. But I also knew I had to find my own answers.

I began to visit the bookstore weekly and combed the aisles of books for the answers I knew had to be there. I was really surprised that very little was available on liver diseases. If I found a book, there would be only a few pages on the liver and that frustrated me. You know, we can't live without a liver so you would think there would be tons of information out there.

One day I was sitting at the table leafing through a medical book and I began to think. Everything we eat has to be filtered through our liver, so why didn't any of the doctors ever ask me about my diet?

I closed the book in my lap and sat back wondering why this thought had never occurred to me before. I was hit with the realization that we all go through life with blinders on. I mean we really don't think. If we're told something, especially from a doctor, we just accept it on blind faith.

I'm a veterinarian and I can tell you that I'm ashamed of myself that I never once thought to question the doctors about nutrition and how that affected my liver. Common sense would tell you that there has to be a correlation. Strangely enough no one ever brought it up to me either and that's scary.

Quickly I jumped up, placed the book back on the shelf and moved over to the supplement aisle. *If everything has to be filtered through the liver, then I need to look at what I can do to give my liver some help.* I soon had a stack of books on vitamins, minerals, liver detoxification, herbs, and trace elements.

When I got home, I piled them on the couch and started going through them. I was on a mission and soon had notes containing names of what I thought would help heal me. The pile of books soon were falling in disarray all over the floor and when Karn walked in, she just stepped over them and went about her business, but I can imagine what she must have been thinking.

I didn't even wait until the next day to go shopping. I grabbed my list and called to Karn and off we went to find everything we could that would put me back on the track to good health. I didn't care how much these supplements cost or how many I had to take. I was going to fix my problem. I bought Milk Thistle and Dandelion Weed because they were emphasized in the few articles I could find on the liver.

Once I went to a herbalist and would you believe I allowed her to inject me with something that I didn't have any idea about what it was or what it would do to me. Imagine that, me a doctor so desperate that I was trying any and everything I could grasp.

For a while I began to feel just a little better, so I downed handfuls of these so-called cures. But I was still not feeling really well and my energy level was growing weaker and weaker. I'd try things for months at a time and if I didn't see any signs of improvement, I'd stop and try something else. I was obsessed with finding a cure.

At the clinic I was diagnosing more and more cancer and was distressed with the pattern of early death among the creatures I had sworn to take care of. It began to add stress and I began to doubt my abilities as a veterinarian for the first time. It seemed that I had spent years studying to become a doctor and taking care of my own body, only to find out that much of it had been off track.

I came across a test where some rats were given Tylenol and it killed them all. So they repeated the test after first giving them Milk Thistle and then the Tylenol. Seventy-five percent of the rats were saved in the second test, thus it was assumed that the Milk Thistle protected them.

Well, I haven't seen a long- term usage study and I had trouble just accepting this correlation. I began to think more and more about supplements. My health was continuing to de-cline even though I was gulping down everything I could find. It dawned on me that maybe I wasn't going in the right direction.

Milk Thistle is supposed to be protective to your liver, but what happens if you use it for a long time? Maybe it does help some in the beginning or for short durations of time, but what happens after extended usage? Maybe it actually does just the opposite, so the more I thought about it, I stopped taking it.

It also got me thinking about how I used to take protein powder and all kinds of vitamins and minerals back when I was lifting weights. I remember the label saying: one serving supplies

100% of your daily requirements. At the time I thought if a little was good for me, then maybe a lot would be even better.

What a fool I've been, taking all that with the best of intentions but all along hurting my liver. I had never stopped to consider that everything had to be filtered through my liver and that mega doses only strained it more and more.

I thought I was improving my strength and stamina when I mixed protein powder with slim fast in a blender with eggs, yogurt, bananas and other fresh fruit. I could down that really fast and go back for more. All the time, I was lulled into the false sense that what I was doing was good for my body. I never once stopped to really think. Now I'm paying the price.

Back then everything had 100% of your daily requirements in it like: milk, yogurt, cereal, vitamins and the list went on and on. You know what I'm talking about. So basically I was not only overdoing the protein powder but I was also getting 800% of my daily vitamin requirements. I was also getting more vitamins and minerals through everything else I ate. Heaven only knows what percentage I had reached.

Vitamin A and D and the heavy metals such as copper and iron are proven to be toxic to your liver and here I had been overdosing in all these areas and at a dangerously high level. No wonder my liver is in trouble.

An example given in class while I was in veterinarian school came to my mind. The professor explained that a group of explorers in the Arctic killed Polar Bears for food. It was noted that eating the regular meat was good for them. But they were startled to find that those that ate the liver from the bears died of liver failure. That was because the Polar Bears have an uncanny ability to concentrate a very high level of vitamin A in their liver and that was toxic to the human liver.

My mind was still reeling from what I had discovered about supplements and humans when I walked into the clinic the next day. I have to say that after I kicked my brain into gear and actually started thinking about my own health, it carried over into my work.

So I went about my day watching and listening to my clients and how they described their pet's health. I was now looking through a new set of eyes and that allowed me to look at the entire **Early Death Syndrome** that had been pla-guing my patients now for years, in a much brighter light.

I stopped just prescribing pills and started asking myself: "*Why?*" Why were so many of the dogs and cats having so many problems? Skin problems were rampant and I was referring an-imals left and right to skin specialists. I had been doing that for years and just hadn't had the time to wonder why.

I began to think back, and when I started my practice I diagnosed cancer maybe once a month, and now I was diagnosing it several times a day on many days. The more I thought, the clearer the picture became. There was also a huge rise in Valley Fever and other immune disorders.

Speaking about Valley Fever, it comes to mind that things aren't always what they appear to be and there's always hope, even when you think there is none. The case that represents that thought so well took place on a really busy day when I hardly had time to catch my breath in between patients.

My examination rooms were all occupied, so I had to see Steve and his dog, Harley, in the surgery room. Steve looked really worried and explained that I was his last hope. He told me that he had come in for a second opinion because Harley had been diagnosed with lung cancer and that there was nothing more that could be done for him.

Most of the time, I thrive on this type of case, because often I find that I can do something. But since Harley had just come from a heart and lung specialist, I figured they knew a little more about it than I did.

Steve had brought the lung x-rays and I studied them carefully. I had to admit that the lungs didn't look very good and on top of that, Harley had pneumothorax (air around the lungs). It didn't look good to me.

I was not working on Harley's problem with a very positive attitude, because I knew the doctor that had just seen him. This doctor was the main man at the specialist veterinary hospital and I had a great deal of respect for him and his work. So I doubted that I could possibly have anymore to offer.

But, I proceeded to examine Harley and I noticed that he was having trouble breathing and considering the diagnosis of lung cancer, I wasn't surprised. At this point it was a reasonable assumption to put Harley to sleep, but I didn't bring the subject up because I could tell Steve was looking for some hope. I wanted to do everything I possibly could for this dog.

I remember being really busy that day and like most other doctors, I just wanted to get on with my job. But the look in Steve's eyes just wouldn't let me move too quickly. I began to look at this problem from every possible angle I could think of.

I thought maybe it could be a heart problem or that maybe he just had a hole in his lungs. Maybe it was as simple as an infection or maybe it was cancer just like the specialist had said. All I knew was that I couldn't just give up, so I spent another sixty minutes trying to find answers, even though I knew my waiting room was overflowing.

This is the part of my job I hate the most. I am trying to save this dog, but at the same time so many others are waiting and the people must be thinking what an inefficient clinic this must be.

I can see clients from morning until night and that doesn't bother me, but people having to wait and becoming irritated in the process, stresses me to no end. It literally turns my stomach inside out. This day was a perfect example of just that.

As I worked on Harley, an eighty-nine year old woman got tired of waiting after about an hour and she started yelling down the hall, "I got to go." She didn't just yell it once, but kept on yelling, "I got to go." Now that I think about it, maybe she had to go to the bathroom, that would have at least made sense, but no, she was just tired of waiting.

Have you ever noticed that older people become more impatient the older they get. They always seem to have some place to go and no time to get there. She continued yelling and finally I began to get irritated because it was hard for me to think. I was trying to help this dog and just couldn't concentrate with all the noise she was making. So when she yelled again, I stuck my head out of the door and yelled back, "Well Go!"

She shut up and I got back to work on Harley. It was still looking pretty hopeless and I was getting ready to tell Steve that I didn't think there was anything I could do, when an idea came to me. Isn't it strange how good ideas just seem to appear when you give yourself time to think and get a feel for the case.

"Steve, there is an option. It just might be Valley Fever because it mimics a lot of diseases, especially cancer. It is a 'look alike' for many things and it is really hard to tell the difference. Here in the Phoenix/Scottsdale area, we are at the hot spot for Valley Fever. It thrives in desert climates and the conditions here are perfect for the fungus to produce its spores."

I continued to explain, "The human body and animal body usually are both able to destroy the invasion, but sometimes it manages to cause serious damage if the immune system is compromised. The lungs are a primary target and often the patient ends up with pneumonia. This is al-most always the case in humans."

I pat Harley on the head and go on explaining. "It can go other places and in dogs often grows in bone and will mimic bone cancer. It can easily be misdiagnosed as cancer. I find that the best path to take is to look at the individual dog's history. Valley Fever is usually a disease of the young, while bone cancer is a disease of older animals."

Steve sat down in the chair and I continued, "It's not that cut and dried, however, and blood tests often give a false reading. If the blood work turns up positive for Valley Fever, we know what the problem is, but sometimes, the blood work doesn't reveal the Valley Fever until much later. It is natural for a veterinarian to diagnose bone cancer in such a situation."

I was really running all of this through my own mind trying to inspect all the possibilities as well as explain them to Steve. "It is sometimes difficult to prove Valley Fever, even with blood work and x-rays. In Harley's case, these x-rays you brought with you look like cancer and the blood tests have been negative for Valley Fever as well."

It still didn't look good, but at least I could think better without someone yelling down the hall, and I hadn't given up on Harley yet. After a little more thinking I told Steve, "We do have one option."

He perked up, because he was looking for any ray of hope of any kind. He really loved his dog and was willing to try anything that might help him.

"Harley *could* have Valley Fever, in spite of what the specialist has told you, based on his blood work and x-rays. It can't do any harm to start him on Valley Fever medication, but we have to keep him alive for at least eight weeks to give it a chance to work, that is if it is going to work."

Steve told me that he had no problem with that and thought it was worth a try and even when I told him that the medication was very expensive, he didn't care. He wanted to give it a try.

So we proceeded to treat Harley for Valley Fever and Steve checked in with me weekly. I was hoping and praying for a miracle and it did happen. It took the whole eight weeks, but Harley did pull through and finally even his blood work revealed that it was Valley Fever. Taking the time to search for answers and the willingness on Steve's part to try a long shot paid off and Harley is alive and well today.

Steve was connected with the Phoenix Hockey Team and when my brother-in-law, Doug, (a total hockey fan) wanted to meet Wayne Gretsky, it was no problem. When he came to visit, we were all treated to excellent seats at a hockey game and at the end we were taken to the locker room where Doug received a puck, a hockey stick, and an autographed picture with Wayne Gretsky. Doug has been flying high ever since and so has Harley.

Things aren't always what they seem. Even in our darkest hour, there can be hope, but only if you're looking for it. You must maintain an open mind and take time to use it. The greatest sin committed in medicine today is not taking the time to come up with a reasonable diagnosis after considering *all* the options, even if they seem hopeless.

Second opinions are also great and I love them. One of two things will happen when someone seeks more than one opinion: you will learn something new or you'll look good. I don't mind looking good, but I absolutely love to learn as well. It's been my forte for the last thirty-five years and why I am who I am today.

By the way, the eighty-nine year old lady who kept yelling down the hall did apologize. So did I for her long wait. She got one full hour of my time; in return, I got a big hug and kiss. She even added that she loved me. "Ditto," I replied.

During the time with her, besides answering her questions, I also asked a few myself. I am doing that more and more, especially with older clients because if they've made it to that age, they must have been doing something right. Even if she had been impatient, she wasn't stupid and she really did help me with my quest for better health, and the hug and kiss weren't bad either.

Things are not always like they appear. One morning Carol Taggart rushed into the clinic with her cat, Tiger. He was a very pretty, or should I say, handsome cat with bold, tiger stripes all over his body. It was easy to see how he got his name.

Knowing that history was critical for any diagnosis, I asked her what she knew about her cat's problem. She explained that her husband, Tag, (his nick-name) had gotten up that morning and found Tiger in severe respiratory distress. He couldn't even get comfortable by lying down because he couldn't breathe.

Tag was afraid that Tiger was going to suffocate, so he woke Carol up. They both realized that they had a serious emergency on their hands, and that it was critical that they get Tiger to a veterinary clinic as quickly as possible. Since her husband had to get to work, it was up to Carol.

She put Tiger on the front passenger seat and ran around to the driver's side and jumped in. She told me that she even broke the speed limit because she knew she was walking a tight rope between life and death for her beloved cat. She ran into the clinic screaming for help!

It was easy for me to see how much trouble Tiger was in and I knew what to do. I needed to know what was going wrong in his chest, so I placed a stethoscope on it and could barely hear his heart, but what I could hear sounded normal.

I did a stat x-ray of his chest and immediately prepped his chest just in case I needed to draw fluid out of it. The x-ray came out within two minutes and it clearly revealed that his chest was full of fluid.

I quickly started thinking about what could be causing his chest to fill up. What came to mind were: dog or cat fight, feline infectious peritonitis, heart failure, cancer etc. At this point, however, it didn't matter what had caused it, for now, I needed to get the fluid out before he suffocated.

I didn't want him to panic when I stuck the needle into his chest, because I knew that any added stress would for sure finish him off. But, he was in such distress, that he didn't even move when I stuck the catheter through his chest wall.

The amount of fluid that came rushing out was amazing. He was only a twelve pound cat and I literally pulled out 200 cc. The relief on his face was immediate and he could finally lie down and breathe normally. I don't think Tiger had realized how wonderful it was to be able to breathe until then.

The crisis was over, but now I needed to find out what had caused it and how to treat it. It was a whole new ball game. The fluid that I had drained out of his chest looked like milk. I had never seen that before and had never included such a thing in my differential diagnosis. But I knew what it was because I had studied about it in veterinary school. However, little did I know how difficult the treatment was going to be.

I referred back to my books trying to figure out what to do. The easy part was the diagnosis: Chylothorax, which happens when a duct, carrying chyle (which comes from fat digestion) ruptures into the chest. The chyle is supposed to dump into the circulatory system. It's the way fat gets into the body so it can be utilized for energy.

Every time Tiger ate a fatty meal, the fat was absorbed into his lymphatic ducts and dumped into his chest, instead of his circulatory system. The simple way to fix this problem is to tie off the ruptured ducts, but as it turned out, it wasn't that simple.

There are multiple lymphatic ducts running through the chest and it's difficult to figure out which one to tie off. At this point in my career, I had just been out of school for two years and there were no specialists, except maybe at a veterinary school. I knew on paper that surgery looked like a plausible cure, but in actuality it wasn't going to work, at least not by my hands. So I drained Tiger out completely and he was doing okay. I wasn't sure what the future held for him, but I knew I would probably have to eventually turn to surgery.

Carol took him home and he continued to do great, but I had to drain his chest every seven to ten days. This was not a great way to live, but

Tiger had no other choice and neither did I. This procedure went on for a couple of months and I was starting to get more than a little discouraged because it wasn't fun for Tiger and I couldn't see an end in sight.

It became old hat draining Tiger's chest, but I wasn't worried about infection because with chyle present, it was almost impossible for him to get an infection. I guess knowing this fact, I became a little careless and didn't do it as aseptically as I should have, but it seemed not to matter.

As it turned out, Tiger did get an infection and it didn't look good for him. I began kicking myself for being even a little careless and I knew that Tiger's end was near. He began running a high fever and didn't look good at all. I gave him the best antibiotic I had available. I rarely used Gentamycin because it can affect hearing and kidneys adversely, but at this point, I really had nothing to lose.

I felt somewhat responsible, but also knew that Tiger was destined for trouble because the draining of his chest couldn't go on indefinitely. I wanted to tell the Taggarts that they needed to quit because Tiger had been through enough, but because I had caused his infection, I felt that I had no right to bring that up. Besides, I could see that Carol wasn't even close to making such a decision.

I proceeded with daily injections of Gentamycin and started to pray. I wanted Tiger to get well and I didn't want to be the cause of his death. After five days, I could tell that Tiger was getting better. I was relieved that if he did die in the future, it wouldn't be because of my conceived carelessness.

I continued the injections for two more days and I knew I was pushing it because of possible side affects, but wanted to get him well. When Carol brought him in for his last shot, he was totally uncoordinated and I knew then that, in fact, I had pushed the antibiotic too long. It was now affecting his inner ear, which controlled his equilibrium.

I couldn't win and it was about time to drain his chest. At this time, I don't know if I was praying for him to get well or praying for Carol to give up. I was beginning to feel like Dr. Death.

Carol wasn't about to give up, so I did the only thing I could do and that was to stop the antibiotics and give him fluid. It was truly one of the low points in my career. I knew I had not caused his original problem, but now it seemed like I had caused the problem that was ultimately going to finish Tiger off after all.

I told Carol to take him home and to call me the next morning. I really only had one thing left to do and that was to pray, so I did and I was hoping for a miracle, but in my heart, I knew it wasn't going to happen. Why is it that even when you try so hard, things go so badly.

In my thoughts, I began to question if I was even much of a doctor. I think we all do this. When things are going badly, we trash ourselves totally. We don't "keep the faith." Maybe God's plan isn't exactly our plan. Maybe He's trying to show us something about ourselves. Maybe He's simply looking for us to have a little trust in him.

I hadn't completely given up on Tiger, but I was hanging by a thread. My only string left was trusting in God. He has come through for me so many times and I wondered if it was possible that it could happen just one more time.

I received a call from Carol early the next morning and I figured that it would be the day she would finally give up.

I asked, "How's Tiger doing?"

She responded, "A lot better."

I couldn't believe my ears.

"The dizziness and head tilt went away and Tiger is acting normal again." She said.

All I could say was, "Thank God."

Even though he was doing well, I truly expected to see him in the near future and that I would have to drain his chest again. I knew that if I did, I would be ultra-aseptic. I didn't know how long Carol would continue to hold out, but at least Tiger wasn't going to die because of something I had done.

The amazing thing is that the chyle never came back and Tiger actually lived to be a ripe old age with **no** ill affects from the disease or the treatment. It just goes to show that when you think things are totally hopeless, they're not.

The way I look at it is that God orchestrated the whole illness and now, when I get to the point of hopelessness, I remember that there is always hope. I've gotten there with my own illness and I have reached that point. When I do, I think of Tiger. Until our heart stops, there is always hope. Our perception of life and death are not always what they seem. I've learned that if it looks like a duck, quacks like a duck, and walks like a duck, **it's not always a duck.**

It's amazing what a change in perception can do for your health. Before, I saw myself dying and now I see myself living everyday to its fullest and I keep getting healthier. Our bodies listen, so be careful what you're telling yours.

I don't know how long I have to live, but I no longer think about it. I just enjoy each day that I have. I'm not caught up in my illness. Nobody can tell you how long you're going to live either. I didn't think Tiger had one more day and with my perception, he didn't have one more day.

I helped Tiger get through his illness and now he's helping me get through mine.

The easy way out is not always the best. Weather the storm because you have so much to live for. Life is good and it is worth sharing with our two legged and four legged friends. I am so happy that I've gone through what I've been through, because I do see the light and that light is a gift from God. Embrace it! God's light will never let you down.

On an interesting note, Tag was a doctor who specialized in treating cancer patients with radiation. He had done me a favor one time when I had a very special friend named, Alberta. She owned an Australian Shepard named Bud, (probably because she enjoyed a Budweiser from time to time.) Bud had a serious form of cancer of the mouth, Squamous Cell Carcinoma.

There wasn't much I could do about it because it was very advanced, so I called Tag and asked him if he would try radiation treatment. To my surprise, he said that he would. He lined me up to bring Bud into the treatment center once a week.

I would anaesthetize Bud and Tag would do the radiation treatment on his mouth. It worked fairly well and we were able to keep Bud alive for another year. Alberta was so grateful that she had us over to dinner all the time. She couldn't feed us enough.

I'm sad to say that Alberta died a few years later due to a similar oral cancer. She was one of the nicest, most thoughtful persons I've ever run into.

She would do anything for anyone or her dog. She had a heart of gold and I'll remember her to my dying day and look forward to seeing her on the other side. I figure God loved her enough to take her sooner rather than later.

Life wasn't easy for Alberta. She worked hard and cared hard for everyone. It really didn't matter who it was. I salute you Alberta!

Just to let you know what kind of person Alberta was, Herb Drinkwater had a tree planted across from the Scottsdale Convention Center, in her honor. Even after her life on this earth, her presence and influence are still with us all.

Another example of how things aren't always want they seem, is the following story about a very lucky cat named Sammy and how his life was totally turned around by two loving people and how that love was returned ten-fold.

Joyce and Jeanette stood in the examination room with a white cat that had serious ear problems. Both ears, at the tips, had squamous cell carcinoma. That's a very malignant form of skin cancer due to over exposure to the sun. It was an easy diagnosis.

The girls had found the cat in Mexico, along the beach. They could tell it was in terrible shape, but the cat wouldn't leave them alone, and it followed them everywhere. Cats are good at adopting people. They were vacationing and having a great time, but this cat, as bad as it looked, kept looking to them for food and affection and they responded accordingly.

When it came time for them to go home, they didn't know what to do about the cat. They had fallen in love with him, regardless of his terrible condition. It was so hard for them to leave him behind and he wasn't going to make it easy for them.

They were packing their car and they became more distraught by the minute. They knew that nobody was going to take care of this cat after they left. He was too big a mess for anyone to want him.

The girls knew that they couldn't get him across the US border without a health certificate, and they were certain, with his appearance, that they weren't about to get one from any veterinarian. So, they continued to pack and the cat kept stroking their legs and purring up a storm.   As they started to step into the car to leave, Jeanette looked at Joyce and said, "There's no way I'm leaving this cat behind."

"We can't get him across the border." Joyce answered.

"I know, but I'm going to try anyway." Jeanette said in a determined manner.

Becoming concerned, Joyce answered, "How are you going to do that?"

"I'll hide him in our beach bag. Joyce, we have to try. Please."

"Okay, Okay." Joyce sighed, and proceeded to help her with the plan.

As they drove off, they were both sweating and worrying about getting back across the border and thinking that they might even end up in a Mexican jail. As they drew nearer the gate, all kinds of thoughts raced through their minds as if they were trying to smuggle drugs instead of a cat.

As they approached the border, they put Sammy (they had named him) in the beach bag and covered him with a towel. They were praying that he wouldn't move or purr as Jeanette rolled down the window to speak with the border patrol officer. He asked if they were American citizens and wanted to see proof.

The girls had everything ready, so it would take less time to be processed. They handed him their passports and the officer glanced through the car, handed the papers back and waved them through. I can almost see the grins on their faces as they got a short ways down the road, knowing that they had made it. I am sure that they breathed a big sigh of relief.

They arrived in Scottsdale about five hours later, but it was too late, so they waited until the next morning to bring him to the clinic. That's where I enter the picture. I am sure that Sammy thinks he has died and gone to heaven and that life couldn't get any better than this. His life amounted to one boy cat and two good looking women who would respond to his every desire.

The problem was that Sammy was just like the rest of us. Just when he thought he had it made, he finds out that he has cancer. It can be a cruel world and if we had taken everything at face value, his days would have been numbered and we would have put him to sleep. That's pretty much what we would have done.

Sammy had obvious cancer of both ears. It was squamous cell caricinoma, which is one of the most malignant forms of skin cancer and it was fairly advanced. I was amazed that Jeanette and Joyce had even wanted to touch him, let alone take him home. It wasn't as bad as leprosy, but it was close.

As I explained the situation, I kept thinking what a shame it was to have brought him all this distance just to have to put him to sleep. I could tell Jeanette was especially upset because Sammy had already bonded to her and vice-versa. She was crying and hanging onto Sammy in such a way that I knew she wasn't going to let go. This definitely was not going to be easy.

The situation was no longer about a stray cat found on the beach. It was now the love of her life and she was going to fight to try and save him, no matter what. I looked at her and knew I had to try something, even though it looked hopeless. I really didn't know if it had spread to another location in his body or if I could cut the cancer out.

I suddenly realized that I was thinking that it was hopeless, and that I needed to change the way I was thinking. Otherwise Sammy would have no chance at all. I remembered the saying: "You're only limited by your imagination." Then I began to think about how I could cut the cancer out. It seemed like it was contained to the upper half of the ears. I'd never cropped a cat's ears before, but I thought: "Why not!"

I told Jeanette that there might be a way to save Sammy, but we'd have to cut off the upper halves of his ears. I'm ashamed to say, that I've cropped many a dog's ears for looks, but I've never cropped a cat's ears for health.

Jeanette was ecstatic to think there might be a way out, so we both decided surgery was the way to go. She signed the consent form and left with high hopes for Sammy. I was hoping it would all work out and that I wouldn't be putting Sammy through surgery and then still have to put him to sleep.

When I finished my morning appointments, I was confronted with cutting Sammy's ears off. It was amazing to me how both ears could be equally affected. As I thought about it, it was a blessing that they were, because if only one had been affected, Sammy would have ended up looking totally lopsided. This way I had to cut them equally.

I was thinking that Sammy was not going to look very good, but as I began drawing the cut lines, I could see that they just might look pretty cool. I thought he might look like a new breed of cat with a similar look to a Pit Bull. I figured that maybe Sammy wouldn't mind the tough guy look, especially because he had two good looking women to protect. By the time the surgery was done, I could tell that Sammy was going to look great. Jeanette and Joyce couldn't have been happier with the results.

The relationship between Jeanette and Sammy became stronger and stronger. Jeanette developed serious health problems where she could barely get around. She got to the point that she needed help even coming into the clinic, but Sammy never left her side. It was an unbelievably strong love affair between this Pit Bull Cat and this lovely young lady.

Their closeness lasted about ten years. It would have been even longer, except that Sammy was about eight years old when Jeanette rescued him from the beach in Mexico. Since that time, he has always been by her side and he helped her at a time that she felt abandoned by others. Joyce was there a lot, but Sammy was there all the time.

Jeanette came in with Sammy because he wasn't eating and he had started vomiting just clear water. I've always hated to hear that history concerning old cats, because it is always kidney failure. Sammy was no exception now. His kidney tests were off the charts and there was no alternative this time.

It absolutely crushed Jeanette when she heard the dreaded news. Luckily, Joyce was also there, because as Jeanette turned instantly pale and started falling, Joyce was able to catch her. She helped her sit down in a chair.

After about twenty minutes of getting used to the idea of having to let Sammy go, Jeanette decided she needed to let him go, rather than to let him suffer. She told me to do what I had to do, but that she had to be there through it all.

I told her it was right that she wanted to stay, because otherwise she would always wonder how Sammy had died and if he had cried or struggled, besides Sammy loved her presence. I've found that if the owners are not there, they always have a version in their heads of the worst possible scenario, instead of the actual peaceful slipping off to sleep that the animal experiences in this procedure.

We laid out a white fluffy blanket for Sammy. He deserved the best and we were going to give it to him. Jeanette was sitting in the chair and petting his head gently. He was purring up a storm and acted very content. Cats always seem to purr the most when they are the sickest.

I had the shot ready and could hear the music on the intercom. Normally I wouldn't notice it at all, but the words caught my attention. A song came on and I was frozen in position as I started giving the shot. I couldn't believe what I was hearing and I looked at Jeanette and I could tell that she was listening to the song too. The tears are welling up in her eyes and her emotions were totally overwhelmed by the beauty of the words. They described exactly what Sammy meant to her. All those years she could barely walk and Sammy was the one who put: *The Wind Beneath her Wings.* How was it that such an appropriate song came on just at that time? It was supernatural and the hair stood up on the back of my neck. I still can't believe it to this day.

From the very start to the very end, God had been there. He knew Jeanette deserved Sammy and that Sammy deserved Jeanette. He knew that she was going to need help to get through her illness and Sammy showed up in the strangest place and then even went through an even stranger surgery. It took all that for the bonding to occur and it did.

Jeanette is doing well today and has another Sammy, but she'll never forget her Pit Bull Cat friend, who pulled her through the toughest of times. Neither of us will ever forget that song. To this day, it is one of my favorite songs because whenever I hear it, it reminds me of how Sammy put the wind beneath Jeanette's wings. That was truly a relationship based on love.

You may have trouble believing in God, but I have no trouble whatsoever. God is truly there for all of us. Sometimes we don't understand why things happen, but later on we realize there was a reason. My liver problem didn't seem like a blessing, but the more I worked with it and as time passed, I could truly see that it has been a blessing.

I don't know what God has in store for me, but I'm going to run with it because I trust his wisdom and I'm starting to see where it is taking me. I have to say I like what I see and as Jack Nicholson said in the movie: AS GOOD AS IT GETS, "You make me a better man." This is what this illness has done for me. All I can say is that if you'll stay on the positive side of whatever happens to you, something good will come out of it. If you get lucky, something great might happen!

I have to say just one more thing to my wife, Karn: "You are the wind beneath my wings and just as God does; you make me a better man."

Along with cancer, allergy problems had become one of the most common illnesses. I was seeing on a daily basis. The poor animals would come in with an intense itch and that traumatized their skin to the point of bleeding. Their skin would become inflamed and ooze blood and serum. The devitalization allowed bacteria to grow and with the skin's immune system in disarray, the bacteria would have an easy time reproducing.

When clients would come in with this virtual mess, I would tell them not to worry that I could fix it easily. It just required a cortisone shot and some antibiotic pills. Initially that always worked like a charm and I looked like a miracle worker to them. But it wasn't uncommon for the animal to have some side affects from the shot.

The biggest problem the medication caused was that it made the animals drink and urinate a lot, but there was nothing else I could do. It seemed the shot was the better of the two evils, but it wasn't at all pleasant when it also caused the animal to urinate all over the house.

This type of treatment created enough problems for all dogs, but for male Dobermans, it was even worse. Many would often stand and try to urinate for a good ten minutes. It was a situation where I was darned if I did and darned if I didn't. I began thinking that there had to be some other treatment.

I would like to say that most dogs got well, but there were a large percentage that would have to come back for their monthly injections. The shot would usually last for only three weeks and the side affects were always present.

To add to that problem, after about a year of injections, the dogs would start looking pretty bad. Their hair coat would become very thin, if not bald and they would put on an exorbitant amount of weight.

I had begun referring many to a doggie dermatologist because I just wasn't getting the job done. After years of building a clientele, I was sometimes giving cortisone shots six to ten times a day and referring at least one a week to the dermatologist. I'm sure the dermatologist loved me.

I was really busy and no one could have worked harder than I, and my reputation reflected that. I worked especially hard at keeping people happy and as it turned out, I needed the cortisone shots to do just that.

It wasn't until I got sick myself and started reviewing where I had gone wrong, that things became much clearer. I hadn't been fixing any-thing. I had just been controlling the symptoms and the dermatologist had been trying to fix the problem by desensitizing the animal to whatever showed up on their allergy skin tests.

Sometimes that worked, but mostly the allergy would continue on and on and was a lifetime problem which needed treatment. There is an old saying: you want to be a dermatologist because your patients never die, but they never get well either.

As I started re-evaluating what I was doing and what they were doing, I also looked back on what I had been taught in veterinary school. At that time there weren't as many skin problems, thus there were very few animal dermatologist needed. I remember distinctly that there were two fields in which a veterinarian couldn't make a living and that was as a skin specialist and an oncologist.

Things had completely changed over the years and now I felt like I was walking through doors backwards and still I couldn't find the answers needed for the ever growing problems in cancer and allergies, among others.

Because of my own growing health problems, I started paying particular attention to what I was eating and I did see some improvement. So I decided to start paying attention to what the pets were eating. At first I was looking at holistic organic food and when people tried that for their pets, maybe things got a little better, but not much.

Then I started recommending this type of food in canned pet food instead of dry pet food. I did see a measurable improvement with that change. Initially I was only looking at weight loss, and that was dramatic when they changed.

Then I had people try feeding healthy people food to their pets, with no dog food at all. Things improved exponentially. The skin cases started getting better and the injections of cortisone fell off drastically. I was no longer giving it multiple times a day, and finally, I wasn't even giving any on some days.

Over the last 2 ½ years, I haven't had to give cortisone even weekly and on top of that, I haven't had to refer a single case to the dermatologist. He's probably even forgotten my name.

This breakthrough didn't happen overnight and I wasn't even looking at diet as a way to fix the skin problems. I literally stumbled onto the fact. It has worked so well that even many patients with skin problems, who came back to me from the dermatologist, could be healed by changing their diet. I have been able to fix them by stopping dog food and feeding only healthy people food.

Those of you (or your pets) who are on cortisone for your allergies might want to try a diet change, because with my experience, it is very likely to cure your problem. What do you have to lose? Also, cortisone shots are known to be detrimental to health.

I'm not looking for your business. I'm not going to make a dime if you switch, but it could very possibly save you thousands and your animal's health to boot.

Slowly as the answers became clear about skin conditions, I was still trying to find answers for the huge increase in cancer. I kept playing with the idea of diet and was beginning to find some help with eliminating dry pet food, but I was still recommending some canned.

I often talked with Carol about things and so I called her into my office. "Carol there is something strange going on."

"What?" she said.

I repeated, "There is something strange going on. You've been with me for twenty-five years now and you've seen the changes in the health of our patients I'm sure."

She nods her head and I continue, "Remember when dogs lived to be fifteen or even eighteen sometimes? And when they did die, it was from old age complications like kidney failure."

"You have a point there."

"Well, there have to be some common elements that are causing this rise in early death and disease." I shake my head.

"You're right, now that I think about it. What do you think it is?" Carol asks.

"I've been thinking about it a lot. You know all about my liver condition and how I've been looking for answers for myself. Well, I've come to the conclusion that everything we put in our mouths affects our health. And you know what? I think it is true for animals too. I think the common thread is diet."

That night, Karn slipped off to bed as I sat huddled beneath the table lamp just poring over article after article. My quest to find answers gave rise to a hidden strength.

The body works in micro quantities not mega quantities. What you think is healthy, may not be.

Chapter 10

God lends a helping hand

Your faith in God is a part of your health. It's a part of how you focus on yourself and the world around you. It has everything to do with how you treat yourself and everyone else, including your animal friends.

It's because I see God in you that I'm willing to do just about anything for you, including save your pet's life. When I see how much you care about your friend I'm not going to walk out of the room and turn my back on you because you can't afford to pay. I have performed many surgeries that I have never been paid for, but the look in someone's eyes has always been my reward.

You may wonder why I pray to God or even mention him in my story. Well, it's because

I know there's a God and that He is a focal point in our lives, whether we like it or not. As a youngster I was always looking for some proof that He existed. I wanted a sign, but it doesn't seem to be that simple. It's like He wants to see if we believe in Him first.

If I look back over my sixty-one years of life, I've had plenty of signs. Because of your love of animals, I'd like to share some stories with you:

A client came in with a dog, that was experiencing abdominal pain. He was depressed and not eating. I could tell that his abdomen bothered him, so I decided to x-ray him. When I looked at the x-ray, it was obvious that there was a sewing needle stuck in his liver.

The only way it could have gotten there was that he had obviously swallowed it and after it made its way to his stomach, the contractions shoved it through the gastric wall into his liver. The liver lies next to the stomach so that is a very reasonable assumption.

I showed the owners the x-ray and told them I'd have to do surgery to remove it. I explained that it was fairly cut and dried and that it definitely didn't seem like a big deal, even though I'd never seen this particular problem corrected before. I thought to myself how hard could it be?

We anaesthetized the animal and prepared him for surgery, while the concerned owners waited in the lobby, not about to leave until everything was finished and their pet was okay.

Well, the surgery was fairly simple because all I had to do was expose the liver and pull the needle out. I made my incision, exposed the liver and proceeded to look for the needle. Over an hour passed and I could not find it.

Knowing the couple was in the waiting room, I was beginning to dread the idea that I might have to tell them that I couldn't find it. Can you imagine after telling these people that it should be no big deal and then after one hour of surgery, have to walk in and tell them that I was sorry, but I couldn't find it.

I began to sweat profusely and I became dizzy and a little disoriented. I knew I couldn't close him up without finding the needle. I sat down and started to pray. I spent about five or ten minutes praying. I really don't remember exactly how long, but it was a reasonable amount of time.

I can't imagine what the surgical technician must have thought watching me. When I re-approached my surgical patient, I took a couple of deep breaths and I was still begging for some guidance from God. The next thing I knew was that my finger went straight to the needle and I pulled it out. I thanked God profusely and closed the dog up.

He made an uneventful recovery and I owed God one more time. I've had several experiences where He has helped me. So I no longer need a sign of his existence. I'm just so very thankful He is always there.

Another time when God came to my rescue was when I was in a terrible mess with a Doberman who came in with severe neck pain. He was extremely uncomfortable and would scream if you even touched his head.

He was seven years old, which is the perfect age for "wobblers" to show up. Wobblers is a condition where Dobermans get subluxation of their cervical vertebrae. Basically the joint between the two vertebrae is stretched out allowing the vertebrae to slip, which puts pressure on the spinal cord, thus putting pressure on the nerves that come from the spinal cord.

Needless to say, it was very painful and the worst thing is that it requires extensive surgery to even try and fix it and it isn't always successful. But, this dog was in so much pain that I decided I would x-ray him to establish the diagnosis. I had to anaesthetize him first, so I gave him a shot to knock him out and then I was going to carry him to the x-ray table.

The whole time I was thinking that I was in a whole lot of trouble for a lot of reasons. I knew these people were deeply religious and had a wonderful family. I knew they would do anything for their dog, but I also knew they couldn't afford the surgery. I normally would help them out anyway because in this kind of situation, I would do the surgery for nothing. To top it off, I'd never done this type of surgery before.

I knew at the neurological center they would charge $3,000 to $5,000 to do that surgery; that thought kept rolling through my mind. Apparently I had so much on my mind that I got careless. When I picked the dog up, I literally dropped him on his head. In thirty years of practice, that has never happened to me.

I can't tell you how embarrassed I was at that moment. There's no way I would do that. He wasn't too heavy and I was in great shape. It was like someone pulled him out of my arms.

Totally red faced, I picked him up and proceeded to carry him to x-ray. I left the owners behind with their mouths open and I'm sure they were just as shocked as I was. I took the x-rays and then read them. The whole time I was visibly shaken. The x-rays revealed what I thought, he had Wobbler's Disease.

Normally I wouldn't even take the x-rays because I pretty much know what's wrong and I refer the client to the neurologist. But this case was different because I knew they couldn't afford the specialist, so I wanted to see if I could help them out. What a mistake!

In the meantime, the dog is waking up and I'm talking to the owners. I am apologizing profusely and I'm praying like crazy that I didn't make the condition worse. *Oh God help me. I'm such an idiot!* The whole time the dog is coming too, I can hardly continue my job so I sit at my desk and pray.

He finally wakes up and he's not crying at all. I move his head and he doesn't cry. He doesn't act like anything bothers him. I'm totally shocked, but pleased. Later after they had taken the dog home, I called to see how he was doing and they said that he was doing great.

He never had another attack and he never needed surgery. It's hard to explain what exactly happened on that day, but the outcome had more to do with what God did than what I did.

A similar case where I was very clumsy and negligent was when a young lady came in with her Dachshund who also had neck problems. It was a similar story, but her problem was caused by different reasons. This Doxy had an obvious slipped disc in her neck and she was in excruciating pain and definitely needed surgery. This breed often has horrible neck and back problems.

I knew this dog needed surgery and I told the owner and she told me that she couldn't afford it. I looked at her and having been under a lot of stress myself, I felt horrible at that time. It was at the time when the doctors were deciding that I needed a liver transplant. I was not having a good day and I wanted to be home in bed. When she told me that she couldn't afford the surgery, I was almost relieved. Normally I would have gone ahead and done the surgery anyway, but I just felt too bad.

I did x-ray the dog and established that it was definitely a cervical disc herniation, which basically means that the disc between two cervical vertebrae has ruptured out and is putting pressure on the nerves leading to the neck and front legs.

Usually with a cervical rupture, you can fenestrate the disc, allowing the soft disc material to rupture and ooze downward away from the spinal cord. When it's a disc in their mid to lower back you have to decompress it, which means you have to cut the bone away from the spinal cord to take away the pressure. You create a slot that is 1/4" wide to 2 to 3 inches long. It's a very technical and time consuming surgery which can last up to three hours.

This was going to be a disc fenestration which takes less than an hour except I didn't feel good and she couldn't afford it. I looked for the easy way out and decided to give the dog a shock dose of dexamethasone, which should help the pain and buy me some time to feel better.

I went into the lab and reached for the bottle of injectable dexamethasone. A shock dose is 1 mg per 1 lb. The dog weighs about twelve pounds so I draw up 4 cc which is 8 mg of dexamethasone. I could go as high as 6 cc but I didn't want to overdo it. I also wanted to make sure it was enough to do the dog some good.

I walked back in and gave the shot I.V. After I gave the shot, the dog started twitching. I couldn't imagine what was going on because dexamethasone doesn't cause that. I ran back into the lab and looked at the bottle. It was not dex. It was equine Baytril-LA (large animal), which is a very strong antibiotic, and I had just given a 12 lb. dog the dose for a 500 pound horse and I had given it intravenously. I have honestly never had this happen to me before.

The two bottles looked very similar, so similar that I'd always told everyone to keep the bottle of equine Baytril-LA in the emergency kit so no one could get them confused. I never use that medication anyway. The other doctors I work with use it, but I don't.

I didn't know what to do. As far as I was concerned, I had just killed her dog. If I had only not been sick and been able to do the surgery, this wouldn't have happened. I figured my laziness had come back to haunt me. I've always said if there's a need, you do it now, because you never know for sure what tomorrow has in store for you. You could end up twice as busy.

Well, the dog starts to seizure and I ran back to get some valium. My world was collapsing around me. I gave him enough valium to control his seizures and then proceeded to tell the owner what I had just done. Now we're both in shock and I don't see anyway to save the dog, so I start to pray. *God, please help me one more time. I know it's asking too much and it's so hopeless.*

In the meantime Dr. Ketchmark decides to call the company that makes the Baytril-LA and see if there's any hope. I'm sure that it's hopeless because it was just too big a dose and I gave it intravenously. The biggest side affect, I thought, would be kidney failure so I figured there was no hope.

About the time I'm thinking that I needed to put this poor animal to sleep, Dr. Ketchmark pulled me aside and told me that the company said the antibiotic diffused into the tissues rapidly. When that happened the seizure would stop and there's a good chance the dog would be okay. I couldn't believe my ears. Could I really be that lucky?

It took about twenty minutes for the seizures to stop and they never came back. I told the owner what Dr. Ketchmark had said and told her there was hope, even though I was having trouble believing it myself.

I decided to check the dog's blood daily and then cut down to weekly. The kidney failure never happened and during this whole time I continued to pray just begging for a break. God answered my plea.

In the end, the dog's neck pain went away the moment I gave that shot and has never come back. She has been totally normal ever since. I figure I've got to be the luckiest man alive and I'm just glad I've got God on my side.

Another case where luck played a great part began one Sunday night around eight o'clock. I received a frantic call from the cement man, Ray, who had poured the footings for my new hay barn in Prescott.

While he tried to explain that his wife had parked his one-ton truck on top of his dog, I could hear him yelling for her to move the truck. The dog was still trapped under the tire as we were speaking. As the truck rolled off of the dog, he told me that the dog couldn't walk and wanted to know what he could do.

I knew he couldn't afford to go to the emergency clinic so I told him to bring his dog, Clyde, over to my place. When he arrived, it was obvious that the truck had flattened his pelvis out.

I treated Clyde for shock and put him on antibiotics. I had a small animal surgery room in my barn, but didn't have x-ray capabilities there. I told Ray if he was willing to take Clyde to Scottsdale that I would have my son, Mike, x-ray him so I could see what had been broken.

Ray left bright and early the next morning for Scottsdale and Mike was waiting at the clinic for him. After the x-rays were finished, Mike called to tell me that Clyde's pelvis was broken on the right and left side and that the main shafts were broken in several places. Both the right and left shafts were broken away from the back bone. On top of all of that the left hip was dislocated as well.

Basically it was going to be a very difficult fix. I had all the equipment needed for this type of surgery and I had fixed many broken pelvises and dislocated hips, but not to this extreme. In Clyde's case, his pelvis was literally destroyed.

I knew it would take a very long surgery and a lot of luck to piece this one back together. I wasn't real happy with the news so I had Mike put Ray on the phone and I proceeded to tell him how bad the situation was and that it was close to impossible to fix Clyde. I suggested that he might want to take him to an orthopedic surgeon, because they deal with these kinds of breaks more often than I do.

There was a long silence on the other end of the phone. I knew how important Clyde was to him and how they went everywhere together.

The ten year old dog was literally his side kick and constant companion. I listened, but still there was only silence on the line.

I knew Ray was very upset, so I said, "I'll tell you what, I'll try to fix him, but I can't make any guarantees." I knew money was a major part of his silence, so I told him that I'd charge him as little as possible, but that it would probably still be pretty expensive because of the seriousness of the injuries.

I could almost hear his relief as he thanked me and told me he wanted me to do the surgery. I explained that we couldn't start the surgery then, because it was already so late in the day and that if he brought him to my surgery room at my barn at eight the next morning, that I would do my best. I could hear his sigh of relief even over the phone.

The surgery room at my barn would rival any small animal surgery room. I used nothing but the best and I had a high quality surgery table and sevoflurane gas anesthesia, just like what is being used on people, in the hospitals today. I had built in a sophisticated venting system so the people in the room wouldn't breathe in the anesthetic, and the room was even air conditioned.

I talked to Mike again and instructed him to bring everything else that we needed for this very involved orthopedic surgery. I especially emphasized for him not to forget the bone plating and external fixation devices we had and also the air drill.

Mike pretty much already knew everything we needed because we have done surgery together many times. Mike is very adept at what he does, and the best surgical assistant I've ever been around. I'm a good surgeon and happy that Mike was already proficient way past his years at veterinary school.

Mike was in his third year of veterinary school and it brought a smile to my face just thinking that he probably knew almost as much as his teachers. I would have loved to have had that experience.

He knew all the latest orthopedic surgeries and could compression bone plate just about anything. He is very good at doing external fixation and he and I both went to Eugene, Oregon to learn the latest anterior cruciate repair, called a TPLO.

Mike had already assisted a doctor in Colorado many times while performing a TPLO and he even taught me how to do that surgery. I actually learned more from him than he did from me on this one. He is, in fact, the only veterinary student who is actually certified to do this special surgery.

Obviously, as his father, I am really proud of him. I love doing surgery with him because he is so meticulous and everything stays very sterile, and that in turn makes the surgery that much easier.

I felt that with Mike assisting me, we had a good chance of pulling this surgery off, but I also knew it wasn't going to be easy. We would need all the luck and prayers we could get to do it.

I told Mike not to forget the new toggle that I had just bought. It would be used to hold the hip in the joint. We had never used it, but I was hoping it would be just what we needed. Mike pulled up with all the materials and now we were just in need of an anesthesiologist. We couldn't do without this very important part of the team because if we couldn't keep the patient alive during the procedure, nothing else would matter.

Karn was willing, but I knew she would not be able to handle this because she was so emotionally involved with Clyde. I knew that I would have to continually reassure her that everything was fine throughout the surgery, and I had to focus on my own job that lay ahead.

Then Edie, our neighbor, popped into my mind. She was a hospital nurse who loved surgery, and when I called her, she jumped at the chance. Finally everyone arrived at the barn just before 8 a.m. We were anxious to get on with the surgery because we knew it was going to be a long day.

As I glanced at Edie, I could see how excited she was to get started. Shortly I induced Clyde with rapinovet, intravenously. I imagine Clyde was especially excited to have surgery because he had been in pain for two days and I knew that after the shot, he wouldn't feel a thing.

I intubated him and gave Edie all her instructions. I knew she could handle it and she didn't let me down. She didn't bother me the whole surgery and was quite the trooper, seeing that the procedure lasted from 8 a.m. to 4 p.m. Most people would have folded, but I think Edie could have gone another four hours.

Mike and I decided to fix the dislocated hip first. When we looked at the toggle, it seemed simple enough, but little did we know. It was new to us, but I've never backed away from any surgery. I had it in my head what I needed to do, and with Mike's expertise I hoped it would work.

The basic idea of the toggle works the same as hanging a picture. You drill a hole and then push the toggle through and it will pop open. With the picture, you have a hook on the end and with the hip toggle, a nylon cord similar to fishing line, with a metal bar on each end. In order to put the toggle in place, you drill a hole through the neck and head of the femur and at this point, you push the nylon line through the hole and then connect the line to a metal bar on the other side. That keeps the nylon from pulling back through the hole and that, in turn, keeps the hip in joint.

It seems simple enough, but believe me it wasn't. It took both of us to pull it off. If Mike hadn't been there, I wouldn't have been able to do it. After three hours and a lot of sweat, we got it in and it worked like a charm. Thank God.

Once we got the hip in joint, we had to turn to the broken pelvis. The truck had done a number on Clyde's pelvis and it was broken in many places. It was obvious that we couldn't bone plate it because it was in too many pieces.

I knew my only chance was external fixation. I needed to run two bone pins in each piece, align them up, and connect them to a rod outside the body. The metal rod on the outside would keep the pieces aligned and stable so they could heal.

Once again, it was a lot easier said than done. Mike and I meticulously aligned every-thing up and we used more connecting rods than was necessary because everything was so fragmented.

Four and one-half hours passed and we finally had it all together. Clyde looked like the bionic dog because he seemed to be carrying around five pounds of metal. I gave him antibiotics and pain shots and told Marcy to bring him back in the morning. Mike and I were exhausted, but we felt good because we had pulled it off.

All I can remember about Edie at this point was that she wanted a glass of wine. Karn and Edie went in the house and celebrated our success.

I saw Clyde the next day and he could actually stand and walk just a little, and he looked pretty good, all things considered. Ray and Marcy were dreading the bill. But the way I looked at it was, after our accomplishment I couldn't put a monetary value on it, so I said there was no charge.

Ray couldn't believe his ears and I could see the relief in his eyes. I'm sure at that moment he planned to rip up my bill for his cement work too because I waited for it a long time, but it never came.

Clyde was doing unbelievably well within only four short weeks. He was walking slowly, but he was walking. When they brought him back for his eight week checkup, I removed all the external fixation devices. Clyde had progressed beautifully except for his dislocated hip where the toggle seemed to be bothering him, but I figured it was because it was too tight and I needed to remove it to see if that was the problem.

The next step was to remove the toggle which was much easier than putting it in. It only took about twenty minutes and only involved a skin incision and cutting the nylon line.

I saw Clyde again a couple of weeks later and he had made a total recovery. His case proved there's a lot of luck involved in medicine. Clyde was lucky because he had an owner who loved him so much, and that he happened to be working in the right place at the right time.

We just happened to have the new toggle and Mike and I were lucky enough to pull off the surgery using it. As I think back now, Clyde could just have easily been paralyzed in his rear legs, due to nerve damage. Because of the extent of the damage, infection had been a real possibility as well.

This list could go on and on. What if Edie hadn't been available? What if I hadn't had the surgery room in the barn? The bottom line is that there is a lot of luck involved in medicine and luck is what God provides when we ask for help.

We improve our chances by thinking things through and working at creating luck. This goes back to how you think. I was sure I could pull the surgery off and I did. What if I hadn't concentrated on that thought? If I hadn't, it probably wouldn't have happened and Clyde would be dead today.

Medicine requires a lot of positive energy and your body feeds off of that energy. Positive energy is mandatory to healing and accomplishing what you want. For example, Ray didn't know how he was going to fix Clyde, but he knew he would find a way.

I, in turn, wasn't quite sure how I was going to fix him, but I did. If you approach medicine with a negative attitude, you're in trouble right away. I know that because my attitude was not good when I learned about my liver disease and I was going down hill every single day.

When my attitude changed, everything changed, and I'm healthier. I'm a better doctor and that helps my patients and those around me to be healthier. I no longer look at my disease as the worst thing that has happened to me. I can truthfully tell you it has changed me and is very possibly one of the best things that has ever happened to me.

I no longer fear death and I don't much think about it. Rather, I look forward to each and every day. I've got so many things I want to do, so many people I can help, and so many animals I can fix. I'm on a mission now.

I live life to the fullest and as Jack Nicolson said: "I save lives." It's that kind of attitude that will save your own life. We all need a little luck, but sometimes you have to create your own luck.

In case you don't think I'm lucky. I fell off the roof of my house and landed on my head. I missed the cement sidewalk by two inches with no serious aftermath. How I avoided a broken neck or concussion, I don't know but I do know God was with me then too.

Having this liver condition has improved the lives of everyone around me, especially the animals I work with everyday. It's not important what happens to you, it's important how you handle it.

I have learned a lot throughout my ordeal and now I know better and I'm going to do my best to make you see and believe that **you are what you eat.**

You need to re-evaluate and start thinking about what you are doing and what you are putting into your mouth. Thank You Heavenly Father for being there when I need you!

There are so many stories I want to tell you and here's another one. I can remember walking into the room and seeing this young lady who was overweight and appeared very down trodden. She looked like she had the weight of the world on her shoulders. She had a Pit Bull with her that was the friendliest dog in town. He'd lick your face off if he could.

The dog was limping very badly on one back leg and I knew there was something seriously wrong with it. I put him on the exam table and had a vet tech hold him on his side so I could examine him. Holding him down wasn't the problem. It was trying to avoid his tongue that was the real hazard because it was making me dripping wet.

As I had expected it obviously was a ruptured anterior cruciate ligament, the same injury that snow skiers and football players suffer from all the time. I told the lady about the problem and that it was going to cost about $1,500 to fix it. She just kept staring at the floor. I already knew she couldn't afford it and I knew she was anguishing over it.

It was easy to know what I would do. I would do the same thing my father and my grandfather did before me. I was going to fix it, no matter what. It's the part that is God like. We truly are made in his image and likeness if we will allow it to come out.

I knew without the girl saying a word, and because of her body language, that she didn't have a dime and that the dog was all she had in this world. It was easy for me to say: "I know what's wrong with your dog and don't worry it's not going to cost you a dime to fix it."

You should have seen her eyes light up. It was worth a million dollars just to see it. I've experienced that feeling a lot in my life and I never get tired of it. But it has been tight sometimes for me to pay my bills and sometimes I couldn't pay them all. There was actually a time when I had to pay as I went, but I didn't care, I wanted to help people when they couldn't afford to get their animals fixed.

I believe in God and I don't know if you do or not, but what do you think happened next? A man named Richard showed up with his Yorkshire Terrier called Mogie. The interesting part was the dog had a similar knee problem as the Pit Bull I just told you about.

Richard had just moved from Seattle and a classmate of mine, Jim McGill, had referred him to me. He loved his dog beyond words and he would do anything for Mogie, no matter what the cost. He told me to do everything I could possibly do to fix his dog.

The leg was such that we had no choice but to do surgery. The amazing part was he really didn't know me, but he trusted me just the same. I wasn't about to let him down, but not because of his money, but because of his love for Mogie.

Well, Mogie came through surgery beautifully. He couldn't have done better. The surgery was very complex because he had been born with a medical patellar luxation and he had also ruptured his anterior cruciate ligament. Basically this means that his knee cap was frozen to the medial side of his knee and the middle ligament in his knee was broken.

When I graduated from veterinary school, I knew how to fix one or the other, but not both. The knee cap itself was a whole new ball game.

When I cut the medial collateral ligament to put the knee back in place, there wasn't a groove for it to fit into, so I had to create one. That was enough in itself, but when the knee cap was in place, there wasn't enough joint capsule on the inside to suture it to.

Luckily I was confronted with this type of thing earlier, when I was fixing a dog for my relatives. This dog walked like Chester in Gun Smoke. He was very stiff legged on his right, rear leg. His knee was identical to Mogie's and when I started on him I wasn't sure what to do. When I moved the knee cap over and I could see there wasn't enough joint capsule to sew to, I panicked.

I pushed back my chair and seriously thought I could kiss these relatives good-by and since they were my wife's relatives it was even worse. I really didn't know exactly how I was going to fix it so I started praying once again and tried to visualize a way to fix this problem.

With God's help, I formulated a plan. It seemed a little far fetched at the time, but I didn't have too many alternatives. There was not enough joint capsule on the right side of the knee cap, but there was too much on the left side. So somehow I had to transpose the left to the right.

I know that sounds like no big deal, but it is, because you can't disrupt the blood supply to the piece you cut off. I decided I would cut it in such a way that it would stay connected to the piece of ligament and muscle above it and therefore would not disrupt its blood supply.

Basically I ended up with a flap from the outside that I could move to the inside and sew it all together. Once again I was asking God for a little help. The amazing part was it worked like a charm. The dog did fantastic and never limped again. Once again I was somebody's hero and God was mine.

When it came time to do Mogie, I knew what to do, so I wasn't real concerned about whether it would work or not. The surgery proceeded as expected and Mogie did phenomenally well.

Obviously, Richard was more than grateful which takes you back to how God looks after you. I was having trouble paying my bills and I was pretty much living month to month. When, in walked Richard with a $5,000 check. He told me to establish a fund that would be used to help people who couldn't afford to take care of their pets.

I was a little shocked but very pleased. He told me how he had grown up poor and knew what it was like not to be able to pay. He especially remembered what his mother had gone through. Because of her, he wanted his donation to especially go to help the older women who were living on social security, and who could barely take care of themselves, let alone their pets.

He doesn't think he's very religious or that he has much to do with God. He doesn't realize that the goodness in his heart and soul is what God is all about.

I'm very careful who I offer the free service to and I expect them to at least write him a letter of gratitude. It is a very moving experience for the people he helps and I'm sure it bolsters Richard's spirit too. It's pretty much a win/win situation.

It's especially a win for me because I can now do more and I don't have to hesitate because I can't pay my bills. I'm not always such a good judge of the situation, however, and I remember a ten year old boy who came in with a dog with a broken leg. He looked to me like he couldn't pay so I automatically fixed his dog's leg. There was a lot of my money and my time involved, but I didn't care, I was going to do the right thing. This was before Richard had arrived to save me.

At any rate, I fixed the leg and was carrying the dog out to put it in the car for these nice people. When I got outside, I found myself putting the dog in a brand new Cadillac and realized that maybe I hadn't been such a great judge of character. It wasn't their fault, it was mine, for jumping to conclusions. But it did hurt because I could have used the money.

Ever since Richard and his wife Donna have come into my life, things have been different. We have become close friends and Karn and I both enjoy their company immensely. He always replenishes his fund to help the people and their pets. His annual outlay is approximately $30,000 to $40,000. How many people do you know who would do that? Richard was sent by God when I needed him.

I ended up doing Mogie's other knee, which was just as difficult and just as successful. It seemed like Mogie always had something going wrong. If it wasn't his knees, it was his skin. Then the worst thing happened, he caught valley fever. That was a whole other ball game.

He started having trouble breathing so I did a blood count and an x-ray. Nothing was conclusive so I did the norm and put him on antibiotics, but they were not helping. A few weeks passed and Mogie wasn't getting any better and in fact, he was getting worse. I just knew it had to be valley fever, which is a fungus that people and animals breathe in and it often establishes an infection in the lungs. It is found in desert climates and is a big problem in Scottsdale, Arizona.

Mogie's blood test kept coming back negative and the treatment for valley fever was kind of serious and it could cause a life threatening liver condition. It is a slow insidious infection that gets worse over weeks. And Mogie just kept getting worse.

Richard had his main business in Seattle so he had to go. Mogie always flew first class in his own seat. Richard was happy to give Mogie anything he wanted or needed. When he arrived in Seattle, Mogie was still getting worse, so he took him to see my classmate, Jim McGill.

Jim could tell he had pneumonia, but he had never dealt with valley fever. He did what any vet would do, he put Mogie on a different antibiotic and a bronchodialator and ran more blood tests. I told him to include a valley fever test.

I knew it was going to take a week for him to get all the tests back and Mogie was getting worse and worse. Richard at this point wanted to lease a jet and fly Mogie back to Arizona. He didn't care how much it cost. So I told him not to panic that I was sure Mogie had valley fever and we needed to start treatment for it.

I also let him know that it was going to be a slow fix and that it might take eight weeks for Mogie to be normal again. That sounded like a lifetime for Richard, but what else could he do but trust me.

The worst was that I didn't have a positive blood test and I was sticking my neck out a country mile making the diagnosis without it, but I felt that Mogie might not make it if we didn't start treatment. I told Dr. McGill what to call in at the pharmacy and to start the treatment immediately.

I was back to praying and hoping I had made the right decision. Meanwhile, Richard called me daily, if for no other reason than for a little reassurance that he was doing all he could for Mogie. Without a doubt it was one of the worst times of his life.

THEN IT HAPPENED. The blood test finally came in positive and it gave me what I needed to know to be sure that I could fix Mogie. I jumped about ten feet in the air. I was ecstatic. I knew I could fix Mogie for sure.

I still needed to get Richard through the eight long weeks and we continued to talk daily, even when I was on my vacation at Yellowstone Park. I'd be walking through a store with Karn and sure enough the phone would ring and it would be Richard. He couldn't apologize enough for bothering me, but it really didn't bother me at all because I had been through it many times with other clients. The only difference was he was more deserving in my eyes and besides I enjoyed visiting with him.

I told him just like everyone else that valley fever was the kind of disease where you have to take the owner by the hand and lead them through it and that it would go on for at least eight weeks. Sometimes the animal would improve dramatically in just a few weeks, but in Mogie's case, it took thirteen weeks.

At the end of the time, Mogie was essentially normal and Richard could once again breathe. I know he was holding his breath the whole time and Donna was right next to him doing the same. Thanks to many years of dealing with valley fever and God's help, I was successful.

Did you ever wonder why Mogie had so many skin problems and why he got valley fever when valley fever used to be so rare? I did. For some reason or another it always came back to food.

So as part of Mogie's treatment and also to put him in a better state of health, I changed his diet. It helped immensely, but I never quite cleared up his skin problems until I took away the dry food. All of a sudden his hair coat improved to the point that he would glow in the dark

I really don't remember Richard mentioning any skin problems after that and his valley fever never came back. In the past there have been several dogs who had to be on fluconazole or ketoconazole (medicine for valley fever) their whole lives.

I honestly believe a change in diet would have promoted their immune system enough that they probably would have gotten over it too.

Hind sight is always 20/20, but at least now I know that the diet is as important as the medicine.

If I hadn't gotten sick this revelation never would have come to me. It required me to start thinking things through. There was no medication for me so I had to look at food. What an eye opener that was! It has been an unbelievable evolutionary process that has extended into my professional life.

I can't stop without telling you the story of my brother-in-law, Mike. He also got a Yorky puppy who had the same knee problem as Mogie. He called me from Atlanta, Georgia to tell me that his vet had diagnosed the knee problem, but had told him to wait to do the surgery because the pup was so young.

He was six weeks old and I knew if we let him develop that way, that he was going to end up like Mogie. So I told Mike, no way, just get him here and I'll fix him.

I met him at the airport and I didn't see his puppy anywhere. I asked him where the puppy was and he pulled him out of his coat pocket. The airline he was flying did not allow animals, but he wanted to fix his puppy so he snuck him on board. The puppy was unbelievably small and suddenly I'm going "Oh shit!" I could barely see the dog let alone his leg.

He just came across the country and I was supposed to fix this midget's leg. I wasn't even sure I had sutures that small. Anybody that knows me knows I'll never back down, so I took him to surgery. I had to use double magnification and 7-0 suture material. I had to use a hemostate to even handle the suture material. The surgery took well over two hours. I pretty much held my breath the whole time.

Well, the surgery was stressful, but went off without a hitch and to this day his puppy walks and runs totally normal. I think the word he used to describe his dog was "He's a holy terror."

The day I took him to the airport, he showed me a lump on his own chest and asked me what I thought about it. I could tell it was unusual and needed to be looked at, and told him to have it looked at as soon as possible. He called me a few weeks later to let me know his puppy was doing wonderfully but that he had just gone through a double mastectomy for breast cancer, which is rare in males.

Breast cancer is no longer rare in men, and I consider it to be diet related, specifically related to the hormones in food. We live in different times and we need to be more educated about the things around us, especially our food.

As a side point, I know men think Yorky's are girly dogs and not manly dogs. You need to change your perspective. Richard has probably known this all along, but Yorky's are *babe magnets.* If you don't believe me, go for a walk with one where there are girls around. It won't take you long before you'll understand what I mean.

I saw a Doxie with obvious paralysis of the rear legs. It didn't take a genius to see what was wrong and there was no alternative but surgery. It was easy to see the concern in both the mother and daughter's eyes.

I knew there was a financial problem, so I didn't quote a price. I just said, "What can you afford?" She knew the surgery was more than $2,000 so she told me she could put $2,000 on a particular credit card from the humane society. To this day I still don't know what that was about.

Anyway, I answered, "Is this going to max you out?"

She didn't say much so I said, "How about $1,500?"

She agreed, so I immediately started surgery. A few minutes later the receptionist came in and said there was a problem with the credit card. I told her not to worry about it that I'd either let Richard's fund take care of it or I'd just eat it.

It was nice to know I could help this dog and not have to worry about a client who couldn't afford to pay. I'm telling you that God does answer prayers. Even though I hadn't been feeling very good all day, after the surgery I felt like a million bucks and was walking on cloud nine.

The interesting thing about this story is that while I was doing the surgery, Richard just happened to be in the parking lot talking to the mother and daughter and reassuring them that their dog was going to be okay. Neither he nor the client knew his fund was going to pay for the procedure at that time.

Whenever Richard stopped by the clinic, he never interrupted me and he never liked to be put in front of anyone, so I wasn't even aware he was there. You can call this whole thing fate or call it whatever you want. I call it God's intervention because there were just too many coincidences. If you add up the sum total of that day, it was pretty remarkable and couldn't have just happened by chance.

Thank goodness for Richard and his fund because I knew I could do this surgery and not have to charge the client. Every time I am able to help another animal through Richard's generosity, I thank God. I refer to him as superman along with Dr. Edwyn Harrison from Mayo who has helped me so much with my liver.

Some of my clients that he has helped have dubbed him "Sir Richard." He has entered the realm of knighthood and he deserves it. I've made him a step higher because I think he is a

Saint and I'm sure the many animals he's helped think so too.

The next patient was a Boston Terrier puppy with a broken leg. It was brought in by Patricia, who is the author of a number of best selling mysteries. I don't think she had the puppy a week before it broke its leg. I knew she was worried and that she really wanted her dog fixed.

I used a bone plate which is an internal fixation device to bring the broken piece of bone together. The surgery went off without a hitch and in a week it was hard to even hold the puppy down.

I found out later that my wife, Karn, knew of Patricia and that she had read all of her novels and loved them. I haven't read them, because I've been busy reading about animals and how to get healthy.

When the receptionist at the front desk handed Patricia her bill, she told Carol that she wanted to join our efforts to help others who couldn't pay their bills. I'm not sure how she knew that, but she told Carol to add on an additional $5,000. Then Carol said Patricia stopped for a second as if thinking and then said, "No add on $10,000."

She has sent additional money as well. How many people have you met that would do that? Patricia would sit out in the waiting room watching people and worry if certain ones had the money to pay for their animal's care. I don't think anyone realized what she was doing. I know this because she would come to the front desk and ask Carol if she thought this little old man had enough to pay for his dog, or if that lady had enough to care for her cat.

What a wonderful soul Patricia has. I would be so proud to be her father or mother and to think that I had raised such a caring child. I think Patricia and Richard came from the same mold. Richard is a little rougher around the edges, but he and Patricia are exactly alike.

Don't think that Richard doesn't sit in the waiting room doing the exact same thing as Patricia, because he does! He comes up to me all the time and says, "Do you think they can afford to fix their pet?"

The interesting difference between Patricia and Richard is they both care about the person and the pet, but I know that Patricia cares more about the person and Richard cares more about the pet.

They both possess wonderful soft hearts and have souls that we could only hope for. I salute them both. They are the kind of people that make life worth living.

Another person who has influenced my life is Tony Snow. I recently read an article of his and we both feel that our illnesses have enhanced our lives. The article began with the following lead in: Commentator and broadcaster Tony Snow announced that he had colon cancer in 2005. Following surgery and chemo-therapy, Snow joined the Bush administration in April 2006 as press secretary. Unfortunately, on March 23 Snow, 51, a husband and father of three, announced that the cancer had reoccurred, with tumors found in his abdomen-leading to surgery in April, followed by more chemotherapy. Snow went back to work in the White House Briefing Room on May 30, but resigned August 31. CT asked Snow what spiritual lessons he has been learning through the ordeal." [16]

"Blessings arrive in unexpected packages—in my case, cancer…..The first is that we shouldn't spend too much time trying to answer the why questions: Why me? Why must people suffer? Why can't someone else get sick?" [17]

"Second, we need to get past the anxiety….Third, we can open our eyes and hearts." [18]

When I read some of Snow's comments, I thought about my own life. I have come to realize that I need to live every day as if it were my last. I am getting much more out of life that

[16] Tony Snow. Christianity Today. Cancer's Unexpected Blessings. July 20, 2007. ww.ctlibrary.com/47315
[17] ibid
[18] ibid

way. This attitude even gives me the strength to often get up at night and write, because I know it might be my last chance.

I've put my life in order and I don't owe anybody any money. I have enough money in the bank to take care of things in case of an emergency and I've made sure that my kids will be able to complete their education and my wife will be fine as well.

It took my illness to clarify my life and even if my years might be cut short, my accomplishments far exceed what they would have been if I hadn't gotten sick.

Miracles do happen.

Chapter 11

Breakthrough at my veterinary clinic

At that time, I didn't fully realize the magnitude of the journey I had begun, but my recommendations had worked! No doubt! That's how my understanding started. I began to tell clients to feed healthy people food, but I didn't know then that I needed to get real adamant about the food. As people started putting their dogs on people food combined with raw meat and taking them off of pet food, their dogs and cats started doing better. No matter if it was skin problems, digestive problems, weight problems or whatever, the change in food helped.

Dogs started losing weight and could literally drop 20 pounds, in some cases, in as little as two months and people kept coming in and saying: "It's Like a Miracle."

One day a year old boxer was brought into the clinic. He didn't look very good. At only one year old, he had started gaining excessive weight, his hair was falling out, and he acted like he was eight years old. This client had taken his dog to New York where they had done all kinds of biopsies and had decided that he had irritable bowel syndrome, and would be on a life time treatment of cortisone.

Since the Boxer's owner was an anesthesiologist, he was willing to accept their diagnosis. If it was a long standing problem in people, it makes sense that it would be a long standing problem in dogs. He accepted the diagnosis and the life time treatment of cortisone.

That was a predictable diagnosis because with his symptoms, what else were they going to come up with. The bill had been outrageously high and the dog had been put on cortisone for the rest of his life. The poor thing was getting by, but that was about it.

I again recommended that the client try another diet. He ended up trying rabbit and potato and I think I saw him a few weeks to a month later. He was buying a couple of cases of rabbit and I asked how it was going and he said: "It's like a miracle."

This simple change in diet had straightened this dog out. Now there was only one problem, his other dog had diarrhea on the rabbit diet. So I recommended he try venison for that dog. It seems that dogs are like people. Some do well on certain kinds of meat while others do well on other types. So in this case, it was just a matter of finding what worked. The last I heard, he was giving one dog rabbit and the other venison and they were both doing well. I would now recommend a raw diet.

As I was beginning to feel better myself, I realized that I was onto something with the dogs and cats too. Besides reading, I now talked about health to every client that came in. I began to spend so much time with each one that I couldn't get to all of them and some had to wait too long. So I wrote a sixteen page handout in which I talked about health and diet.

I have some testimonials that I would like to share with you so you can hear from some of my pet owners and get their perspective on diet. There are many more testimonials, but I didn't want to overdo it so I chose the letters on the following pages:

Myrna R. Kahlo
Tonto Verde, AZ

October 5, 2007

Dear Dr. Rick,

I cannot thank you enough for your urging and encouragement to make a change in what I feed my two boxers. Happily, for them and for me, I finally listened!

For almost two months, they have been on a diet of brown rice and mixed vegetables added to raw buffalo meat. They literally run to their food bowls; the younger boxer is a pogo stick jumping up and down with anticipation. They think goat yogurt is dessert!

They are alert......their coats shine.....they are happy dogs!

Thank you,

Myrna

9-29-07

We had just lost our second rottie (from cancer) in January of 2003. In fact, this was our third dog that had contracted the disease.

Dr. Soltero's office called in March. They had received a severely abused rottweiler with a shattered right front leg and the mangiest coat we'd ever seen. We found out later that she had a plethora of internal problems. She was about 2 ½ years old. We decided to take "Bea" and give her the best home possible.

We started to feed "Bea" on the diet dog food we'd fed our other Rotties. "Bea" was vomiting, listless, and in general, a very poor sight. At that point we'd had tests run; she had high liver enzymes.

We gave her milk thistle and other natural remedies to bring the liver enzyme problem under control. It didn't help. In addition, she'd developed tick fever, and at times she could not keep food down and she had a tendency to get bloated. We thought she had a blockage. After another exploratory surgery, we found there was no blockage. More testing was done and we were more frustrated.

It was then Dr. Soltero suggested a different diet. (We knew he had experienced liver problems.) Dr. Soltero had been on a similar diet, and it seemed to help him; it was definitely worth a try for "Bea."

So "Bea" became the lucky dog with a great diet: goat yogurt and pineapple in the morning; wild salmon (canned), mashed sweet potatoes, garlic and ground flaxseed in the evening. Snacks were baby carrots and celery. She ate what we ate.

Over time, she became more alert. Her weight is under control and her coat is glossy and soft. "Bea's" test results are normal. She is seven years old now and is as excitable as a three year old.

We will never go back to dog food for any of our pets.

Cheri & Chuck Craig

9-28-07

I have 3 Argentine Dogos. Neutered males, ages 11, 8 and 6. I was feeding the #1 dry dog food with no fillers or additives. My 11 year old at 135 lbs. came down with gastric hemorraghic enteritis. We found him in the morning with a trail of blood throughout the house. " Shorty" recovered and was suspected to have Cushing's. The emergency center wanted to see him two weeks later.

Instead I brought him to Dr. Soltero about a month later when he was eating again. He was having a very bad time getting up and down. In fact, I was having to use a towel under his belly to get him to stand and to do stairs. His hind legs would fall out apart behind. It was very sad. He was bald and his coat blotchy with hair.

"Kundi" my 8 year old at 150 lbs. was also having difficulties standing and I was having to lift him to his feet with a towel under the belly. He would cry when he wanted to get up so I would help him.

"Murray" the 6 year old was very lethargic, acted older then the other slept all the time and was balding. The 3 dogs were fat and had bloated bellies.

Since I had lost my first Dogo at 9 1/2 years, I just assumed this was an aging thing since these 3 were much larger dogs.

When Dr. Soltero saw "Murray" and "Shorty," he immediately said, "They look like crap. Stop the dry food! Put them on raw buffalo (bison)." Having trusted him for 22 years and fortunate enough to afford it, they went on a diet of 8 oz. bison, vegetables, rice, barley or pasta, in the morning, and the lecithin. Immediately there was a change in them. Within a week, "Shorty" and "Kundid" were getting up and down without assistance. Their stools became formed instead of loose, their eyes brighter, much more energetic. Back to whining to wake me up at 5:30 a.m. to go out for a walk, like when they were young dogs. Their bellies were no longer bloated and within a month "Shorty" and "Murray's" coats were more even and filled in.

"Shorty" who used to have several heavy breathing sessions, which I think is a sign of pain, rarely has them. I had been giving him Pepto Bismol tablets for it.

They never before would eat vegetables. Now they eat them all and seem to enjoy them. They always used to leave some of the dry food and were never really into eating, but now they anxiously gobble and seem to really enjoy it.

I also make them their treats: cookies from oatmeal, oat bran, flaxseed meal, peanut butter, eggs with shells, canola oil and maple syrup.

"Murray" has gained 5 lbs but looks slimmer. His shoulders are prominent and his belly is defined.

"Murray" and "Kundi" are again romping and playing as they did as puppies.

In the past I had several dogs and I only wish I had known to do this with them. I didn't realize how important diet was. I was so ignorant and thought dogs eat anything so you can feed them anything.   I am sure some of my other dogs would have lived longer and enjoyed their quality of life had I only known.

Thank you for figuring this out,

Much love….Ellen O'Brien

October 5, 2007

Dear Rick….
I was so pleased to see you today and have a little time to talk with you. You said some things in

passing that made me think about how our 'teachers' are revealed to us-who and what they are and the myriad of forms in which they show up. I have come to believe that the best I can do everyday is to grow and evolve in some way. To live fully, awake and present in my life, has not always been my understanding or choice. And the more I do this with the choices I make, the clearer and simpler things become. We are meant to be joy filled beings and to not take ourselves so seriously. I am a work in progress, much the way I assume that you see yourself. And this is a beautiful thing! We have huge opportunities and choices each day, and you perhaps more than me, have a very clear picture of just what that means. Thank you for revealing more of who you are and sharing the openness with which you are living your life today. I've always known you to be a special being, long before I really knew what that meant.

Now, for the endorsement.....

I fully believe in the diet that Dr. Soltero prescribed for my dog. It is similar to how I have naturally chosen to eat for over 25 years. I am a firm believer that diet is underestimated as a major contributor to disease and health issues in our culture, and our pets are no exception.

Introducing this diet to "Suki" four years ago has given her more energy, a healthy coat, fewer medical issues, and weight that balanced out to be 10 lbs lighter in the first six months. She is a lean, happy, playful 10 ½ year old lab who is often mistaken for a much younger dog.

Good luck with this book my friend. I am glad that you are writing and sharing your insight and wisdom. I believe that our world can and does change one small action at a time, and you are doing this. I am working at doing the same. With love and very long friendship….

Barbi

I got my dog Peanut in March of 2005 when she was about four months old. She was covered from head to toe in demodex and was basically completely bald and scabby. I finally took her to Saguaro Veterinary Clinic where she was treated for her skin condition. In the beginning I never had an opportunity to meet with Dr. Soltero so I never knew that the dry food that I was feeding Peanut was potentially hurting her, not helping her. Her demodex started slowly going away for some periods of time with the oral medication she was taking, however the demodex managed to reoccur every six weeks or so. The medicine made her sick sometimes and it worried me that she might have to take it for the rest of her life. I decided to take her to a skin specialist where I was basically told the same thing and just ended up spending a lot of money. About eight months later I finally got an opportunity to talk with Dr. Soltero about Peanut. He talked to me about her diet and suggested that I also give her some supplements to strengthen her immune system. I was willing to try anything at this point so I gave Dr.Soltero's diet a try. Peanut's hair coat started looking beautiful after a few weeks. I was sort of nervous to take her for her next skin scrape because I was so ready for her demodex to be completely gone. Sure enough the skin scrape was negative for mites and it was finally time to stop the oral medication. A couple months later we did another scrape to make sure the demodex didn't reoccur and it hasn't since I started following Dr. Soltero's diet. I am so grateful that Dr. Soltero shared his knowledge with me. I never knew something so simple, like changing my animal's diet, would make all the difference in the world. Thank you Dr. Soltero, we appreciate it more than you will ever know!

Crissy

My 8 year old yellow lab, "Ginger," lost 22 lbs. on Dr. Soltero's fabulous diet! She's like a puppy again. Thank you so much......I'm sure this diet added years to her life.

Thanks again, Kandace Rising

Natural, Raw, Organic Pet Food

Although I had been feeding my Dobermans a premium kibble and canned food for over 20 years, it wasn't until I lost one of my precious babies, "Byron" at 3 ½ to heart disease that I really began to look into nutrition to see if I could do better.

When I brought home my present male, "Chester," I fed him what I thought was a better food. But at 2 ½ years I noticed that he was getting a bit chunky and lacked the energy that I thought he should have. About the same time a little female, "Franki," joined our family so I went back to my nutrition research.

I consulted with my vet, Dr. Richard Soltero, who had become keenly aware of the nutritional effects of commercial food on our pets' health and encouraged a more nutritious natural diet WITHOUT kibble. The "cooking" or extrusion process in commercial foods destroys most of the naturally occurring nutrients. Also most commercial foods contain high amounts of "filler" grains which convert to unnecessary sugars. It became apparent to me that a more natural way to feed is raw. It made sense— how many animals "cook" their food?

I liked the idea of raw but was not sure I wanted to deal with trying to "balance" ratios, raw bones and organ meats. I opted for a raw "grainfree" dehydrated balanced food to which I rotate additions of organic egg, canned wild salmon, canned sardines in water, ground buffalo, elk, venison, and goat yogurt. The dehydration process also "kills" bacteria that some worry about in the raw diet but retains the nutrients.

"Chester" and "Frank" absolutely love their food and gobble it down. For treats they are given raw beef or buffalo shank bones. I keep a few bones around to stuff later with a variety of ingredients including green beans, bananas, carrots, raw meat, just to name a few. I freeze the bones and they get them after they eat in an attempt to keep them calm for a while to avoid "bloat." My dogs love the frozen bones and it keeps them occupied for a while as they lick out the goodies like a Popsicle.

I add a few supplements to my dogs' food but they have never looked better since eliminating commercially processed food from their diet. There were so many unexpected results from the new raw diet, lean muscled bodies, increased energy levels and endurance, amazingly clean bright white teeth, fresh breath, and incredibly silky, shiny coats.

Several of my friends have also switched their dog's food with similar results. One of the most remarkable is a 17 ½ year old mxed breed, Sasha, who usually stayed under a desk most of the time. After the diet change she has perked up with clear eyes, an increased energy level and a surprising renewed zest for life.

Feeding "Chester" and "Franki" a natural grain-free diet filled with hormone free meats and organic ingredients has been one of the best decisions I have ever made. Just ask them!
Joyce Hergert

The answers were coming in each and everyday and I knew that listening on both the part of the doctor and the patient was the critical ingredient to good health, only in that way, can a good diagnosis be made and in turn a treatment given. Of course, the patient must then try the new treatment, often a diet, for it to cure the problem.

I had known all along that listening to the history of my patients was a critical piece of information for me, but now I was realizing that listening was the most critical piece. So I started taking more time to listen each day.

I have another story that emphasizes the importance of paying attention to a patient's history: Dr. Thayne Larsen from Mayo Clinic in Scottsdale called me because his dog, Brandy, had been vomiting for days and the veterinarian that he had been going to diagnosed him as having Addison's disease.

I know that most of the diagnosis is in the history so I started questioning him. "How old is your Brandy?"

Thayne answered, "One year old."

"What kind of dog is he?"

"A Golden Retriever."

"When did he start vomiting?"

"Five days ago."

"Does he like to chew on things?"

"Sure."

"Does he vomit every time he eats?"

"Yes."

"What makes the doctor think he has Addison's?"

"Because he has low sodium," he explained.

"Does he have elevated potassium?"

"No."

At this point, I'm positive I know what's wrong with this dog so I say to Thayne, "I think your dog has an obstruction, so you need to bring him in."

He arrived about an hour later and I examined Brandy and could see no visible signs of any obvious illness. I repeated my thoughts, "Thayne I still think it is more than likely he is obstructed. I've never run across a year old dog that had Addison's and usually if he did, his potassium would be elevated."

I patted Brandy's head and continued, "From his history alone, I would open him up and look for a foreign body that would cause an obstruction. If it had been one or two days of vomiting, I would x-ray and do a barium series, but after five days, I would open him up no matter what."

Thayne felt like he had nothing to lose because Brandy had not responded to the treatment for Addison's and he was really sick. I just knew I was right and because he had just been on fluids for four days, I could proceed immediately and open Brandy up to see what was going on. I was sure I would find something.

With Thayne's permission, within twenty minutes I had Brandy on the surgery table and I began. As I made my incision, I was hoping and praying I was right. Most people would have thought I was crazy because I had only known these people twenty minutes and I was already opening their dog up.

I made a small exploratory incision in the hopes I would get lucky. It was less than ½ the size of a normal incision. I fished out a loop of bowel and proceeded to pull out as much as I needed.

I had pulled out about two feet of bowel and it was normal. As I progressed, the ileocecal junction came up so I knew I was going in the wrong direction. Most obstructions are in the duodenum or the jejunum and I had pulled up his ileum. At that point I pushed that part of his intestinal track in and progressed in the opposite direction.

Within a few minutes I had his jejunum and most of his duodenum out and there was no obstruction, so I had to extend his incision forward to get to the descending duodenum. I was becoming a little apprehensive because I hadn't found any obstruction.

As I pulled up the descending duodenum, which comes from the stomach, I could see it. Praise God, there it was. It was an obvious round structure that had totally corked him shut.

I cut over the object through the intestinal wall and out popped a ball. It was a Super Ball. I don't know if you remember them, but at this time, they were very popular.

With ball in hand, I walked out of the surgery room and down the hall, where Thayne and his wife, Carol, were nervously waiting.

I called out, "Hey Thayne!"

He turned toward me and I bounced him the Super Ball. He got the most appreciative grin on his face and I went back to close Brandy up. When he woke up, he was a new dog. He hadn't felt that good in a week. He actually left the clinic an hour later with Carol and Thayne.

He healed up with no complications and was back to running and playing within five days. I thought, "Isn't this a great job!" The diagnosis was in the history. The first doctor had only been paying attention to the vomiting and blood work and not to the history.

It's true that Addisonial dogs can be sick to their stomach and have a low sodium, but they are usually much older and have a high potassium. I already knew why the sodium was low and that was because he had been vomiting for five days. Excessive vomiting will cause the sodium drop.

Most doctors could have picked this up, but only if they had been paying attention to the history. I didn't mind if Thayne and Carol didn't know this because I enjoyed bouncing that ball down the hall because it felt great.

I was more convinced than ever that the simple act of listening to not only history but also to what others had to say was extremely important. I especially respected some of my elderly patients like the eighty-eight year young lady who came in looking great.

So I asked, "How did you get so healthy?"

"If you have your mind, you have your health. You have everything." She said as a matter of fact.

"Do you have any health problems at all?" I asked.

"Nope."

"What's your recipe for being so healthy?"

"I read a lot and do my crossword puzzles and play bridge. As far as food goes, I eat mostly fruits and vegetables. My grandma taught me what to eat."

"You probably don't even realize the good you do yourself. I promise you if you don't use it, you lose it. Were you a big meat eater?" "No, but my husband was and he died of cancer," she answered.

"How long were you married?"

"Thirty-three years." She smiled.

"So that was a good one. You know you have all the secrets for us and you don't even know it. We don't know how to live or how to eat, but I'm learning. You have your mind and I'm sure you're doing something serious or meaningful." I said.

"Yeah, I stay busy and I feel great."

"I'm finding out that too much exercise isn't good either. I have a shoulder problem and a friend, who is a doctor, said that I should quit lifting weights. He told me that about a year ago. While trying to build my muscles, I guess I was tearing other things down. Too bad I didn't listen to him. Have you ever noticed how we're all too busy to listen?"

She grinned at me, "It's all about moderation."

"You're absolutely right. Now let's see what we can do for your dog today."

After that, I made it a habit to talk with every elderly person who came through the door. I wanted to know why they were so healthy. We should all start listening because older people have a lot to say.

As I ate lunch, I sat at my desk thinking about everything that had happened. I hadn't expected that the answer could be as simple as food and even though it took a shock in my own life to get me on the track of finding answers, I was so surprised when things began to get clearer and clearer.

I became very proactive as far as my health went and also dealing with my patients. I started looking at what I had been doing. I realized that I had been treating symptoms and not the causes. You can't treat the disease without knowing the causes. It seems that modern day medicine has become a bunch of pills that alleviate symptoms, but does nothing to fix the real problem.

I figured that if someone couldn't give me a diagnosis or if I couldn't diagnose one of my patient's problems, it didn't mean there was no cure. So I kept looking for answers and trying different things. After many of my patients responded so well when I took them off of dry dog food and put them on people food, I started recommending the diet change more and more.

After finding that supplements didn't help me, I wasn't big on them for animals either. When a client brought in a cat or dog with a problem, s/he would tell me their pet's symptoms and then I would say: "What are you feeding him?" I would check them out thoroughly but in the end, it always came back to diet.

The obvious is not always obvious.

Chapter 12

Feeding raw meat

After some success with cutting out dry pet food, I later found that canned was not very good either. So I began to read about feeding raw meat to both cats and dogs and am now recommending it highly. This chapter deals with some of the facts concerning raw meat and I included it so you could read and decide for yourself.

Some articles talk about certain bacteria in raw meat. The bacteria they mention are Escherichia coli, salmonella, klebsiella, and clostridium. Everyone talks about the potential for problems: in pets eating the meat, in you handling it, and in how your children could be exposed from touching the meat and/or your pet. All I hear about is the *potential* of a problem, but not about actual serious outbursts from feeding raw meat.

On the other hand, the U.S. Food and Drug Administration warned,   "On March 15, FDA learned that certain pet foods were sickening and killing cats and dogs. FDA found contaminants in vegetable proteins imported into the United States from China and used as ingredients in pet food." [19]

I for one see this as a major issue because the recall is not for just a few pet food companies, but rather involves pages and pages of the brand names we all know. If you want to read for yourself, the FDA notes, "This compiled list represents several related pet food recalls. If and when new information is received, this list will be updated." [20]

I find it very interesting that I've doubled my efforts to find reports about outbreaks of salmonella food poisoning in animals. I've even been looking for articles that talk about salmonella being transmitted from pets to people.

My son is at Kansas State Veterinary School researching literature on this subject. I told him that I especially wanted anything he could find on the public health aspects of pets passing on E.coli or salmonella.

[19] U.S. Food and Drug Administration, "Pet food Recall/Tainted Animal Feed". (http://fda.gov/oc/opacom/hottopics/petfood.html). (5/31/2007).
[20] U.S. Food and Drug Administration. "Search for Pet Food Recalls". (http://www.accessdata.fda.gov/scripts/petfoodrecall/. (updated 5/30/07).

I also asked for any studies that anyone had conducted to show the dangers of raw meat. Maybe something like taking a certain number of dogs and putting them on raw meat for a period of time and what the serious side affects might be. So far he hasn't found *any* such reports and neither have I. He did send me a couple of articles that involved salmonella outbreaks in people, but neither had anything to do with pets eating raw meat. Read for yourself.

"CDC is collaborating with public health officials in Pennsylvania and other state health departments and the US Food and Drug Administration to investigate a multi-state out-break of Salmonella serotype Schwarzengrund infections in humans. These human illnesses have been linked with dry pet food produced by Mars Petcare US at a single manufacturing facility in Pennsylvania." [21]

".....Illness related to this outbreak has not been reported in pets. However, the outbreak strain of Salmonella Schwarzengrund was isolated from fecal specimens from two dogs that ate dry pet food in the homes of two of the ill persons." [22]

[21] CDC (Safer, Healthier People) "Salmonella Schwarzengrund Outbreak Investigation. August 2007.
http://www.cec.gov/salmonella/schwarzengrund.html
[22] ibid

"The Pennsylvania Department of Health (PADOH) conducted environmental testing in this pet food production facility. One of the environmental samples collected by PADOH yielded the outbreak strain of Salmonella Schwarz-engrund. In tests by the US Food and Drug Administration of unopened bags of finished dog food produced by this facilty, two brands yielded the outbreak strain of Salmonella Schwarzen-grund." [23]

"Investigations are ongoing to determine why human-illness, especially among infants, is associated with dry pet food. Factors under investigation include handling and storage of dry pet food, hand-washing practices, exposure of children to dry pet food, and location in the home where pets are fed." [24]

As I kept reading, another report along the same lines that I found interesting and informative was from the Centers for Disease and Prevention in Atlanta, Georgia. Please read for yourself what they had to say about Salmonella and where it is found. "Public health officials in OutbreakNet (the network of epidemiologists and other public health officials, facilitated by CDC, who investigate out-breaks of foodborne, waterborne, and other en-teric illnesses nationwide) are investigating a multi-

---

[23] ibid
[24] ibid

state outbreak of Salmonella Wandsworth infections. Salmonella Wandsworth is a rare strain of Salmonella." [25]

"A multi-state case-control study demonstrated a strong association between illness in people and consumption of Veggie Booty, a snack of puffed rice and corn with a vegetable coating. CDC OutbreakNet staff shared this information with colleagues at the Food and Drug Administration (FDA) on June 27. After being informed about the outbreak by FDA, the company that manufactures the product issued a voluntary recall on June 28." [26]

"The outbreak strain has also been isolated from sealed bags of Veggie Booty by the FDA laboratory and the New York State Department of Health Wadsworth Center Laboratory. Preliminary testing suggests that the seasoning mix used in Veggie Booty may be the source of the contamination." [27]

I think it is really ironic that it is the dry pet food industry that is toting the dangers of raw meat and how it causes salmonella in dogs and cats. But I've not been able to find one article

---

[25] Center for Disease Control and Prevention, *Salmonella Wandsworth Outbreak Investigation. June – July 2007.* http://www.cdc.gov/salmonella/wandworth.htm

[26] ibid

[27] ibid

where a child has contracted salmonella from handling a pet on a raw meat diet.

Don't feed chicken by-products. Chickens have been associated with Salmonella for years. I don't recommend chicken but not because of its association with Salmonella. I think there are better choices of raw meat available.

Buffalo is a perfect example because it is not genetically engineered like chicken. They are grass-fed and not likely to have been on hormones and antibiotics. They are usually loose in a pasture and stay active. They are not overly crowded and get to live the way God intended.

Chickens are treated pretty much just the opposite. They have a pecking order of 90 and beyond that, they lose their minds. So I will never recommend chicken for people or pets. No animal on the face of the earth deserves to be treated the way chickens are.

We should look at our food supply the way Native Americans have in the past. They view animals as sacred and that they give them life and enable them to exist. If handled properly they offer good health to us and it is appalling that humans torture them in return.

Getting back to the raw meat diet for dogs and cats, I still have not seen any evidence that it is a threat to you or your family and certainly not to your pet. I've found just the opposite. Raw meat offers our family pet a new lease on life and seems to be the 'cure all' for most medical problems.

I'm sure that it's possible that an immune suppressed person or animal could be at risk from contaminated food, but I haven't even run across an incident where it has been life threatening for a pet. These bacteria may be a threat to you, but not to your pet that is genetically different than you.

I've read articles that expound on the risk of raw meat, but there is nothing to prove their claims. I haven't really seen any examples of it causing Salmonella, E.coli, or Klebsiella. I haven't seen any examples of animals dying from eating raw meat either. Maybe there are a few incidences of diarrhea or vomiting, but no deaths.

However, I've seen many deaths of pets associated with canned or dry pet foods, but even they are not usually associated with the meat in the product. The last outbreak that caused many cats and dogs to die was the food additive for thickening food.

"Pet food manufacturers have voluntarily recalled more than 100 brands of dog and cat food across the nation since March 16, 2007. The recall was prompted by reported cases of cats and

dogs in the United States that developed kidney
failure after eating the affected products." [28]

"FDA first learned of a problem with pet
food manufactured by Menu Foods, Inc. after the
company reported illnesses and deaths in cats and
dogs that had eaten some of its 'cuts and gravy'
style products. The Canada-based manufacturer
supplies cat and dog food to numerous pet food
companies that sell it under various brand
names." [29]

"...FDA consumer complaint coordinators
around the country began taking calls from pet
owners and veterinarians who reported illnesses
that may have been associated with the
contaminated pet food. FDA received over
14,000 such reports in the first four weeks—more
than twice the number of complaints typically
received in a year for all of the products the
agency regulates." [30]

"A New York State laboratory reported
finding aminopterin, a form of rat poison, in some
pet food samples. FDA's Forensic Chemistry
Center could not confirm these findings. What
the center did find, though, was melamine in the
pet foods and in the wheat gluten used as an
ingredient. Subsequently, FDA's field labor-
atories found melamine in over 130 of more than

---

[28] U.S. Food and Drug Administration, *FDA's Ongoing Pet Food
Investigation* 10/18/2007. www.fda.gov/updates/petfoodrecallup.html
[29] ibid
[30] ibid

210 samples of pet food and wheat gluten. In addition, Cornell University scientists found mela-mine in the urine and kidneys of cats that were part of a taste-testing study conducted for Menu Foods." [31]

"....the association between melamine in the kidneys of cats that died and melamine in the food they consumed is undeniable" [32]

After the initial recall it wasn't over. The U.S. Food and Drug Administration gave another consumer update: "FDA is investigating an imported shipment of rice protein concentrate that has been found to contain melamine. The rice protein concentrate may have been used as an ingredient in some pet foods. Melamine is the same industrial chemical that was found in wheat gluten imported from China and used in pet food made by Menu Foods, which recalled 60 million cans and pouches of dog and cat food in mid March 2007...... FDA investigators have obtained records showing distribution of the rice protein concentrate to 5 pet food manufacturers in 7 locations. Investigators are currently inspecting all 5 manufacturers and collecting additional samples for testing." [33]

---

[31] ibid
[32] ibid
[33] U.S. Food and Drug Administration *Contaminant Found in Second Pet Food Ingredient.* March 2007.
http://www.fda.gov/consumer/updates/petfoodup042007.html

Erik Mueller is the contact person for the following recall – press release: St. Charles, Missouri - April 19, 2007 - Royal Canine USA is announcing today that the company has determined there is a melamine derivative in the rice protein concentrate in some of its dry pet food products." [34]

I recommend feeding raw meat to cats and dogs and I've never diagnosed any serious bacteria problems from it. I appreciate other's concerns but to me it looks like a smoke screen created by the pet food industry. Randall Fitzgerald quotes Richard Pitcairn, a veterinarian who said, "Since I graduated from veterinary school in 1965, I've noticed a general deterioration in pet health. We now see very young animals with diseases that we used to see only in older animals…..Without the perspective of several decades, veterinarians just coming out of veterinary school think these degenerative conditions in younger animals are 'normal'. They do not realize what has happened over the passage of time. I believe that, along with poor quality nutrients, the *chemical additives* in pet food play a major part in that decline." [35]

---

[34] Royal Canin USA Press Release *Royal Canin USA Announces the Voluntary Nationwide Recall of its Dry Pet Food Products Containing Rice Protein Concentrate.* FDA release. April 19, 2007.
[35] Richard Pitcairn , Natural Health for Dogs and Cats, Rodale Press, (1995) As cited by Randall Fitzgerald, The Hundred-Year Lie, Plume, a member of Penguin Group (USA) Inc. (2007). p. 110.

I have witnessed the similar findings at my practice and I diagnose cancer problems daily. These cancer rates did not exist 35 years ago. I agree with Dr. Pitcairn in that I too rarely see a dog dying of old age anymore. They are dying younger and almost always due to cancer or some immune related problem.

Randall Fitzgerald explains further, "Many of us who have pet companions, particularly dogs and cats, have either seen first-hand or heard stories from other pet owners about how the animals contract illnesses, allergies, behavioral abnormalities, or disease when consuming some commercial pet foods, only to miraculously recover once those processed foods are taken out of their diet. Given how pet foods are produced, we shouldn't be surprised. Four of the five largest U.S. pet food companies are subsidiaries of major multinational corporations that also produce processed foods for humans. American pet owners spend an estimated $11 billion annually on animal foods made in part or whole from the scraps, rejects, and wastes - known as 4-D meat - collected and set aside by plants producing human food. This 4-D category stands for dead, diseased, dying, or disabled."[36]

---

[36] Randall Fitzgerald, The Hundred-Year Lie. Plume, a member of Penguin Groupd (USA) p. 110-111.

The question is: Why would such harmful ingredients be placed in pet food? David Brown, Washington Post Staff Writer, explains: "Why Someone Would Spike Pet Food….Usually, the nitrogen in pet food comes from protein, which is made of chains of amino acids. There are 20 amino acids, each containing one to four nitrogen atoms. High nitrogen levels imply high protein content. Adding a nitrogen-rich compound such as melamine or cyanuric acid (or both) would boost nitrogen levels to make food appear more nutritious. Most current testing of pet food ingredients measures nitrogen content but does not distinguish between nitrogen from protein and nitrogen from other sources. Consequently, the addition of melamine or other nitrogen-containing compounds might not be apparent…and How Scientists Try to Detect It. In the urine of the dead cats, crystals were found with a particular infrared spectrum. At the University of Guelph in Ontario, scientists mixed melamine and cyanuric acid in cat urine and produced crystals matching those found in the dead cats. This led scientists to theorize that when the compounds are eaten by a cat, and then concentrated in urine, they can form crystals and cause kidney failure." [37]

---

[37] David Brown and Laura Stanton . *How Two Innocuous Compounds Combined to Kill Pets.* Washington Post (Science Section) Monday, May 7, 2007. (AB) (Some information from staff research, University of Guelph. Journal of the American Chemical Society.

It appears clear that 'making money' is the driving force behind commercial pet food companies and not your pets' health. United States Senator Dick Durbin explains another aspect that plagues the dog food companies. "Many cats, dogs, and other pets, considered members of the family are now suffering as a result of a deeply flawed pet food inspection system. The FDA's response to this situation has been wholly inadequate—we need to establish standardized inspections, impose penalties on companies who delay reporting health problems and increase communication between the FDA and the state inspectors so that we can catch potential problems more quickly. These sound like basic steps but the FDA has failed to put them in place." [38]

I think that the only reason people wouldn't see the obvious improvements from raw meat diets would be because they haven't tried them. The changes are unbelievably obvious such as: marked improvement in mental demeanor, obvious weight loss for overweight animals, improved vitality, markedly improved hair coats etc. It's become my main drug of

[38] Dick Durbin, United States Senator, *Durbin Calls For Better Oversight Of Pet Food Inspections; Tougher Penalties For Companies.* April 12, 2007.
http://www.drubin.senate.gov/record.cfm?id=272317.

choice for any dog or cat's illness. It's called *good food* and the main staple is *raw meat.*

If we're going to start cultures where serious bacteria problems might come from, let's start culturing public toilet seats. God only knows what hangs out there. There're many more possibilities of serious illnesses for your children when they touch these filthy seats and then put their fingers in their mouths.

Most bacteria and viruses are species specific so that dog bacteria don't usually cause illness in people and vice - versa. But people bacteria coming from human excrement is a lot more dangerous.

I don't know any cases personally where children have gotten sick from their pets. I know it can happen, but I haven't run into it. Along with that, I've not seen dogs getting intestinal bacteria problems from eating raw meat. To date, everything has been just the opposite. All I see are dogs getting healthier and healthier. The worst I've seen is occasional vomiting and a very transient diarrhea, that stops quickly with a bland diet.

I have had some clients who have asked about feeding cooked meat instead of raw meat. Cooking meat does not make it healthier. It makes it safer for you to eat, but not for your pet. They have evolved eating raw meat. But, feeding cooked meat is still highly superior to feeding dog food of any kind.

Dry food is dehydrated, denatured protein and is much more contaminated than raw meat. The dog food companies don't care how contaminated the meat is because they're going to cook it to the point of sterilization. Dry food has obvious rancid fat which has been associated with cancer. Just smell dry or canned dog food and you'll see what I mean, because it smells putrid. How can anything that smells that bad, be that healthy?

The fat that went rancid was the essential fatty acids which humans and animals all need to be healthy. They are called essential for a reason. All the vitamins in dry food are synthetic and synthetic vitamins aren't necessarily bioactive. Plant and meat sources of vitamins are much more active because of the synergistic activity that goes on with the other nutrients in the plant or meat.

I'm a big proponent of raw meat and I recommend human grade first. It obviously is not as contaminated as the meat meant for dogs and/or cats, but I am not afraid of that either. I would try to minimize exposure to contaminated meats, but I'm not going to lie awake at night worrying about it.

Think about it, dogs eat manure all the time. It's totally contaminated. We can't do that because we're built differently. They evolved eating contaminated food, we didn't. To compare the human digestive tract (which is much more susceptible to contamination) to a dog's is silly.

If dogs' and people's digestive tracts were so similar, why don't we eat dry dog food? Well, we don't eat it because we wouldn't expose ourselves to such vial food. Dogs can get by on it but they can't flourish.

I've talked a lot more about dogs and raw meat, but cats thrive on it too. A fellow veterinarian told me about a study at Colorado State, where they took twenty diabetic cats and put them on all meat diets. Eighteen out of the twenty became non-diabetic.

Those were pretty impressive results so I began using it as the first line of treatment for all the diabetic cats that came into my clinic. I was delighted that, out of the diabetic cats that I switched to all meat diets, not a single cat remained diabetic, except my own cat, Pesty, who just wouldn't change to the different diet. He simply refused to eat anything other than dry food, which he had been raised on.

I was treating Pesty with insulin two times a day for five years and he finally died at the age of 12. That means he had developed diabetes at the age of seven, and in my mind, there is no doubt now why he developed it. It's too bad he was so finicky because I could have saved him.

It is much easier to change a dog's diet than a cat's, but most will prefer raw meat hands down.

My other two cats made the transition to raw meat. One was not very friendly due to a lame leg from birth. I managed to splint it and it came back straight, but the entire trauma from that experience had really turned her sour. Along with the lousy attitude, both cats had terrible dandruff and shedding problems. No one could even sit down on the couch because of the hair.

After only a few weeks on raw meat, their coats turned shiny and beautiful and they stopped excessive shedding. One dropped from eighteen pounds to thirteen pounds and began to look great. They began to play like kittens again and old 'grumpy' began to crawl up into my lap and purr. Some want to know: "Where's the proof that a raw diet is safe and healthy?" All one has to do is open your mind and your eyes. It's so obvious even a caveman could see it. To say that dog and cat foods are safe and healthy, is to deny what all the papers are printing about the number of cats and dogs dying from it.

So don't tell me they're living longer and healthier lives. There has been a marked increase in digestive problems, weight and skin problems as well as cancer. There are also all kinds of unidentified liver problems. We continually see elevated liver enzymes for no good reason in middle aged dogs.

We do our blood tests, ultra sounds, x-rays and biopsies to no avail. We have degenerated liver problems for no good reason until we look at the food. We take them off of dry and canned dog food and over a couple of months the liver tests improve dramatically. All of a sudden the answer is obvious: It's the dog food.

I've seen dramatic changes in just about any condition you can mention when I have taken animals off of pet food and put them on healthy people food, including raw meat. I've opened my eyes and my mind. What's your problem? Maybe you're too busy or too tired to care. At least that's an honest answer.

Commercial pet food manufacturers throw up a smoke screen in front of everyone's eyes so they can't see. I don't want scare tactics; I want good solid proof. There's more proof that a raw meat diet is healthier for pets than conventional pet food. The last two years of continual reports on the news and in your local paper about pet food should be proof enough.

Ward Johnson, President of Sojourner Farms along with Cathy Sinning, DVM of Minneapolis, Minn. pointed out: "One must remember that the pet food industry created the Association of American Feed Control Officials (AAFCO) and thus the chemical analysis procedures used to evaluate a food's nutritional adequacy. Rather than relying solely on chemical analysis, why not study the animals' health? Using only a chemical analysis to determine a food's nutritional adequacy also ignores crucial information on the biological availability and digestibility of a food. It has been proven that digestive enzymes found in fresh food enhance biological availability, whereas extreme heat (common to the preparation of commercial pet foods) leads to the depletion of enzymes and depressed levels of digestible energy." [39]

If my diet is so deficient of vitamins, minerals and proteins, then maybe I should reevaluate what I'm doing. One thing I'm sure of is that what I eat is a lot healthier than what is in pet food. Frederick Kaufman clearly points out the major problem with pet food, "Dogs and cats are fed for our convenience and in accord with our crazes. On that, a $15 billion business feasts." [40]

All we need to do is be sure what we eat is healthy and adequate to keep us healthy. "Dogs and cats are living longer and growing fatter and more dyspeptic, and, like their owners, they have to watch the calories." [41]   But if we chose healthy

---

[39] Ward Johnson and Cathy Sinning, DVM, "Letters to the Editor: Differing opinions of raw food diet research". Javma, Vol 218. No. 10, May 15, 2001.
[40] Frederick Kaufman, The New York Times Magazine.They Eat What We Are. September 2, 2007.
[41] ibid

food for ourselves and our pets, we will both live longer. As far as our pets go, besides healthy people food, we need to add in a good source of raw protein (60 to 70% of their diet). Also I would like to direct your attention to The American Society for the Prevention of Cruelty to Animals (ASPCA) so you can be informed about a few foods that we as humans can eat, but that might be harmful to our pets. "Foods to avoid feeding your pet: alcoholic beverages, avocado, chocolate (all forms), coffee, (all forms), macadamia nuts, moldy or spoiled foods, onion and onion powder, raisins and grapes, mushrooms, salt, yeast dough, products sweetened with xylitol." [42]

When you start to feed your cat or dog healthy people food, it opens the door to millions of different kinds and there is no way I can list every single thing you might decide to feed. We need to start using the brain God blessed us with. We need to think and stop listening to people who just want to make money. We need to stop taking what doctors say, as gospel. We need to think for ourselves for not only our own health, but that of our pets.

You can't improve on what Mother Nature provides.

---

[42] ASPCA. *A Poison Safe Home.*

Chapter 13

Stories of pets on raw meat diets

I have to tell you a story about Bea and how changing her diet changed her life. It all started on a certain day that Chuck came into the clinic. I can remember it like it was yesterday. I could tell he was extremely worried because he was normally all smiles and full of life. But this day he wasn't smiling and he spent most of the time staring at the floor.

He had just come from the liver specialist who had not given him much hope for Bea, his dog, and he wanted to perform a liver biopsy that would cost $2,000. Chuck wanted a second opinion.

Chuck had originally gotten Bea from us. As I remember it he had just lost his other dog and I felt that I had the perfect dog for him. Actually I knew I had the perfect dog for him because she was 1 ½ years old and the sweetest Rottweiler I'd ever laid eyes on and all the girls had literally fallen in love with her.

We had received Bea from another clinic. She was young and very friendly, but she had a broken leg. The girls at the other clinic loved her dearly but the veterinarian whom they worked for wouldn't fix her leg. The girls at the clinic wouldn't give up on her so they started calling around to see if anyone would fix her.

They got lucky because they got a hold of Carol. Carol is a lot like my wife in that neither of them will ever give up on any animal, no matter how big or small. I don't know if she planned it out in her head, but she knew just what to say to get me to fix this dog's leg.

She came back to me and told me that there was a young Rottweiler over at another clinic with a broken leg and that it had been there for a whole week and nobody would fix it.

I was pretty sure that she was picking her words carefully, because she knew when she explained how long the dog had been suffering with the broken leg that I would fix it. Maybe it was a week or maybe it was a couple days, but she knew if she said a week that would do the trick.

I think if the week hadn't worked, her next approach would have been: "I'll pay for it!" She had me one way or the other.

I replied, "Do you mean to tell me that this poor dog has been waiting to get its leg fixed for a whole week? You've got to be kidding me!"

Carol answered, "No, I'm not kidding you. It's been over there a week and the girls there absolutely love this dog and would not let their doctor put Bea to sleep.

"Carol, tell them to get her over here and I'll fix her." It's not often I get to look that good in front of my girls and the other doctor's girls. It was kind of like playing superman and I love surgery anyway. But secretly I was worried how badly the leg was broken, because if it was shattered, it would be almost impossible to fix.

Well, Bea showed up with the x-rays of her broken leg. I could see it was going to take an internal compression bone plate to fix it, but I could fix it. It wasn't going to be cheap and there was probably nobody to pay, but it was worth it for me because there's a lot of good involved in doing something like this and it always gives me a high that can't be bought. I can honestly say I've never turned a broken leg down and I've never had to amputate a leg because I couldn't fix it.

I always refer to "we" when I say we took Bea to surgery because it was a team effort. My team for the last twenty years has been my wife (Karn), Carol and Marilyn. There have also been interludes of wonderful vet techs such as Marsha and Candace, Katy I, Katie II as well as my sons Mike and John, my daughters Jodi and Lia, and many others whom without their help I'm nothing. I couldn't have done the things I've done without them.

We took Bea to surgery and plated her leg without a hitch. It took several hours and a lot of sweat, but it happened. She did so well that she was walking almost normally in a week. If you fix it good enough, the body doesn't know it was broken.

Well we (the team) had solved the first part of the puzzle and now we needed to find an owner for Bea. It was lucky for her that Chuck had been in a couple of days earlier to put his terminally ill dog to sleep. So I called him and asked him if he would be interested in meeting the friendliest dog in town.

Surprisingly enough, he said, "Yes."

It was surprising because most pet owners go through a prolonged grieving process when they lose their best friend and in Chuck's case, he had definitely lost a good friend.

So, Chuck shows up and instantly falls in love with Bea. By the way he's the one who gave Bea her name. Chuck and his wife have been crazy about her ever since. In hind sight I'm not sure if I did him a favor or not because Bea's had a long history of medical problems right up until I changed her diet. She hasn't been sick since. It's hard to explain but you can really see it in their eyes. It's always the first thing I look at when they come through the door.

Bea had been through several medical problems for the last four years which included a broken leg, a severe eye problem, an autoimmune disorder, surgery for an obstruction, tick fever, and an unidentified liver problem. Now you know why I said that I'm not sure I did Chuck a favor.

Bea's liver tests were normal on 9/01/04. They started climbing in 12/03/04. We had fixed her leg sometime in June of 2003 and she had an episode of tick fever on 9/2/04. At the time I thought her liver elevations were because of the tick fever.

She responded beautifully to the Doxycycline to treat the tick fever but her liver tests never returned to normal. What's worse she just kept developing additional problems.

I know Chuck has a lot of faith in me but at this point, I'm not sure he should even like me. A redeeming feature was that we always seemed to be able to clear her up, but there was always something else happening.

One day Chuck came in with his wife and Bea. I'm in the process of treating another one of

Bea's illnesses when Chuck shows me his hand and says, "What do you think?"

I always wear a magnifying loop on my head so I pulled it down and looked at the palm of his hand. There was a swollen area about the size of a quarter and a small hole in the middle of it which was draining a sticky, clear fluid.

"How long have you had this?" I asked.

"Oh, about a month."

"Why haven't you gone to a doctor?"

"Because I just haven't had a chance," he answered, "by the way, this swelling appeared just a few days after I had picked up some broken glass."

That's when the light bulb turned on. There had to be a piece of glass still embedded in his palm for the wound to not have healed over a month's time. I know I'm not a human doctor and maybe I shouldn't have messed with it, but I couldn't resist. I also knew that Chuck trusted me totally, so I pulled out a small needle and proceeded to open the wound up.

I went out of my way to make sure it wouldn't be painful. As I worked at opening it little by little I could feel my needle bumping a hard object. The hole just kept getting bigger and bigger and the next thing I knew out popped a chunk of glass that was about 1/8th of an inch square. Chuck was totally relieved and thanked me profusely. His medical white knight had come through one more time.

So now you know why Chuck came in to see me one more time. Because of my own illness and unavailability, he had seen other veterinarians from time to time. He had even gone to a liver specialist and he had been beaten down totally and was literally whipped.

I had just gone through a year of liver evaluation myself. I had also spent the last year reading everything I could about livers and was totally amazed at how little I could find. There wasn't that much literature on how to heal a liver and the doctors knew even less. There were all kinds of advice, but no solid facts. The one thing they all knew was how to take a liver out, but no one knew how to fix it.

When Chuck came in with Bea, he told me he just wanted to know what I thought. I could tell he wasn't thinking that I could do much and I wasn't sure if I could either. But, I reviewed the records and the main thing I picked up was that it was a slow progressive liver disease and every single time I would do liver tests, the counts would be consistently higher and I mean every time.

I also reviewed the liver specialist's assessment of Bea and he stated that in spite of all the blood tests, x-rays, ultrasounds etc., the best he could come up with was a nonspecific hepatitis of unknown origin and he recommended a liver biopsy.

I didn't even know all of this was going on because I had been sick myself. The thing that amazed me the most was how it mirrored my own condition. If I hadn't gone through all this myself, I would have told him to go through the biopsies, but not now.

I had been through three liver biopsies and not one gave any real clue and more importantly not one told the doctors how to treat my condition. To my dying day, I know that last liver biopsy caused my colitis, but when you're panicked, you'll let them do anything to you. So I had immediately agreed and thought the sooner the better.

As I lay on the operating table with an IV in my arm, I was full of anxiety and really worried. I didn't want to die.

When the doctor came he said," I'm going to do an intrajugular liver biopsy on you."

His words almost jolted me out of bed. "You're going to do what?" I almost yelled.

He repeated again, "I'm going to do an intrajugular liver biopsy on you."

I'm no liver specialist but I know if you're looking for cancer, you're not going to find it via a jugular vein unless you're extremely lucky. If you're looking for cancer, you use an ultrasound to find the bad spot on the liver and then do an intercostal liver biopsy because you can stick the needle directly into the area you're concerned about.

I looked at the doctor, "Why a jugular and not an intercostal?"

He answers, "Because there's less bleeding."

"But aren't you looking for cancer? I don't think you'd do it this way if that's what you're looking for." I said.

"You're right; this is not the procedure to do if we're looking for cancer." He responds.

By now I'm paralyzed and upset, but he proceeds with the biopsy, meaning that he injects me with a sedative and insists that's what he's going to do in spite of my objection.

That liver biopsy was done two years ago and I've paid for it ever since. I progressed from severe bloody diarrhea for one solid week to intermittent blood and mucous in my stools. I never had this problem before the biopsy.

My condition has steadily improved to the point that I can control it; but I promise you prior to that liver biopsy, I did not have that problem. This problem is continuous now. I guess he had to justify his life. I've lost a lot of respect for him and doctors like him.

There's a close synergy between your liver and your colon. If you disrupt this synergy I can promise you that you'll spend the rest of your life wishing you hadn't and that is exactly what that doctor did to me.

Getting back to my story, the dog and I had similar conditions and I'd already been there. I told Chuck, "They might be able to give you a diagnosis, but they're not going to be able to give you a treatment. Why don't you take the $2,000 that you would pay for the biopsy and go out and buy some decent people food and feed that to Bea and see what happens."

At this point, I hadn't really worked with the food much, but I was starting to think it might make a big difference. I had seen a lot of dogs through the years who had elevated liver enzymes for no good reason and the best I could tell these people was that their dog had a degenerative liver problem or cancer. That was another reason I knew they weren't going to help Bea.

Chuck trusted me so he left and followed my advice to a tee. He came back about two months later and the moment I looked into Bea's eyes I knew she was fixed. Chuck was grinning from ear to ear and once again I got to be his hero. It was easy to tell she was well because her total demeanor was different.

I ran her blood tests and found that her liver enzymes had essentially dropped to normal and I knew I was on to something. That's when I sat down and wrote a handout on diet that would make people think about what they eat and what they feed their animals. It made me double my efforts to see what was going on.

Then Chuck really proved my point because he came back in six months and I could tell once again by looking at Bea's eyes and demeanor that things were not right.

"Chuck, what are you doing different?" I asked.

He looked at the ground sheepishly and said, "Well, her stools weren't as firm, so I put her back on dry food."

I'm thinking what is there about older people that they get so hung up on stools. I turn to Chuck and say, "You've got to be kidding me. After all her problems, you put her back on dry food?"

I guess he wasn't totally convinced about what I was saying, so I drew a blood sample from Bea and told him I'd get back to him in the morning.

When her blood test came in, all her enzymes were up again, so I called Chuck and gave him the results and told him to put her back on people food. He told me that he would and I told him that I wanted to check her blood again in a month or two.

When the time came, he brought her back in and once again I could tell she was back to normal. Since then, I've checked her blood yearly and it's been normal each time. Finally

Chuck became a believer and swears he'll never go back to dog food.

In case you still aren't convinced that diet matters, I have another case I'll share with you. I had a six year old Springer Spaniel who came in about four months ago. Her name was Trixie and she had a horrible nose problem where the skin was dying and sloughing off.

Trixie had been undergoing treatment for over two years for an autoimmune disorder. Usually it's referred to as Lupus because everybody relates to that. Trixie's owner, Mrs. Stevenson, was fairly distraught and totally exhausted. She had been to the dermatologist and was basically told that it was going to be a life long battle.

I have to admit that it was a terrible mess and I was thinking that I might not be able to help her much either. At that point I was just really starting to see what a raw meat diet could do, so I went over it with her. I spent a good hour with her going through the pros and cons because I didn't want anyone to scare her off by bringing up Salmonella, E.coli or tapeworms.

Sometimes when a diet is changed, a dog gets a little diarrhea, so I didn't want this lady to back off from raw meat because this might occur. I explained how easy it was to fix that. I also told her that I would rather deal with Trixie's possible diarrhea than her nose problem.

At this point I could not expect too much because the disease had advanced pretty far, but at least we had something to try. I wished I could tell you that she left with new hope, but I'm not sure if she did. All I knew at that time was the best that I could do was to give her another shot of cortisone and put her on more antibiotics, along with a totally different diet. I wasn't sure if she bought into the diet theory, but what did she have to lose.

The only thing I did different than the dermatologist was to take Trixie off of dog food and put her on raw meat and people food. But Trixie was already so bad it was even a stretch for me to think that it would work.

I went about my business and had pretty much forgotten all about Trixie because I didn't hear anything else from her owner. But, four months later, she brought her in for her yearly physical.

I didn't even realize who she was. I proceeded with the normal check-up and everything about her was perfect. My attention was not even directed towards her nose because it was perfectly normal. I told Mrs. Stevenson that Trixie looked great and I saw no problems whatsoever.

She looked at me bewildered and said, "You don't remember us, do you?"

I didn't say a word and I referred directly to her chart and started reading. I should have done that in the first place, but Trixie looked so good that I didn't think there was a need. As I was reading her chart I suddenly realized who Trixie was.

I blurted out, "You've got to be kidding me! Holy smokes, how fast did her nose problem clear up."

Mrs. Stevenson said, "Almost immediately when I changed her diet. Each week I could see a difference and after two months, she was normal."

"This is unbelievable because her nose was so bad, that there should be scarring. But look at her, she is perfectly normal and there is no hint of a problem."

We looked at each other and the words came to mind: It's like a miracle. So why wouldn't I be high on a raw meat diet, which healed her in two months when drugs couldn't do it in two years. It also cured it instead of just controlling it like drugs do.

I had a client come in a week ago with her cat, Garfield. He was literally driving her crazy. He was itching and had diarrhea and she went on and on about his symptoms. She told me she lived by herself and that she couldn't stand to watch her cat itch and she was tired of cleaning the carpet.

When I tried to talk to her about her cat's diet, she didn't want to hear and quickly told me that she had already tried it and in fact, she said it had given him diarrhea. She explained that she had him on a special food which seemed to be controlling the diarrhea. But the itching was still driving him and her crazy.

She even alluded to getting rid of the cat, but she said that she just couldn't because she loved him so much. She was upset and just went on and on until I began to get exhausted trying to help her.

I finally said to her, "Just what do you want me to do? You won't listen so we're in a no-win situation and if I begin to talk to you about his diet, you jump all over me. You tell me he needs his fiber and that he can only get it from the dry food because the canned food gives him diarrhea."

I already know she hasn't even given the raw meat a chance, so I tell her, "Your options aren't too good here. If you won't listen, then I have nothing to offer you."

At this point she settled down. I guess she could tell that I was ready to throw up my hands. Seeing my chance to maybe reach her, I continued, "You're going to put your cat in the bathroom so if he has diarrhea, I won't be in trouble. The first day I don't want you to feed Garfield anything. On the second day he can have a teaspoon of raw ground buffalo two times. Then I want you to call me in the morning every single day until we get this problem worked out."

She agreed and she took Garfield home. As she left, I thought she would follow my instructions simply because she was so desperate. She called me the morning after she had tried the two teaspoons of buffalo and Garfield was holding his own, but was a little hungry. So I increased the buffalo meat to three teaspoons a day.

The next day he was just fine, so I told her that she could increase it to one tablespoon, twice a day. At this point, he was doing great, but he hadn't had a bowel movement. Didn't I know this was coming? It's now constipation she was worried about. I reassured her and told her not to panic. I explained that there is not a lot of fiber in meat so he would have less frequent and smaller stools.

She called me one evening and now she was really worried because Garfield hadn't had a stool in five days. He didn't have diarrhea and he didn't itch, but he was definitely constipated.

You would probably begin to worry at this point too, but I wasn't. Usually what happens is, that just about the time an owner is really worried, then the pet has a stool. But I'm not taking any chances so I tell her to give an extra tablespoon of meat and bring Garfield in the following morning.

I've been there too many times. You'd be surprised how many people bring an animal in for diarrhea. I treat it that day and the next day I get the phone call complaining that their pet is now constipated. It happens all the time. You would not believe how this subject is such a concern for many clients.

Constipation is a rare problem in dogs and it's only an occasional serious problem in cats, which is usually associated with the lack of nerve supply to the large colon of older cats, but I could guarantee her that was not the case with Garfield. I held my breath because owners panic more times than not.

I knew if she panicked and put him on another diet or gave him an enema that his diarrhea would return. I hoped she would stay the course and knew if she did that Garfield's itch and diarrhea problem would be gone and she would be pleased.

Just the other day, I got a call concerning how Garfield was doing. She explained that his stools were normal and that he was not itching. Surprise! Surprise!

Diet has improved my life immensely and it has improved the health of the animals I treat. In almost all chronic conditions it seems to have cured them. For the first time in my life, I actually feel like a real doctor and I know I'm making a difference.

For those who say: "Where's the proof?" I know they haven't tried it because if they had they wouldn't be asking the question. There are a lot of people that go through life with closed minds. I know because I was one of them. It took my illness to open my eyes. It didn't happen overnight. It was a slow awakening, but when it happens it is so refreshing. It's wonderful to look at life and medicine in a whole new light.

I can finally cure conditions not just control them. I no longer have to threaten animals' longevity and quality of life by relying on cortisone and antibiotics. My energy level is high and my mind has never been clearer. I am the one that supposedly needs a liver transplant, but I can tell you right now the transplant is not likely to happen.

If you're not willing to try something new, how do you expect things to be different? You can't fix a chronic condition using the same old treatments. That's why it became chronic in the first place.

If you don't like what you're seeing, change the way you're thinking.

Chapter 14

More discussion on pet diet

Animal nutritionist, Pat McKay, reports that animals, especially dogs and cats along with all the other carnivores, have a well designed digestive system to handle raw meat. He's just an-other of the many people who have not seen serious problems with pets eating raw meat.

People are omnivores and are not as well equipped to deal with the problem of eating raw meat. Dogs and cats are carnivores and they have been eating raw meat as long as they have existed. Their GI tract evolved in such a way that they don't have the same problems with contaminated meat as we do. We obviously don't want to go out of our way to feed contaminated meat, but if it happens our pets are more than likely going to be okay.

I haven't seen a life threatening case of food poisoning in a pet. As far as I can tell, you might risk vomiting or diarrhea or a tapeworm. But I can treat and cure diarrhea and eliminate a tapeworm without much trouble, but I can't cure most cancers. So I would encourage you to start focusing on the real problem.

I am hoping that your pet's raw meat comes from the butcher or the grocery store. I'm not looking to feed them road kill. One needs to try to be reasonable. I know how expensive you think it is, but we've gotten so attached to our animal friends that some people will spend thousands at their local veterinarian hospitals to cure them of all types of problems.

I think you should put your money up front by purchasing good food so they don't end up at the hospital. There's a distinct possibility that all these degenerate conditions we see may not have happened if the animals had been on a healthy diet from day one. Even if that was not the case, improving their nutrition can certainly help them.

Martin Goldstein, D.V.M. has strong feelings about commercial pet food and says, "You can boost your pet's health profoundly by making one simple decision. All you have to do is to change his diet from unhealthy commercial brand fare to something you may never have imagined giving him: "*real food*!" [43]

Dr. Goldstein goes on to explain, "The pet food industry appears to be a cynical one, focused mainly on the corporate profits its prepackaged product lines bring." He talks about the ridiculous idea of commercial pet food companies adding color to their dried feed, mainly to impress owners. But he goes on to say, "Synthetic flavorings, on the other hand, are only for pets. Phosphoric acid, for one, makes animals' tongues tingle and so acts as an artificial appetite stimulator, especially in cats. Beef digest, poultry digest, salt and sugar are also used to perk up tasteless food; barely a nutrient among them."

Goldstein gives the following situation: "Imagine waking up in the morning and coming down to the kitchen to make yourself breakfast. You take some soybean grits, mix them with some tainted cattle-meat meal, throw in a few beaks and feathers, and smother your concoction with processed sugar syrup and chemicals, then sprinkle on a few preservatives and dyes. Pressure-cook the hell out of it, let it cool—and dig in! What if you were told that this is exactly what you'd eat at every meal for the rest of your

---

[43] Martin Goldstein, D.V.M. , The Nature of Animal Healing, A Ballantine Book by The Random House Publishing Group. 1999. (pgs. 54-57).

life? Is it any wonder: our pets have degenerative diseases, that so many get cancer, that so many die before their time?"

I too think that healthy people food is far better for dogs and cats, but I take it another step further and recommend raw meat to go with it. You can take any condition your dog or cat has; put him/her on 60 to 70% raw meat and 30 to 40% of whatever you deem as healthy food for you and then see what happens. You may have already spent hundreds if not thousands of dollar and in most cases, just controlled their symptoms. But you have not cured them.

You need to try a raw meat diet. Introduce it slowly over two weeks and figure you have to do it for two months. See what happens. Most people who try this say, "It's like a miracle."

Usually the worst you're going to see is possible diarrhea. If it happens, give them an appropriate amount of Pepto Bismol and hold them off food for a day. You can then introduce a blander diet such as mashed potatoes and hard-boiled egg whites. Once things are better, reintroduce the meat, giving less or just try a totally different type of meat.

I'm not saying you won't have problems, but they will be less trouble than what you have now. If you're not willing to try something different, then how do you expect things to get better. It's such a small price to pay when you consider it involves the life of your pet.

If you begin feeding a raw meat diet, you might not want to leave it out for hours. If your pet doesn't eat it in five minutes, he's not hungry anyway. Just pick it up and put it in a zip lock bag and refrigerate it. Free feeding is not a good idea anyway because pets tend to overeat and that isn't healthy. It is the same as humans eating a big bag of rancid potato chips with a bunch of questionably viable synthetic vitamins.

You can feed your pet dry food if you want, but I never will again. There should be a label on pet food that says: Feed at your pet's risk!

As far as canned pet food goes, apparently it is not a lot better. I don't feel the need to expound on it, because I think the latest news-paper articles about food intoxication and the death of all those precious pets has already done the job.

This cry about salmonella and parasites is a joke compared to what's gone on in the pet food industry. They have lost our trust and they deserved to lose it because they try to make us think that they're giving us the best, only to find out that it's no better than road kill and in some cases it is road kill.

I'll risk store bought raw meat any day. I no longer trust any food that's sold for dog or cat food, be it raw, canned or dry. I came to this conclusion when I bought some frozen packaged buffalo meat intended for consumption by dogs only.

I can now see how dog food manufacturers are cheating with raw meat. Buffalo is a dark, red meat. You shouldn't be able to see much fat in it at all. It's much redder than hamburger. It appears more like the color of liver.

When I received the frozen prepackaged ground buffalo, I couldn't believe my eyes. Instead of liver colored ground meat, it looked like flakes of meat packaged with a bunch of white beans. I thought it was a pre-packed diet with a lot of things in it, especially white beans.

I read the package and it said it was 100% buffalo with a minimum of 5% fat. How stupid do they think we are? I don't want to know the minimum, I want the maximum.

They know you're going to see 5% fat and think that's good. Give me a break. Basically off of what they're saying, it could be 100% fat and in this case, it looked like they included every-thing but the meat. It stated 100% ground buffalo, but it wasn't meat. I don't know what all the white stuff was, other than tendons, ligaments and butt holes, but I couldn't possibly feed it to a dog or cat.

I won't sell it and I can't, in good conscience, even give it away. So I use it as an example of what not to buy. If you can, buy human grade meat because I know now there is some-thing wrong with the dog grade or they would be selling it as human grade.

If you buy a one pound can of premium dog food, you pay the same price or more than you do if you buy one pound of ground turkey or beef. If you watch for sales, fresh meat is often even cheaper

The first raw diet was chicken and chicken by-products. I knew from day one that it was not a good way to go, because it consisted of chicken backs, chicken necks and 'innards'. When you consider how chicken is processed and how little meat is on their necks and backs, I couldn't possibly recommend it.

The by-products are worse because of obvious fecal contamination and its relationship to Salmonella bacteria. How could you possibly want to feed it or eat it yourself?

I've just learned to be suspicious of any food product sold for dogs or cats. I initially could see that dry food was not healthy, but as this evolved, it became clear that canned food wasn't much better. As I progressed I could see that raw food, sold for animals wasn't a whole lot better, but I still consider it better than dry or canned pet food. The pet food industry is losing people's faith by leaps and bounds. They're the one's killing their own industry and the sad part is they're taking your pet with them.

When I saw how they were trying to sell raw buffalo and misrepresent it as meat and then smelled a can of cat food that finished me off with the pet food industry. I see no redeeming qualities. I don't have a single good thing to say about them anymore. Your food (hopefully food that is healthy for you) is your pets' only chance at a healthy long life.

I've tried to find as many articles as I could about the pros and cons of commercial dog food versus a home made diet, especially if it consists of raw meat. As I read, people tried to make the line between the two simply black and white.

The commercial dog food advocates continually throw out scare tactics. They tell you that your dog is going to get Salmonella and very possibly die if you feed raw meat. They talk about three or four other bacteria that you need to worry about. And if that isn't enough, they explain that if the bacterium doesn't get them, then some nutritional disease such as Ricketts will.

They try to be somewhat subtle but they know you'll get the point. They say things like: "We can formulate a balanced diet around an animal's medical condition." They just try to plant a seed of doubt about homemade diets and let your mind do the rest.

It's not hard for them to shoot down a homemade diet because we have been indoctrinated from day one, especially your veterinarian. The commercial dog food advocates don't even need to use a sentence to scare you. They just need a word such as: food poisoning, unbalanced, tapeworms, Salmonella, rickets, osteoporosis, E.coli, and vitamin deficiency etc. Your immediate reaction is "Oh my God. I don't want that for my pet."

They can close your mind down in a second. You're no longer willing to think. They count on that, and it is so easy. Who are these people? I figure they are one of two types. They are subsidized by the pet food industry or they've been totally brain washed in veterinary school. They believe what they say all right, but they're definitely not thinking.

Let's try to sort this thing out. I've been in practice since 1972 and I was just as brain washed as everyone else until I developed liver failure. I wasn't eating anything that I felt was unhealthy. I didn't have some dread virus and I sure wasn't drinking alcohol or using drugs. In fact, I was a health fanatic. Why would I develop a liver condition?

It should have been just the opposite. My diet had everything in it to make me healthy, especially vitamins, minerals and a more than adequate source of protein, which included eggs, lots of fish and good red meat. I worked out for hours every single day of the year. So when my problem popped up I thought, "Liver failure, you've got to be kidding me!"

I now pay attention to supplements, food additives, excessive vitamin usage, coffee, excessive protein in-take, etc. There was a myriad of problems with my diet that I had ignored.

Your animal is what you feed it as well. You can feed just the way some veterinarian tells you, but all you see is your pet slowly falling apart, just like I did. I don't care what condition your pet has: obesity, severe skin problems, allergies, autoimmune disorders, digestive problems, cancer etc. They are all related to diet.

If you don't believe me, just try a two month trial period of feeding your pet nothing but what you consider to be healthy people food and raw meat. What do you have to lose? You will see what I've seen and suddenly realize that commercial pet food is not what everybody thinks it is.

There have been more pets that have died on commercial pet food than all those other diseases combined. It could be 10 times to 100 times greater, I don't know, but I know without a doubt that the real danger is in commercial pet food.

The pet food industry didn't start because they wanted your pet to be healthy. Someone was trying to make some money with all the by-products of the meat industry. They try to make you worry about contamination, but in fact they're the ones continually fighting the problem of contamination.

How many animals have died in the last two years because of tapeworms, Ricketts, osteoporosis, Salmonella, etc? None that I know of and I run an extremely busy practice. There have been hundreds if not thousands of deaths due to the pet food industry. If you throw in their link to cancer, which to me there is no doubt (I'm 100% positive), there have been uncountable, suspicious deaths, but not one single one that I've run into from homemade diets.

You need to remember that the pet food industry is motivated by profit. They are going to use the left over stuff, contaminated or not. They have one of two choices: use the leftovers as dog food or as fertilizer. What do you think they do with it? Money talks and it has nothing to do with your pet's health.

There are several reasons why healthy dry pet food doesn't exist. In the process of drying the food the protein is denatured, which makes it less valuable. They have to add in essential fatty acids in order to call it a complete diet. The problem with adding essential fatty acids is that they go rancid.

Our bodies and our pets' bodies need essential fatty acids, especially for our immune systems. Fatty acids are involved in the integrity of the cell wall. Without it your immune system can't function properly. Without an effective immune system, we get some immune mediated problem such as lupus or cancer or a disease such as valley fever that's extremely difficult to treat.

The bubble baby proves that point. He was born without an immune system so he lived in a bubble until he was thirteen. At that point, he was losing it mentally, so they decided to give him a bone marrow transplant from his sister and then take their chances by letting him out of his bubble. He was dead in a year due to cancer.

It's not bad enough that your pet doesn't get viable fatty acids, in reality, you're feeding rancid fat. There has been a long time association between rancid fat and cancer. Dried pet food is actually sprayed with essential fatty acids which go rancid rather quickly. You can't win. To me it's an obvious cancer producer. There is a direct correlation from the fatty acid deficiency and there is an indirect correlation due to the rancid fat.

You ask anybody in the know, just how long the fat sprayed on the surface of dried dog food will last before going rancid. They would tell you maybe days, maybe just hours and that liquid fat will oxidize the fastest.

Fish oil and flax seed oil are both sold in bottles kept under refrigeration in the grocery

stores. If they were merely sitting on the shelf, they would already be oxidized. So that is why it is often sold in gel caps and dark bottles. If you abuse fat, it will abuse you and the end result will very likely be cancer.

If we're going to talk facts, the commercial food industry has nothing to brag about. Its forty year history should be reevaluated as to how much good it has done. There's a very important point I would like to make. In most cases, the meat used in commercial dog food comes from rendering plants and it doesn't matter how diseased or contaminated it is. Let's face it; the best thing you can say about pet food is that it's convenient.

As far as vitamins in pet food, you need to remember that most, if not all, are synthetic. Their bioactivity is questionable and don't compare with the vitamins and minerals obtained from raw meat or vegetables.

You might ask how I came up with all these revelations. Well, it was so easy. All I did was start to use that wonderful God given gift called a brain. I started thinking about what I was doing and questioning age old ideas of what was healthy or not. I stopped taking people's biased recommendations.

If you think cancer is not an epidemic in the human and animal world, you are sadly mistaken, especially if you find out that you or someone you love has it. Thirty five years ago I used to diagnose cancer **six to twelve times a year**. I now diagnose it daily.

Last Monday, out of my first five patients, I diagnosed four with cancer and I could only help one of them; that made me look further into my own failing health. I was doing what I thought were all the right things and I was going down the tubes. You might think I am exaggerating, but I'm telling you I'm not. If anything, I'm understating the problems.

At this time I was thinking that my biggest fault was all the stress I was putting my body through. To alleviate stress, I'd exercise daily for hours but it didn't help. I was still losing my health. When they finally diagnosed my liver problem, they had no treatment. I knew I was a goner. There was no help in sight. I was going to die of bile duct cancer in a matter of months.

I tried to fight back by taking all the health aids and supplements like milk thistle and dandelion that I could. I tried a number of ways to detoxify my liver, but I wasn't getting any better. I prayed a lot and got ready to meet my maker. It's amazing how an illness draws us to God. He must get tired of talking to sick people. All the healthy ones are out there doing their thing. They don't have time for God and I was no exception.

When I realized how much I needed Him, I started praying and began to feel good about my relationship. I kept hoping for a miracle, but that part didn't happen then. It is like a joke I heard about a guy who was sitting on the roof of his house during a terrible storm. Everything was flooding and the man would surely drown, so he prayed for a miracle. Meanwhile, a boat comes by and tries to rescue him, but he turned the help down because he knew God was going to save him. A short time later, a helicopter swooped down to save him, but he said, "No thanks because God will be along shortly."

The water level kept rising and sure enough he drowned. When he got to heaven, he was pretty upset with God because he hadn't been ready to die. He had so many things on earth that he wanted to finish. He approached God and chastised him for not saving him. God looked at him in amazement and said, "What are you talking about. I sent you a boat and a helicopter and you turned them both down."

When I read that joke, it hit me right between the eyes! I realized that the help is out there for all of us, but we have to look for it. I knew I had to use my brain and reevaluate everything. That is when I stopped feeling sorry for myself. I began searching and reading. I worked on eliminating stress in my life and took a long hard look at what I was eating. But most important, I changed the way I was thinking.

It became clear that I had fallen into believing any and everything I had been told and I had started acting accordingly. When the doctors told me that I was going to die, I believed them. When they told me I would probably end up with cancer, I believed them. I began to think death and cancer and I began to act like I had it. It affected how I ate and what I did. I think that if we think something long enough, you'll eventually end up with it and oblige your doctor by dying.

Now, as I began to change my way of thinking, my eyes were open and my brain was functioning. I could see the light. God's miracle was so simple. I just had to change the way I was thinking and everything changed. I began feeling better and better with each passing day. I concentrated on watching out for stress.

My diet had changed to the point that I was weighing the pros and cons of everything I put in my mouth. I patrolled my mind to make sure that I was thinking good thoughts. The big bonus was that my mind started working. I could actually see and I reached the point where I felt good all of the time. I knew then that I didn't have cancer because I was putting weight back on and walking four to six miles every day.

So the doctors who had told me that they were 100% sure I had cancer were wrong. They told me that two years ago. I'm not sure how good a sixty-one year old person is supposed to feel, but I can relate to thirty-five year olds and I can keep up with them too.

It is interesting how easy it was to change my diet, once I started thinking for myself. I used to think that milk, meat, and potatoes were a great meal. Now I'm into water and black bean burritos mixed with lots of fresh vegetables. To me, food tastes much better now than it did before.

Every now and then, I'll cheat and try to enjoy a good steak or prime rib. The funny part is that it doesn't taste as good as it used to and the whole time I'm eating it I am worrying about how it will affect my health.

Your body communicates with you all the time and you can tell by the way you feel if something you eat doesn't work for you. It is easy for me to know that red meat isn't for me. It certainly doesn't make me feel better and in most cases it makes me feel worse, but I can eat a black bean burrito and I feel like a million bucks.

The feeling is strong and I urge you to start paying attention to what your body is telling you and to eat accordingly or you will start to hurt your health as I did. I realize that it is not easy to change your way of eating, thinking and living, but if you can't do it for yourself, then do it for those you love.

Your pet has to eat what you feed him or her. The pet food and fast food industry are not worried about going out of business because they think the public is too lazy and too stupid to catch on. We are a nation that wants our conveniences and that feeds the greed that is killing us and our pets.

I have a friend that owns several fast food restaurants and he told me that people aren't willing to pay more for healthy food and that he wouldn't even consider offering it. Have we degenerated to the point that we are willing to give up our health and the health of our pets just for convenience and cheaper prices? You're going to spend the money one way or the other. Buy good food now or pay your veterinarian or doctor later. I can guarantee you that a doctor or veterinarian is more expensive in the long run.

We are blaming our genes or saying that our problems are simply our destiny and we can't change that anyway, so we might as well eat whatever. Our pets are simply doomed by our closed in-thinking.

What we feed our pets really does matter.

Chapter 15

Outright frightening facts

Day after day, I continued to work on my own health and that of my patients. As I was having success, I looked for even more answers. I became obsessed with finding the truth and continued reading daily. It was crystal clear now that my own attitude played a major role in my health, be it good or bad. I began to pray daily and ask God to help me in my pursuit.

To say the least, as I read I was enlightened, appalled, upset, disgusted, elated, shocked and even sickened by what I found. I began to see that we as humans don't think nearly enough. Sometimes I wonder if we think at all. We tend to follow along without asking questions or looking for solutions, especially if we've learned something in school. We have grown up in a society that throws pills, shots, and supplements at every possible health problem.

Many of the so-called new inventions are proving to be hazardous to our health, especially all the new chemicals that they have introduced into our foods, not to mention all the new plastics that everything comes in. These plastics are known to release toxic substances on our food and in our water. Lack of exercise caused by television and computer games is plaguing our youth. The decline of the interaction of close family life is taking a toll. The fast food industries and additives and hormones and pesticides are ruining our food supply. We need to be concerned about this kind of terror in addition to outside terrorist attacks. Our food is killing us.

Even more sadly, greed is the motivating force that is causing the loss of our healthy food supply. We are caught up in a world where we are victims many times over each and every day. We are in a whirlwind and can't seem to find our way out.

I thought about how people used to eat long before we had all the fast food joints, TV dinners, canned soups, packaged dinners etc. People used to eat very simple diets which often included home grown vegetables and fruits as well as pork, beef and chicken which they raised.

Now, I know not everyone was raised on a farm or ranch and that you might never have even visited one. But the poisoning of our food supply evolved slowly over the years. The more traditional way of gathering and preparing food gave way to "convenience."

The more the public demanded faster and easier ways to feed their families, the more traditional farming started to change. The old family farm today has a very hard time surviving in an environment dominated by agribusiness and factory farming. It is disappearing at an alarming rate because of big business, and so is our good health. Obviously, greed and huge profits have become the driving force, not peoples' health.

Out health is now determined by CEO's both of the food industry and of the health care industry. The deciding factors are all profit motivated. It's not possible for any good to come out of this kind of system. You had better take notice and start demanding changes, if not for your sake, then for the sake of your children.

As I spent hour after hour literally pouring over all the material I collected, more and more thoughts, ideas, and startling revelations occurred. At home, I used Karn as a sounding board and at work Carol and my clients. I wanted to repeat out loud what I had been reading and thinking about. I wanted to see what others thought about my findings, especially those I held in high regard.

Karn and I were walking along the beach in Del Mar and my mind was flooded with what

I'd been reading. I looked at her and she knew what that glance meant and she smiled back as if to say, "What are you thinking?"

So I said, "Karn, obviously greed and huge profits have become the driving force in the food market for people as well as in the pet food industry. I'm sure of that."

"Rick, I couldn't agree more and sadly caution and health has taken a back seat."

I continued, "I found something really disturbing today. You remember Diethylstilbesterol (DES)?"

"Yes, wasn't that a synthetic female hormone?"

"Listen to this article from the National Cancer Institute: "DES (Diethylstilbestrol), a synthetic form of estrogen (a female hormone), was prescribed between 1938 and 1971 to help women with certain complications of pregnancy. DES has been linked to an uncommon cancer of the vagina or cervix (called clear cell adenocarcinoma) in a small number of daughters of women who used DES during pregnancy. Daughters of women who took DES during pregnancy may have a slightly increased risk of breast cancer after age 40."[44]

"Remember it was later found to increase the risk of miscarriage and it was then tested in a

[44] Nation Cancer Institute. U.S. National Institutes of Health. *Fact Sheet.11/29/2006.*

'morning-after' pill. Children born from such pregnancies were actually referred to as the DES babies." I looked at Karn.

"Didn't they ban that?"

"Here's the catch. In 1973 it was banned from human use, but they continued using it to accelerate growth in beef cattle. Well, that was also banned in 1979, but under the ban, the cattle industry was permitted to continue using existing stockpiles of DES."

I ran onto another article dated 2000. Bruce Silverglade, CSPI's director of legal affairs stated: "The food industry likes to claim that our food supply is the safest in the world. The use of an illegal cancer-causing drug and USDA's failure to uncover it demonstrates why that mantra is nonsense. It's sad that we have had to rely on health officials from another country to discover the problem." [45]

"You know, Rick, it's just horrible how things like this can happen and continue, especially in this day and time."

"I know. I don't know what has to happen for these practices to be stopped. I mean look at the progression of breast, uterine and prostate cancer. Hormones added to just about everything

---

[45] Bruce Silverglade, Center for Science in the Public Interest. Common Dreams progressive newswire. *CSPI Urges USDA to Determine if U.S. Beef is Tainted With the Hormone DES. U.S. Sold Beef with Cancer-causing Hormone to Swiss.* February 2, 2000.

we eat are causing a major health epidemic. I think we all expect to get cancer if we live long enough. But it hasn't always been like that."

We walk along the sandy beach with the wind blowing gently. We stop and watch a seagull as it swoops down and skillfully picks up a small fish. As it flies off with its prize, the water crests time and time again until the white foam laps at our feet. For a short time we forget all about everything else and we just take in the beauty all around us.

We decide to move back out of the water and sit on the beach for awhile. I'm supposed to be relaxing, but my mind pushes on trying to find answers. I pull out a book and start reading.

"Karn, this is a really informative book."

"What's that?"

"*The Hundred Year Lie,*" I flip the book over, "and it's by a guy named Randall Fitzgerald. It's interesting how he actually lists the years starting with 1900 and what some of the problems or lies were." I turn through the pages until I come to 1947. "See what we were just talking about. I quote, "Sex hormones are first introduced into livestock production to add more fat and weight on the animals. One of those hormones, DES, is hailed as the most important development in the history of food production. Several decades later DES will be found to cause cancer. Even after the FDA bans this substance, cattle will continue to be administered illegal doses of DES."

Karn digs her toes into the warm sand as she speaks, "Well, I know so many people now who have cancer. It's everywhere you look."

"It gets worse. Fitzgerald says, "From 1950 to 2000 the overall incidence of cancer in the United States will rise by 55 percent." I look up at Karn before I continue. "He also explains that most of the nation's cattle used to spend their time grazing in open spaces until slaughter time. But then, by the 1970s, three-quarters of U.S. cattle spend most of their lives in crowded feedlots, being injected with antibiotics and hormones."

"It's hard to know what to eat anymore."

"One thing is for sure; there has to be a direct correlation between what we eat and our health. And it is the same for pets." I close the book and stick it back into my backpack, "How about some water?"

"Great."

I hand Karn a bottle and I drink down half of mine. "I had a client come in just the other day and we got to talking about brain tumors. She works at the Children's Hospital. I asked her if she saw many brain tumors in children these past few years. Immediately she told me 'you wouldn't believe.'

"In children?" Karn's face hardens.

298 It's Like a Miracle

"I'm convinced that there is a strong correlation between growth hormones and brain cancer. Now that I think about it, over the last year, I've heard of five children who have been diagnosed with brain tumors. And that's from my own clients. One has already died. It makes sense that children would be more susceptible to brain tumors because their brain is still developing and the constant exposure to hormones cause the brain cells to act differently. The change causes them to grow uncontrollably. It's all very subtle but I'm sure it happens. To me there's as big a correlation between growth hormones and brain tumors as there was between smoking and lung cancer. Everyone knows it, but no one could prove that either for some time."

"Makes sense to me."

"And it's not just cancer our diets are contributing to. Take our granddaughter and her urinary infections. You know, she's had this problem for well over a year now. She's been on antibiotics and had all kinds of tests done. They haven't found one reason why. But the scary part is: they've never once asked about her diet, just like my doctors. And you know she eats garbage. If it doesn't have sugar on it, it's not food. You always try to get her to eat fruits and vegetables, but it's an uphill battle. Remember, a full meal to her is one chicken strip or should I say cancer strip."

"Okay Rick, but calm down, you're right, but you're getting all worked up."

"Well, someone has too. You know the urinary tract is more than capable of handling a urinary infection as long as it has a healthy immune system. Why do you think humans have survived as long as we have? It certainly isn't because of hormones and antibiotics. They didn't even exist seventy years ago. Humans survived because they had good immune systems."

"I know." Karn motions for me to lower my voice.

"Well, I'm just worried about our grand-daughter and I know it's her diet."

"Come on Rick, let's walk some more."

I smile and know she's right. But I continue to run things through my mind. It just won't let me rest. Not until I have the answers. Karn takes off down the beach knowing full well that I will come along. She has a knack for knowing what I need.

I manage to keep some of my thoughts to myself for the rest of the afternoon as we sit down to listen to a little music. The time is restful and everything should have been perfect, but there is no escaping the fact that I am in the fight of my life and I don't have time to waste.

The phone rings and Karns goes to answer it. In a few minutes she hands it to me, "It's Richard." (Richard and Donna have become our best friends and we spend as much time as possible with them. They own Mogie that I've already told you about.)

"Hey, how's it going….oh fine….yeah….tonight?...well yeah that'd be fine ....what time? ..great ….see you then."

"Richard and Donna are coming over around seven."

"Oh, great. We haven't seen each other for some time. Uh, I think I'll go do a little shopping with Donna while you and Richard talk. Do you need anything from the store?"

"Not really." I smile deep inside because I know she called them. I guess I've been a little testy these past days.

After Richard arrived it didn't take long before we were in a deep discussion. I felt like a vessel just overflowing with emotion.

"You know Richard, I've learned a lot about myself and about doctors through all this. I have been grabbing at straws just hoping I'd get lucky and get well."

Richard just nods and lays his arm on the back of the chair as if knowing our discussion would be a long one.

"First I tried to take every possible supplement I could find. Now I find out I actually made myself worse. You know me, I'm a pretty driven person and when they told me I was going to die, I seemed to go out of control. I tried everything.

I was even willing to sacrifice my sons. Richard, I never thought I could do anything like that."

"Now Rick, wait a minute. You're being too hard on yourself."

"No, let me finish. They started checking my youngest, John, to see if he could be a liver donor. He was like a lamb going to the slaughter and happy to do it. For a moment I thought he was so mature and handling things so well, as he went through the tests. I actually was proud to have raised such a great son. But Richard, I was ready to let someone cut part of his liver out - *for me*."

"Rick, they do liver transplants everyday. The doctor told you it would be fine. They told you your son would do fine and that his liver would regenerate. Now isn't that what you were told? As well as the message they gave you that you were going to die without the surgery. Hell, I'd have done the same thing."

"Well, I don't know about that. There was so much frenzy, and the doctors didn't have time to talk to me. Well, I thought John was okay and mature enough to handle it, and maybe he was, but he didn't really know what he was getting into. He wasn't prepared. You know John just got back from the Army where he spent three years, included several trips to Afghanistan and Iraq. He'd already been through enough and he thought he was stepping up to the plate for me.

When they started showing him pictures of post operative patients and the scars on the abdomens' of patients who had gone through the surgery, I think he thought of it as a scar of honor."

Richard listened as I talked on, "But let me tell you, when they showed him a picture of a patient with a catheter stuck in the jugular vein in his neck, I could see him just staring at it. I broke down because I knew the reality of the surgery had just hit him. And the reality hit me that I was doing this to him. I was so blinded that I was grabbing for anything that might save me and I had forgotten how precious my son was to me."

"How about we go have a little bite to eat? I'm starved. You know that little restaurant just down the street?" Richard motioned toward the door.

"Yeah, that'd be fine. Just a minute, let me change my shirt."

As our guests left later that night, I sat down at the table and began to read again. "Karn, I like the way this book, *The Hundred-Year Lie* gives a chronological list of some of the things we need to be concerned about. I think I'll go through it again and shorten some of the items on the list that pertain to what I'm dealing with today. I may work with it and add some things too. What do you think?"

"I think it's a good way to organize your thoughts. Good luck. In the morning I'd like to read what you have come up with. Now, I'm going to take a nice long bath."

So I began to read and reread and the following is a partial list by Randall Fitzgerald as well as my own comments:

Randall Fitzgerald writes: "At the outset of the twentieth century our food supply became an initial testing ground for innovations in the emerging 'better living through chemistry' belief system. Chemists work with food processing companies to create artificial sweeteners, a butter substitute, taste-enhancing additives such as MSG, and the first partially hydrogenated vegetable shortening. These synthetics set the stage for the revolution in food processing that are to come." [46]

As the light of day dimmed, I turned on more light and settled back to read and take notes. This is what I came up with, and it will help us talk more about the health issues for humans and pets:

In 1900, in the USA, cancer was the tenth leading cause of death (3% of all deaths) and diabetes affected 1/10 of 1%, but now combined they represent around

_____

[46] Randall Fitzgerald, The Hundred-Year Lie (Plume, a member of Penguin Group USA, 2006) p. 63-87.
Direct quotes will be so noted, but as an author I have also chosen to expound on some of the topics.

40% of all deaths in the USA. That's a major switch from 3.1% to 40%.

In 1911, heart attacks as a result of growing artery disease were almost unknown.

In 1921, a total of 20 reports of endometriosis were noted, but by 1990, 20% of women of child bearing age were affected.

In 1931, "In this year a girl named Virginia is born; she will become the oldest child diagnosed with the new disease called autism; her birth year is also the first year that thimerosal is used in vaccines." (Fitzgerald). I would like to explain that thimerosal is preservative containing mercury which was used in childhood vaccines.

In 1935, the first case of cancer was reported among the Inuit Tribe of Alaska and Canada. Fifty years later, after adopting processed food diets, the cancer rate exploded and now rivals the USA.

In 1941, "The FDA approves DES for use as a treatment for menopausal women.

Later the FDA will extend DES use to a variety of conditions associated with pregnancy." (Fitzerald)

In 1947, "Sex hormones are first introduced into livestock production to add more fat and weight on the animals. One of those hormones, DES, is hailed as the most important development in the history of food production." (Fitzgerald). I would like to add that a decade later, DES was found to cause cancer and even though it was banned, cattle continue to be given it illegally and it may still be used today.

In 1949, breast cancer doubled.

In 1950, most of the cattle are grass fed, but by 1970, 3/4 of them live in crowded feedlots. They are injected with hormones and antibiotics and fed diets that include processed sewage, poultry litter, shredded newspapers, sawdust, fat tallow and grease. From the 1950's to 2,000, the overall incidence of cancer in the United States rose by 55%, breast and colon cancer by 60% and testicular cancer by 100%.

In 1968, scientists discovered that MSG caused widespread brain damage in immature and newborn animals.

In 1971, "An association is found between mothers who took DES and a rare form of vaginal cancer in their daughters. Apparently the DES taken during pregnancy affected fetal development." (Fitzgerald)

From 1973 to 1991 there was a 126% increase in prostate cancer, a 26% increase in childhood leukemia, a 25% increase in breast cancer and a 41% increase in testicular cancer.

In 1974, FDA banned the commonly used pesticide Eieldrin that had been used since 1921, as a dangerous carcinogen. It was found in 96% of all meat, fish, and poultry as well as 85% of dairy products.

In 1976, "The director of the National Cancer Institute, Arthur Upton, tells a committee of the U.S. Congress that half of all cancers are caused by diet. The Journal *Scientific America* reports that the diet a chicken is placed on in poultry production is "almost totally foreign to any food it ever found in nature. Its feed is a product of the laboratory." This diet includes antibiotics, hormones, sulfa drugs, and even arsenic compounds." (Fitgerald)

In 1985, Smithsonian Institute reports: outbreaks of cancer in fish only began after the widespread distribution of synthetic chemicals in the early 20th century.

In 1993, BGH (genetically engineered bovine growth hormone) was approved by the FDA to increase milk production.

In 1994, FDA approves the marketing of genetically modified foods even though they haven't been proven safe. Food processors now use ingredients from transgenic corn and soybeans in 60% of all processed food.

In 1995, "The United States now uses five pounds of pesticide active ingredients every year for every person in the nation." (Fitgerald)

In 1997, "Testing conducted by the United States Department of Agriculture finds 72 percent of fruits and vegetables produced in the United States contain detectible levels of pesticides." (Fitgerald)

"A study in the medical journal *Pediatrics* reports the results of a survey of 17,000 girls that finds that **by the age of eight, about one in seven white girls and one out of every two African-American girls are starting puberty,** with breast growth and pubic hair. Even more startling, one out of every one hundred white girls and three out of every one hundred African-American girls show these characteristics at the age of three! The explanation for this **early onset of puberty seems to be in their diets.**" (Fitgerald)

In 2000, (Fitgerald) "The incidence of testicular cancer is now estimated to be **four times higher** than just fifty years earlier.

In 2003, (Fitgerald) "As of this date, 80 percent of the soy and 38 percent of the corn planted in the United States are **genetically engineered;** derivatives of these two crops now show up in 70 percent of all **processed foods.** The Centers for Disease Control and Prevention reports that of all babies born in the United States in

2000, at least **one-third will become diabetics.**"

In 2004, "The Science journal *Public Health* prints a study revealing that the incidence of **death from brain diseases**, such as Alzheimer's and Parkinson's, **more than tripled** during the period of 1974 to 1997. (Fitzgerald)

"A study in the medical journal *Archives of Disease in Childhood* reveals that four hundred children were tested for the effects of **food additives and artificial preservatives** on their behavior. The results demonstrated 'a substantial effect' of these synthetic **stimulating hyperactivity and behavioral problems.**" Fitzgerald)

In 2005, Southern California Coastal Water Research Project found that 2/3 of some species of fish possessed both male and female reproductive organs due to contamination of estrogenic chemicals.

I sat back in my chair still holding the sheets of paper in my hands. The facts raced around in my mind and pieces of the puzzle began to connect. It is scary to realize what I, along with so many others, have been eating.

Then I thought about children and how we as adults are setting them up for health problems and some of those are showing up earlier and earlier.

It was also clear that pets are not spared either, because we have been letting them down dramatically as well. I believe that a lot of the blame should fall on us as individuals who should strive to educate ourselves on healthy nutrition. But then again much of the blame has to go to the food industry and pet food industry because they have done us all a major disservice by exposing us to obvious cancer producing hormones and pesticides all in the name of making a profit.

With our busy lifestyles we have become complacent when it comes to our own awareness to which we have fallen victim. We are bombarded now with so much wrong information that it is difficult to sort through the smoke screens which lead us astray. But I know we must all put forth all the effort possible if we want to live healthy lives.

I turned the light off and made my way to bed, promising myself that I would continue my own education and that I would share what I found with others.

Keep reading and searching for answers.

Chapter 16

Beware of the experts

Don't fall victim to the quick fixes, protein powders, supplements, vitamins, diet drinks, processed food and fast foods. Don't let the large greedy food producers of the world con you into believing that the use of pesticides, hormones and antibiotics are an improvement in our food supply.

There is no substitute for real, down to earth fresh food. Read for yourself what is happening to society because of what we are putting into our mouths. There is no denying, the obesity problem, cancer deaths, and heart problems have all escalated. Take a hard look at the tons of new chemicals which have been developed and how they are used in our food supply.

Look at the numerous pet food recalls in the recent months as well. Think about what you, your family and your pets have gone through. You are reading this book because you see the problems and you want to know what you can do. You want answers and you already know that health is everything. I am sure you are either fighting a major battle in your life, a close friend or relative is, and/or your pet is.

Don't wait until the problem is too big. Take action now and be proactive with regard to your children and, in the future, your grand-children. Take action now for the lives of puppies and kittens yet to be born. Look at the greed all around you and realize that it is dictating our very lives and the lives of our beloved pets.

Stop listening to the sales gimmicks you are bombarded with each and every day on television, labels, and even at our doctor offices and veterinary clinics. Start thinking, reading and educating yourself so you can make informed decisions. Remember you not only have to take care of yourself, but you must take care of children and your innocent pets.

I am not recommending any so called diet. I am not selling any product. I am not getting a kick-back from any product. I am simply telling you my own life story because I am just like you. We are victims of our time and the greed of industries that do not have our best interest at heart.

There are no recipes in this book. There are no supplements or magical pills for you to try. All there is here for you is common, down to earth sense about what we are facing. I am not trying to scare you or hit you over the head with my thoughts.

But I am telling you what happened to me and why I am now fighting a serious liver problem. I want you to know how it happened and how I found some answers for myself. I also want to tell you that the pets of the world have been victimized terribly and they don't deserve that. I am admitting to you that I didn't have all the right answers for my patients, but I do have proof now that I am sharing with you about returning them to their natural food.

It has always been known that fresh fruits and vegetables, whole grains and meat in moderation were good for us. But the kicker is that over the years, hormones, pesticides, antibiotics and other chemicals have been added to the simple wholesome diet, and that has altered everything.

Organic would certainly be better if you could prove the product really is organic. The National Organic Standards Board defines "organic" as: "Organic agriculture is an ecological production management system that promotes and enhances biodiversity, biological cycles and soil biological activity. It is based on minimal use of off-farm inputs and on management practices that restore, maintain and enhance ecological harmony.

Organic is a labeling term that denotes products produced under the authority of the Organic Foods Production Act. The principal guidelines for organic production are to use materials and practices that enhance the ecological balance of natural systems and that integrate the parts of the farming system into an ecological whole.

Organic agriculture practices cannot ensure that products are completely free of residues; however, methods are used to minimize pollution from air, soil and water.

Organic food handlers, processors and retailers adhere to standards that maintain the integrity of organic agricultural products. The primary goal of organic agriculture is to optimize the health and productivity of interdependent communities of soil life, plants, animals and people." [47]

---

[47] The National Organic Standards Board Definition of Organic. The definition was passed by the NOSB at its April 1995 meeting in Orlando. Fl.

However, you need to look out for yourself by reading labels. Manufacturers play around with words which are sometimes confusing. "Natural and organic are not interchangeable. Other truthful claims, such as free-range, hormone free and natural, can still appear on food labels. However, don't confuse these terms with 'organic.' Only food labeled 'organic' has been certified as meeting USDA organic standards.

You must look at package labels and watch for signs in the supermarket. Along with the national organic standards, USDA developed strict labeling rules to help consumers know the exact organic content of the food they buy. The USDA Organic seal also tells you that a product is at least 95 percent organic."[48]

I am sure if you could find healthy food without any additives that you would certainly prefer them, so it is worth your time to be sure of what you are buying.

Look at all the hidden ingredients in all the processed foods and know if you can't even pronounce them, that they certainly aren't natural or good for you. I like to say that if I can't identify it, I don't eat it.

My problem with organic is that the meaning and all that it entails, is still too vague.

---

[48] The National Organic Program. *Organic Food Standards and Labels: The Facts.* January 2007. http://www.ams.usda.gov/nop

It's a lot like cage free chicken. They use these words because they know you will read more into it than what is really there. To you, cage free means chickens in their natural environment, eating what they normally eat. It also implies they are leading normal lives. That couldn't be further from the truth.

Cage free just means they are not in a cage. The chickens are on the ground, but they are still in some kind of enclosure and it may be 500 feet by 500 feet. That might be fine if there were only 200 together in the pen and they might even be able to find some natural food on the ground, but that is not the case.

There are often 10,000 to 20,000 chickens crammed together and they are forced to eat whatever is put in front of them, and many times it is a concoction of whatever cheap waste products that is available. These are mixed with antibiotics and probably growth hormones.

These birds still can't exercise because of the gross numbers, and they are knee deep in chicken shit. That's not what I would call a natural environment. Health officials are now finding more contamination with cage free versus chickens in a cage.

It is big business and they are going to do and say whatever it takes to make a buck and they're happy to let you read into the situation whatever you want, because you make their case for them.

If cage free is that abused, I have to figure that organic could be just as abused. I don't trust the word because it is not that specific and you are still allowed to read into it as much as you like.

If it says hormone and pesticide free, I figure, it probably is, especially if it is associated with a health food chain. Stores such as Sprouts, Wild Oats and/or Whole Foods are probably a safe choice in such stores. These markets also sell meat that they label hormone free and I tend to believe that too because these specialty places would be put out of business if anyone could prove otherwise.

They're not as concerned about your health, however, as they are about staying in business. Making money is the American Way and they won't jeopardize their business. For that reason only, I do trust them, until proven otherwise. We need words that are very specific as to what they imply. The words today are vague and allow countless abuses.

Since they are not worried about our health, we must continue searching for the truth and going back to what is healthy, or we are all going to see the rise of more and more deadly diseases. I believe we can stop that trend if we focus on it.

I've thought a lot about doctors and how and what they prescribe. Just last month, I encountered an experience that exemplifies how vulnerable we all are when we place ourselves under the control of modern medicine.

My sister-in-law recently underwent a colonoscopy and upper (gastric) endoscopy. The reason for the upper endoscopy was to examine the condition of her G.I. tract and stomach because of her long-term use of 'heartburn relief' medicines (i.e., Tums, Ranitidine). Lab results indicated the presence of Helicobacter pylorus bacteria.

He decided to put her on a two week regiment of antibiotics. About ten days into the treatment, her mouth began bothering her, so she returned to see the doctor. She found out that she had thrush (an oral yeast infection brought on by the excessive use of antibiotics).

This is a typical case where you jump from the frying pan into the fire. Let's think about it. They had cultured out a potential pathogen that so far had not caused an obvious problem. I believe these bacteria can be found in normal conditions and that there is a certain number of people that have no problems with it. In other words, it could have been a normal part of her stomach flora.

We all have staph bacteria on our skin. And it is a potential pathogen waiting to strike. If we disrupt or damage our skin, the staph will be able to set up an infection, but under normal circumstances the skin has a good defense mechanism. So I don't think it is a good thing to prescribe or take antibiotics just because we have staphylococcus aureus on our skin.

I don't know why it would be any different for the Helicobacter pylorus in the stomach. I do know that there is a large percentage of people who will culture it out that have no symptoms or visible lesions.

Let's give Marlene's doctor the benefit of the doubt and say that Helicobacter pylorus is not supposed to be in the stomach. You have to question what condition arose that allowed it to grow. There are many things that can create an environment which would predispose you to a gastric ulcer and secondary infection with the bacteria.

Diet and stress would be the main ones. Both of these will increase your gastric acidity thus predisposing you to ulcers. Marlene was already taking Prilosec because of a history of gastric cancer in her family or she was having stomach upset. I really don't know for sure why.

Taking the antibiotic would hopefully kill Helicobacter pylorus, but it has done nothing to correct the condition that allowed it to grow there in the first place. An obvious place to start was to evaluate what she ate and work on eliminating stress in her life. As far as I know these weren't even talked about between she and her doctor. She was just put on antibiotics.

What's to stop the Helicobacter pylorus from coming back? They haven't changed a thing so there's no reason why it wouldn't come back. I would think that initially the doctor would try and find out why she was taking Prilosec in the first place before even considering putting her on antibiotics.

Prilosec is a medication one takes to lower gastric acidity. Chronic use would lower the acid in her stomach, but it could also change the normal environment of the stomach which may have allowed Helicobacter pylorus to grow in the first place. Personally I would have tried to get her off the Prilosec and make sure she was eating an appropriate diet as well as eliminating stress as much as possible.

Marlene is an avid reader and thinker and it is very possible that she becomes very emotionally involved during certain activities. It happens to all of us. It could be a good book or movie that puts you on the edge of your seat which ultimately drives your gastric juice upward.

My point is there are conditions that allow these bacteria to exist. The doctor has done nothing to change those conditions so there's no reason why the bacteria won't come back unless its environment has been changed. Something different must be done. You can take all the antibiotics you want and all you've accomplished is that now you have another problem such as thrush. Quite possibly you have even made the bacteria more resistant to future antibiotics.

Another problem with the antibiotic use is that you can't measure the amount of damage you are doing and it has a domino affect. It is easy to see such things as thrush and it is common knowledge that healthy bacteria in the G.I track is also killed off. But it is more difficult to see the overall affect on the immune system as well as the rest of the body. There are physiological problems affected too, that just can't be measured.

If Marlene had been suffering from an ulcer, it would have been crazy not to have treated it, but she didn't have one. All she had was a bacterium that may have been a risk or it could have been normal flora for her. So the doctor started with a clinically normal patient and he put her on antibiotics and now she has a problem.

It doesn't make sense to approach the situation in that manner. Why not work on improving her health so her immune system could eliminate the problem? Why not try to get her off of the Prilosec to see if that was the problem? Why not reduce stress in her life so she wouldn't need the Prilosec? Why not use healthy bacteria found in probiotics to crowd out the Helicobacter pylorus. Unhealthy bacteria and yeast have a difficult time existing when there is an abundance of healthy bacteria.

As far as I can tell, modern day medicine often attacks the symptom and not the problem. It is relatively easy to eliminate gastric discomfort with antispasmodic and antacids, but a little more complex to find and attack the cause. Marlene and her doctor both need a different perspective on life.

She's just as guilty as her doctor because she needs to evaluate how she thinks. *If you don't like the way you're feeling maybe you should change the way you're thinking.* Know that it can be very subtle and that it might lie beneath the surface, but if you're willing to really look, you will find that this critical thinking is just as important as what you eat.

We all know that diet is important, but that it is difficult to correct. Doctors often don't even mention it because humans are so addicted to food that they wouldn't try to change their eating habits even if a doctor warned them that their health was suffering. So the villain here is our own frailty or weakness toward food. I think our addiction to food is even worse than smoking or alcohol.

Take Marlene for instance, she worries about what artificial sweetener she's going to use in her coffee, instead of the fact that it is quite possible that her coffee is the culprit that is creating her gastric acid. That has thrown her into a vicious cycle of having to take Prilosec which in turn is probably allowing the Helicobacter pylorus to grow.

When it comes to food, coffee is not the main culprit, but it is a major player. I know how addictive it is because I lived on it for thirty years and literally worshipped it. I'd have a large latte in the morning to get me going and I would stay on that high for much of the day. I could accomplish so much more at work because I was alert. Then in the afternoon I'd often get a frappocinno on ice to give me that buzz. No wonder so many 'coffee shops' have grown up so fast, we're an easy sell.

But none of us looks at the down side of some of these addictions until major health issues arise. Dr. Chattman told me over twenty years ago to stop drinking coffee. It went in one ear and out the other. I thought to myself to quit coffee would be like cutting my life line off and besides everyone drinks coffee, so it couldn't be that bad.

But then, Dr. Chattman was sterner with me when I began having bouts of chronic diarrhea. They progressed to pretty much every single day. I began living on Pepto Bismol, Immodium, and Pepcid AC. Ultimately I was con-fronted with my liver problem. At this point, I still refused to even consider that coffee might be playing a part in my overall health.

But when I reached the point where doctors were telling me I needed that liver transplant, I finally realized that I needed to improve my diet. Only then did I stop drinking coffee. It became very apparent that coffee added to my diarrhea because when I stopped it I got better, and if I fell off the wagon, so to speak and drank coffee, the problem was immediate. The relationship was very clear.

It wasn't easy to quit because just the smell of it made my mouth water. I also missed the stimulation. But after thinking it through, I realized that although it gave me a high, that it also gave me a low. A body doesn't let you cheat and I knew that continuing to drink coffee was making me lose my level ground.

Did coffee cause my condition? I doubt it, but did it contribute to it? Yes, the caffeine is a stimulant and it definitely made me hypertensive, which may very well have contributed to the constricting action of my bile duct. I could envision how it could also contribute to a stroke or heart attack and I'm living proof of what it does to your gastro intestinal tract.

As far as I'm concerned you are playing Russian roulette if you drink coffee and that there's a chance it might not hurt you but there is also a chance it will. The problem is not limited to coffee, but includes everything we put in our mouths.

Doctors need to look at and treat the whole patient and not just the local symptoms. But of course, they won't be successful if the patient isn't willing to listen and make changes in their lives.

Not until I was in bad shape did I begin to make changes not only in my own lifestyle, but in the way I looked at and treated my patients. The change in my own thinking has helped me numerous times when dealing with difficult cases.

The most unusual case I think I've ever had involved a diagnosis that was totally theoretical and full of hypothesis. But I am sure if I hadn't been open to seeking answers for the cause instead of simply treating the symptoms, this dog would have died.

Steve and Carol came rushing into the clinic with their three year old Airedale, Barkley, who was literally suffocating. He was named after Charles Barkley who was a hero to many people in Arizona at that time, especially my mom and dad because they were basketball fans.

Well, Barkley was in deep trouble because it was all he could do to breathe. Steve explained, "Dr. Soltero, he started having a little trouble breathing about two weeks ago and it has gotten progressively worse. We kept thinking it was nothing and that he would get better, but today I didn't think he was going to make it to the clinic."

I began to check him out and I knew there were several conditions that could cause this type of reaction, Valley Fever being number one. But that didn't add up because his condition spiraled downward too quickly. Diagnosing is filled with elimination of each possibility, one at a time.

I rushed him to x-ray, all the while trying not to stress him further. Within a short time, I was explaining what I had found to Steve and Carol. "His chest is full of fluid and I mean full. I'm going to tap his chest to draw off some so I can see if it looks sterile or infected."

They watched as I proceeded. The fluid came out blood tinged but clear. I knew if he had been a cat that the problem would more than likely be a case of feline infectious peritonitis caused by a virus. But I dismissed that thought because dogs don't get that. My mind was searching for answers.

"If he were older it could be a heart base tumor or be congestive heart failure because of the huge amount of fluid. I can barely see his lungs." I explained.

I didn't have much time and I needed to make a decision so he could breathe. I drew off more fluid, relieving the pressure a little and making it easier for him to breathe. This bought me a little more time to think.

I have learned from my early days of practicing medicine that the diagnosis is always found in the history, so I pulled Steve and Carol aside and began to quiz them further. I needed something to get me started on the right track, but that was fruitless because they said nothing out of the ordinary had happened.

He was too young for this type of problem, so I kept thinking that something else must have happened. I started thinking about the fact that he was a male and that possibly he had tried to get to a female in heat. "Has he been out of your yard that you know of?" I asked.

Carol looked at Steve and said, "Well, now that you mention it, he did get out of the yard, but that was a least a month ago."

My mind started racing because now I at least had a possible hypothesis. "Maybe Barkley got hit by a car when he was out. If so, he might have ruptured his diaphragm and his liver and stomach might have been pushed into his chest. That would cause the symptoms we are seeing."

"But wouldn't we have seen something if that were the case?" Steve asked.

"Not necessarily, because the damage would be on the inside with no visible signs on the outside, except for his obvious breathing problem now."

To me, this hypothesis seemed reasonable and it was all I had to go on at the moment. Barkley was breathing a little easier, so I had a little time to prove or disprove my hypothesis. I took him back to x-ray and gave him just a little barium because I couldn't risk stressing him too much. Just turning him on his side, in his condition, was bad enough.

The barium would delineate his esophagus and stomach so I'd be able to see if his stomach along with his liver were pushed into his chest. When we went to take him to x-ray we had to work really fast because he was in so much trouble.

When the x-ray came out, the stomach was exactly where it was supposed to be and the liver too. So much for that hypothesis, I thought. The thought went through my mind to refer him to a specialist, but the reality was he couldn't make it that long.

I had done several chest surgeries with the open heart team in Billings, as I've explained to you earlier, but I wasn't sure about the cause in this case. I live by the old saying: "That you'd better shit or get off the pot." I knew my hypothesis was not substantiated by anything at this point, but I knew this dog wasn't going to make it if I didn't try something.

I turned to the couple, "I still think that he was hit by a car and that a piece of his liver is shoved through the diaphragm. It might be so small that the x-ray didn't detect it. But I think I'd better open him up and see what I can do."

I went on to explain that if I was right, the reason they hadn't noticed anything for a month was because if he had been hit by a car, maybe it had created a really small hole that would only allow a lobe of the liver to stick through. Then the diaphragm had started to heal over, but in doing so it had slowly constricted the piece of liver to the point that the arterial blood (higher pressure) could get in the liver, but the veinus blood (lower pressure) couldn't get out of the liver. That lobe of liver would swell and form congestion and start seeping fluid.

I realized that my hypothesis was a little far out, but it was the only way I could explain what I thought and we had to do something or watch Barkley suffocate. I looked up at Steve and Carol, "If I get in there and can't fix him, we'll have to put him to sleep."

The immediacy and complexity of the situation was clear to Steve and Carol, so they agreed to the surgery, including the need to put him to sleep if necessary. Armed with at least some hope, but knowing that my hypothesis was my best guess, I went into surgery.

Anaesthetizing him was going to be the real trick because in his condition, he could easily die in a matter of seconds. I had the tracheal tube and everything else ready and close at hand. I was holding my breath the whole time.

In those days we used Suritol (an ultra short acting barbiturate) that you would inject and then immediately intubate and hook the patient up to gas anesthesia. In this case, that was a lot easier said than done. On top of the Suritol, it would depress his breathing even more and death would be ever so close.

There was a reasonable chance that when I gave the Suritol, that he was going to turn blue and die right there.   The pressure was truly immense, but I couldn't think about that because I needed to stay focused. I just knew that I had to be fast.

Initially he did turn blue so I quickly intubated him and hooked him up to ventilation. His color slowly became pink. While Marilyn prepped his chest, I took a deep breath because step one was done. I didn't know which side to go in, but I figured the right side would be the best. I told Marilyn to prep the whole chest just in case.

We were both literally flying in all directions at once and Barkley's color was remaining okay, but not great. I knew I had to work fast and that the minute I cracked his chest and let all the fluid out that his color would improve.

I wasn't looking for too many landmarks. I just knew to go between the two ribs that parallel the diaphragm. I found what I felt to be a good location and made a quick incision into his chest. The pink tinged fluid came boiling out of the incision all over everything.

Barkley's color improved and I felt better in that I could settle down and look for the problem. As I started to probe, I couldn't find anything. Now I'm starting to sweat and anyone who knows me knows I rarely do that. But the urgency of the situation was wearing on me.

I tried to keep a cool head, but knew that if I couldn't find anything, I'd have to put Barkley to sleep. I continued and just started extending the incision longer and longer. I practically cut him in half just hoping for a break. I blinked my eyes. There it was! The lobe of liver caught just like I had imagined. I was absolutely consumed with joy realizing that my hypothesis had been a long shot….but the right one. Now I knew I could save him.

The diaphragm had healed so tightly and was so constricting that I had to open it more just to place the lobe of liver back into the abdomen where it belonged. I sutured up the diaphragm, closed the chest wall and installed a Heimlich chest drain to get the rest of the fluid and air out of his chest.

I have to stop for a minute here and give credit to my whole team because it takes all of us working together. During this tricky surgery, we all did our own jobs and depended completely on each other. If that hadn't happened, Barkley would have been dead. So when explaining to you about what took place, it wasn't just me, but all of the team who saved him.

To finish the story, Barkley healed completely and lived to a ripe old age. You can call it skill or you can call it luck, but all I know is that it was a remarkable chain of events. I truly believe that **the most important part of any diagnosis is the history**. I am so glad that I listened to Steve and Carol and that I was open to seeking answers to the cause instead of just trying to treat the symptoms. If I hadn't been in that frame of mind, Barkley wouldn't have made it.

I believe today that it is critical that a doctor questions the patient or owner until he or she can get a feel for the case. Doctors have blood work, x-rays, and ultra sound etc. but out of all these aids, the history remains the most important for a proper diagnosis.

History remains the starting point for all diagnoses.

Chapter 17

With Loving Memory of Mogie

Mogie, a special Yorkshire Terrier brought Richard into my life. The little guy had survived two different knee surgeries as well as a bout with Valley Fever. But he now felt like a million bucks and looked like it too. I wasn't surprised because Richard and Donna loved Mogie and he always had the best of care.

Then, Richard called me one day when I was in Del Mar. He was panicked. He apologized profusely for interrupting my vacation, but said he didn't know what else to do. He told me that all of a sudden, Mogie couldn't breathe so they had rushed him to the emergency animal clinic. Richard explained that it was all Mogie could do to just breathe enough to stay

alive. He and Donna just knew if I was there,
that I could save him.

    With emotion, he told me that money
would not be an issue. I think he would have
spent as much as a million dollars. I know you
don't believe this, but I'm telling you that he
would have.

    I've known people that would have hocked
their homes to have saved their four legged
friends. That's how deep love runs. Others would
have eaten corn flakes if that's what it would
have taken to save their pet. If you can't relate to
such devotion, it's probably because you haven't
been there and experienced such a bond with an
animal.

    It's the same bond you may have
experienced with your parents, your spouse, or
your best friend. If you have ever lost anyone
important to you, a part of you died too. It is a
bond that stays with you for the rest of your life.
I even doubt if that bond will be broken in the
event of your own death. Hopefully we will all
be reunited with our loved ones after death.

    Such a bond with an animal is created
because the animal has always been there for you,
especially during the hard times you've gone
through. We all have such days. It could have
been a time when you felt most alone, or a time
when you had a serious illness. It might have
been through a painful divorce or financial crisis.

We all have different experiences and I don't know what you have been through, but I do know that your friend was there with his/her kind eyes and loving tongue, offering you affection and warmth. These devoted creatures literally carry on a twenty-four hour vigil until you get through whatever is disrupting your life.

In Richard and Donna's case it was probably Mogie's companionship that they enjoyed so much. Mogie was always there making both of them happy. They had been inseparable for thirteen years. He was always with them and if they went on a trip, Mogie always had his first class seat on the commercial airlines. There was no money spared when it came to Mogie's comfort.

Richard even bragged about that all the time. He didn't care how big his veterinary bills were. He just wanted Mogie well. Mogie had it made, but it was a small price for them to pay for the love and comfort he gave back in return.

When I got that call from Richard, I could hear in his voice how serious the situation really was. I told him not to worry that I would meet him at the animal emergency clinic in six hours.

Karn and I packed our car quickly and headed for Scottsdale, Arizona. We arrived exactly six hours later. I was hoping and praying that it wasn't as bad as it sounded. I rushed into the intensive care ward, where Mogie was in an oxygen cage. But it was obvious that he was in a life threatening battle and wasn't going to make it.

He couldn't catch his breath and in spite of the oxygen cage, he was turning blue. He had a characteristic hump to his breathing, coupled with the speed that it came on, I knew what had happened. He had ruptured one of his cordae tendonae and there was no saving him.

A cordae tendonae is a cord that holds your heart valve in place. There are several of them. When one ruptures, it's like cutting the string to a kite. All the kite can do is fall to the ground. The heart valve can no longer do its job. It can't open or close. It just flutters. There was no saving Mogie and I knew it.

The real problem was to make Donna and Richard understand the gravity of the situation. This was going to be difficult. It was hard to know where to start because I knew Richard and Donna's lives were now whirling out of control.

They had the means to fly Mogie anywhere in the world if that would save him. Possibly someone could change his heart valve with a pig heart valve. There was such a surgery, if you could find it. I knew it was being done in California, but there was only one problem with that idea: Mogie didn't have that long to live no matter what we did.

I knew Richard would do anything or give up anything that he had if it would save Mogie so he could look into his precious eyes and feel the softness of his tongue, or cuddle up next to him at night. Richard had spent all of his days at work with Mogie. We used to laugh and talk about Mogie probably thinking he was running the business.

But, all of our thoughts didn't change the fact that there was nothing we could do for him. Death was inevitable and all I could do was try to make it as easy as I could for everyone. I needed to help Mogie the most because he was actually experiencing suffocation and there was little time to lose. Richard and Donna had to let go.

There are a couple of reasons people need to let go. The number one reason is that their friend is truly in pain and you know you can't save them. The second reason is if you prolong the inevitable, you also prolong the memory of that day.

Since there was no hope, I knew what I had to do. I wanted to save Richard and Donna the agony of drawing the whole thing out longer than it had to be, thus creating more sad memories. I wanted them to live with the many happy memories of Mogie.

At a point like this, I always put myself in the position of my patient and think about what I would want for myself. I looked at Mogie and he could hardly catch his breath and I knew that I would not want to die that way. I would want it to be over quickly and with that fresh in my mind, I knew what I had to do.

Richard and Donna could see how bad it was. They knew their Mogie and they knew in their hearts that he was going to die. As painful as it was and believe me, it was probably the worst and most difficult decision they've ever made as a couple. They told me to do what I felt I should.

They ultimately left the decision up to me because when you love someone that much you are never going to say, "Put him to sleep." The most I could look for was for them to nod their heads or give me a look from their eyes and they did.

Mogie passed away within seconds. It was totally painless because at that point Mogie wasn't really conscious. He had essentially passed on before the shot. All I had accomplished was to stop his body, but his brain had already gone, due to lack of oxygen.

Richard and Donna were totally devastated. I worried about them while driving home. I knew they weren't even looking forward to going home because there were so many memories of Mogie all around their house. They just didn't want to be there anymore. They became like zombies and life had lost its meaning. Donna told Richard that she just couldn't stay in the house and that she wanted them to move.

I'm telling you that unless you've experienced this kind of pain, you don't understand what they were going through. I knew it because I've felt it and I also go through it with other patients on a weekly basis.

It's not putting these wonderful pets to sleep that bothers me, for I consider that a privilege because I truly stop their pain and misery. It's watching the owners that suck the life out of me. A person should only have to witness that every now and then. But it's a part of life as a veterinarian.

When you love people like Richard and Donna as I do, I choose to go through it to help them. I don't actually want to, but I do. I've often said that if stress kills, I'm dead. It doesn't matter what the situation is: fixing a broken leg, or other problems all the way up to euthanasia, everybody needs reassurance. Is he going to live? Is he going to be all right? Is he in pain? Will his itch stop? Will his cough stop? How fast? On what day? It goes on and on.

If I didn't like my job so much, I would just quit. With my present liver condition, I probably should quit, but I can't. I'm hoping my reward comes on the other side. Here I am whining when I've got the best job in the whole world. Do you know how many people wish me well and pray for me? If prayers work, I'll never die and I'll never quit practicing because that's what people are praying for.

Do you know how all those well wishers bolster my immune system and give me a high? I should be superman and there are days that I am.

If your kids want to be veterinarians, encourage them. There really is no better job. I've been able to live my dream and do what I've always wanted to do: help people and work with animals. I've always loved the line that Jack Nickolson used in a movie. He said, "I save lives."

After putting Mogie to sleep, I knew that Donna and Richard would worry about how Mogie was handled after death. I knew they would want his ashes and would worry if the ashes they would receive would really be his.

There was only one way to solve this problem and that was for Richard to be at the cremation. So I took Mogie to the clinic and arranged for Richard and I to witness Mogie's cremation. It was a very solemn day as I took off work and we left the clinic for the crematory. It was actually a human mortuary, but they had a building just for pets too.

It was refreshing to see how well they treated Mogie. The people who did the cremation were very considerate and helped Richard get through it as best he could. Richard watched Mogie being put into the crematory and he actually pushed the button to start it.

We then walked outside, but the door was open so we could see the crematory the whole time. We talked and shared some of our life experiences. It was a time when we grew very close to one another. These were precious moments that I will never forget. I am sure they have bonded Richard and I together for the rest of our days.

The cremation took a good hour and at this point we were waved inside where we observed the ashes being removed. Every last, little, precious ash was reverently placed in the urn. Richard couldn't thank the person who had done the cremation enough.

One thing I know for sure is if you've ever done anything for Mogie you are Richard's friend for life. You may wonder why anyone would care this much or go through this much for an animal. All I can say is if you have to ask that question, you haven't been there but hopefully some day you'll experience that kind of love.

Richard and Donna had unconditional love for Mogie and they understand. I'm sure, in the end that one-half of Mogie will rest with each of them when they die. All I can say is God bless them for loving Mogie that much. We would all be better off if we knew how to love like that.

It was not easy for either Richard or Donna after Mogie's death. They were lost and felt hopeless. Richard couldn't work and I doubt if Donna was sleeping very much. I could see and feel their anguish. They even wanted to sell their house and move because they had lost a little bit of their will to even live. Everybody around them could see how devastated they both were.

I knew how long it could go on. It takes years if not a lifetime to get over a loss like this. It was apparent they were going to take a long time to get better. I just knew we had to do something to ease their pain. I didn't want to risk my friendship by stepping over the line by messing around with the memories of their blessed friend.

I know there is a mourning period that people need to go through and that I needed to respect that in this case. The hard part, however, was knowing when to step in to soften the pain. But I finally got to the point that I couldn't stand to watch Richard and Donna suffering anymore. I had to do something.

So I told Carol, my receptionist, to take a check from the clinic and to find a Yorkie puppy for Richard and Donna. Little did I know that she would do such a good job. She drove at least eighty miles round trip to find the cutest little Yorkie puppy you've ever seen. He was unbelievably quiet and had phenomenal manners. Thank you Carol!

Karn and I were meeting Richard and Donna at the horse race track at 12:30. I wasn't planning on giving the puppy to them at that time. It was hard to know when we should present the puppy because I knew that it might not go well.

We were all sitting at the table with Carol and her daughter, Freddie, just waiting for the race to start. A short time later, Freddie got up and walked away. Then she showed up with a shopping bag and plunked it in the middle of the table. All I could think was, "Oh shit! Not now!"

Even I was afraid to approach the subject, but it was too late. As I look back on it now, I'm not sure there would have been a good time. But, at any rate, we had to try and make the best of the situation.

So I looked at Donna and Richard's faces and I knew it wasn't going well. They were trying to be nice and so asked what was in the bag, but I could tell they really didn't want to know.

Freddie opened the bag and out came the most beautiful Yorky puppy any of us had ever seen. Donna screamed in terror and Richard pulled back as if to say keep that thing away from me.

I started apologizing profusely about the bluntness of the whole thing and that I hadn't planned it to happen in such a way. Richard's face was red and tight and I knew I'd screwed up. I really didn't know what to do. It was obvious that the day was shot and that they weren't ready to think about another pet.

I have always tried to tell people in such cases that they were not replacing their pet, but just adding another wonderful memory to their lives and that each and every pet brings its own joy and love.

At any rate we were for sure screwed! Things hadn't gone anything like I'd hoped. After about ten minutes, Richard decided that he would like to see the puppy. He held it and petted it almost like it was Mogie. Donna watched her husband and then decided that she might like to hold him as well. As she tenderly touched the pup, I could see her loosening up just a little.

He was such a good puppy and never made a sound the whole day. Dogs are not allowed at the race park, but in this case it didn't matter because he was so cute that no one was going to say anything, including the waitress or the people around us. He helped by being so quiet.

By the end of the day, Richard and Donna decided that they would try him for one day. I already knew that's all it would take for them to fall in love again. They felt it was a slow process and even threatened to get rid of him for days, but it never happened.

They ended up naming him "Doc" after me and I know they love him dearly. It did get them out of their grieving process but don't worry, they'll never forget Mogie and neither will I. I don't think they should have named the new puppy "Doc". I think he should have been named, "Lucky". How lucky can you be to live with Richard and Donna? It doesn't get any better than that.

God bless you Richard.

God bless you Donna.

May Mogie's memory never die.

May Doc keep you happy and healthy because you deserve all the love your four legged friend can offer and we know he will.

You're loved by all of us for a reason, because you deserve it!

We could learn a lot about love from our four legged friends.

Chapter 18

Lessons from the heart

"The secret of the care of the patient is in caring for the patient."

Dr. Francis Weld Peabody of Harvard Medical School in 1923.

I found this quote and it reminded me of the attributes and attitudes of my grandfather and my father. Sadly, this way of thinking and practicing medicine is not as common in the medical community today.

On a personal note, of all the doctors I've seen since my liver illness reared its ugly head, there has been only one that I felt truly practiced this philosophy: Dr. Edwyn Harrison at the Mayo Clinic. I am totally convinced that the way he worked with me and showed that he truly cared about me was as important as any of the procedures he performed.

When someone is facing a life threatening disease, they are emotionally distraught and scared about what is happening. Before a doctor can begin any treatment, s/he must convey that they really care about the patient. If there is no trust or hope for the future, the patient's attitude will negatively impact any and everything the doctor might try.

Medicine is a science and an art and there are so many doctors who have the knowledge, but don't realize that the patient needs to feel reassured and cared for. It seems they don't know how to make it all work, or at its worst, they don't care enough to take the time.

It doesn't surprise me because only students with a high grade point average are accepted into medical school. That is a measure of their brain capabilities but not the size of their heart, and both pieces are needed for a doctor to be successful. Dr. Harrison definitely has a heart.

Another problem lies in the fact that as more and more doctors go into specialty areas, fewer doctors know much about the whole person. After awhile, the person is not being treated; some part of him such as eyes, brain, skin, liver, pancreas etc. is being treated. The spectrum is so narrow that the doctor no longer sees the whole picture and frequently may miss the cause of the problem that he is treating.

Doctors cannot learn enough about a person or an animal in a five to fifteen minute office call to really understand them. But sadly, that is the routine today because of the time restrictions and work loads. No wonder doctors are stressed and patients are not fully treated. Dr. Harrison has always given me as much time as I felt I needed and has never failed to answer each and every question I had.

In the old days when people cared, the doctor-patient relationship was a bonding where the doctor knew the patient and all his/her idiosyncrasies. And the patient knew the doctor and trusted him. I believe this mutual caring aided in the recovery of many a patient.

Some may call attitude just a placebo effect, but all the pieces of a patient's care ultimately come together and affect the healing of the body. I believe there is even a serotonin release for both the patient and the doctor which actually bolsters the immune system. The best part is that it helps the patient heal and it also protects the doctor's health.

If a doctor has been treating a patient and has taken the time to listen and examine him, the doctor gets a feeling for what's going on. He has a very high percentage of the chance that a right diagnosis will come out of it. But if he walks in cold, not knowing the patient, and not taking the time to learn about his history, it is possible that he will take the wrong path and may never find the cause behind the symptoms.

Such errors compound and precious time is lost and ultimately it might end up costing the patient his or her life. There is a possibility that prolonged treatment for symptoms might make the actual problem worse and more difficult to treat in the future.

The first rule for doctors should be to take time to listen to the patient even if they think they know what the problem is. There's been many a time when I already had a preconceived idea of what was wrong, only to find out I was wrong.

The second rule for doctors should be to do a total exam. I have often changed my diagnosis more than once, the more information I gathered. I think a doctor must have a *feel* emotionally as well as physically to come up with the correct diagnosis.

I doubt if most people realize that a diagnosis is a doctor's best guess. It isn't necessarily right and it certainly doesn't have to be a death sentence. What people hear is: "You're going to die and there is no treatment for what you have." But remember that your doctor doesn't know all there is to know and he might be right, but he could just as easily be wrong. If your doctor barely knows you and doesn't take the time to listen and check you out as a whole person, it is possible that he *is* wrong.

Medicine is not an exact science. In order for it to work, it requires a brain to come up with a reasonable diagnosis and a heart that ministers it with loving care. Only then does the treatment have a reasonable chance to work. I salute you, Dr. Harrison.

This is not a condemnation of doctors and I think most doctors would agree with me because they would like to have the time to adequately care for their patients. It is a condemnation of our present hurry- up system that is fed by greed.

I don't blame the doctors and especially don't blame the most loving nurses. I blame the CEO's who control the guts of the operation. They have to show an ever increasing profit. So your doctor is driven and directed by the institution over him as to how he must practice his medicine. Many are paid off of his performance which dictates his salary. He not only has the stress of coming up with the right diagnosis in the shortest possible time, but he also has the stress of making sure he's done everything possible that cost you money. So, that leaves very little room for a personal relationship between doctor and patient.

We need to give doctors the latitude and time to be able once again to get to know their patients and show them how much they care. In my opinion, that will lead to a better diagnosis and more appropriate and timely treatment. All of us doctors and patients alike should not give up even if the diagnosis seems hopeless. Maybe it is hopeless, but maybe not. Just because there is no known treatment for something, doesn't mean there is no treatment. Maybe it just hasn't been found yet.

My prayer is that admissions to medical schools will find a way to come up with students that have a heart as big as their brain and that, when they graduate, they have a chance to go to work for an organization that will increase their fervor for health instead of dosing out their flame with greed.

You may not buy into my comments, but I reveal them to you because I was one of these modern day doctors. It took my getting sick to open my eyes. When my father lay dying of cancer, I remember him telling me that every doctor should have to go through a life threatening illness because only that could make him/her a better doctor. One who had empathy and would take the time to administer to all the needs of their patients.

I've also learned that I've gone through my life treating animals' symptoms and not their diseases. The way I've been practicing medicine slowly has taken away my patients' longevity. I've come up with quick decisions on how to treat patients for which I did not have a right diagnosis. Hurry-up medicine is full of errors.

I needed to reevaluate and adjust what I was telling clients and how I was treating their loving pets. The amazing side affect was that my change in attitude improved my own health as well. It may very well have been because of the serotonin release, because that has been scientifically proven to boost the immune system. My patients are so much happier and healthier than I ever thought possible.

I strongly believe the key word is *think*. I actually started to think, and I was no longer a medical robot. When I started thinking, everything changed because I began to see things differently.

Even though cancer, Parkinson's, Alzheimer's, and many undiagnosed neurological problems are on the increase, there may be a way out. We all need to think more and we need to act. A big part of this is reading. Start reading about whatever condition you or your pet has. Go to the library and the bookstore and get on the internet. Learn everyone's point of view; learn the new information that is coming out. You have the time for your own sake, your doctor simply doesn't.

If your doctor is open minded, s/he can even learn a few things from you. They need to be hearing information from people other than pharmaceutical salesmen. We need to change how the medical profession, including the veterinary clinics, does things. If we all take some initiative, we will find better answers and our health will improve because of the effort.

God has given us a gift of health and we can cherish it and nourish it or we can destroy it. It matters how you think and what you think. No one is going to be as concerned about your health or your pet's health as you. So take an active part in finding the answers. You have to be part of the team.

I need to make another point here because I have fallen into some pitfalls along the way and I want you to be aware of them. Searching for the answers to a healthy existence isn't always clean-cut and easy. Even after the success I've shared with you in my own battle, I just recently made a poor choice.

I was reading about all the toxic chemicals we get in our food, water and air and just the thought of all the harmful things around us, made me order a detox book. I was searching for answers, but I got in too big of a hurry. I began to drink fresh squeezed wheat grass juice. I started with just one ounce. I would hold it in my mouth for five minutes and then swallow it.

Then I would wait five minutes and then drink sixteen ounces of freshly juiced carrot, beet, celery, spinach and apple juice. It wasn't all that tasty, so I would chase it down with sixteen ounces of blended banana, blueberry, pineapple, and apple juice.

For the first couple of days, I thought I was better, but then my intestinal tract, especially my colon started falling apart. When I had started this new regime, I had also gone off my colitis medication. Within ten days to two weeks, it was obvious that I needed to go back on it because I was feeling weaker and suddenly even had trouble picking dogs up at the clinic. My stools had become filled with mucous and I knew the next thing to expect would be bloody stools.

I thought I was helping myself by reading and trying wheat grass, but it is another case of my not thinking things through clearly. I should have considered what I was consuming. The wheat grass is advertised as having 103 vitamins and minerals, which all came from a plant source and at first that sounded really good to me.

I also watched other people ordering two or even four ounces that they would drink in one setting. Some of them talked about wheat grass as being one of the best sources for living enzymes and especially good for vitamins A and D.

Bingo! The light bulb finally went off in my head. What was I doing? I was back to taking a lot of vitamin A and D which I knew was toxic in excessive amounts. I was back to the mega quantities, just like I'd ingested in my earlier years. I'm not saying that vitamins are bad for you, but they can be if you take excessive quantities like I had just done.

For some reason we Americans are born into excess, no matter what it is. We think if a little is good, then more must be even better. We also pay for this mindset in so many different ways. When it involves food, it involves our health. Excessive food and supplementation are not building us up, they are most certainly taking us down.

If I had taken a sip of the wheat grass and one or two ounces of the vegetable and fruit drinks, I might have been okay, but as usual, I had to have the whole enchilada and now I'm paying for it. Will I eventually get well? I have a chance, but not if I continue my cycle of taking everything to excess. I'm on a rollercoaster of feeling well and not so well. I need to find level ground where I do things in moderation.

I think that is the secret to good health. Maybe we should try to get our natural vitamins and minerals from natural sources and in normal amounts. I've found that even the excess of healthy food can be detrimental to our overall health.

At this point in my life, even though I've found the answers to a lot of my own problems and those of my patients, there are so many more solutions that need to be found. So this book doesn't even begin to address all the issues, but I hope it will get you to start your own conscious search.

I hope my own life's journey, which included lots of mistakes but also many successes, will in some way help you find your personal path to a healthier life and one for your loved ones, and your pets as well.

I will continue to look for answers for my own life and that of my patients and I challenge you to be your own master.

You are the master of your own health.

Chapter 19

The Miracle: The gift of caring

I can now say that I've been there and I've done that. For the first time in my life, I feel like I know how to approach health and illness. I've found that our health tends to mimic our state of mind. If we don't have the right thoughts, things in our lives are not going well. That's why I always say, "If you don't like the way you're feeling; you need to change the way you're thinking."

Our health often depends on our state of happiness. Have you ever noticed that the happiest people seem to be the healthiest? What is it that they know and we don't? I've spent a lot of time pondering this question.

I've observed all kinds of people with money and it's easy to tell that money isn't the answer. Many of them go through life acquiring *things* like: houses, boats, cars jewels, etc. It doesn't seem to matter how much they get. If anything, they are more frustrated because all of these things don't seem to satisfy their hunger for even more.

Time and time again, couples think that the answer to happiness is just around the corner and so they continue trying to buy joy, while barely having a good word to say to each other. Their health isn't really even part of the picture. They are so focused on material things and often fighting with each other that they don't even think about each other's well being. Welcome to rich America.

I have a good friend who just lost her spouse. She is so consumed with grief and trying to keeps the business going, that she isn't aware of what she is doing to her own health, or that her own death could be just around the corner.

It all adds up to an unbelievable amount of stress that we are willing to withstand, in order to have and to hold. Stress is going to get us if we allow it to build. It's very subtle to begin with and by the time we catch on, often it is too late. Then, we wish we had paid more attention to the more important things in our lives: health, happiness, loved ones, and our fellow human beings.

If you don't think your wife (husband) and family are as important as your business, just ask those who have lost theirs. They are totally alone and lost. They will tell you that life took on a whole different meaning to them after losing a spouse. In spite of all they have accumulated, they realize that they have nothing at all. All the houses, boats, cars, diamonds etc., can not fill that void.

During this time, often people spin out of control and start heavy drinking, smoking, or taking up other habits which are detrimental to their health. Life turns into a vicious cycle where they can't sleep, let alone eat healthy, and they are so wounded, that they no longer even think about taking care of themselves.

Life doesn't seem to have any meaning. They don't know what to do with themselves, so they just sleep or work. They seem to think they just have to keep the business going. Sometimes the work gives them something to do because they don't like to be alone, but if they continue to press too hard, their health suffers greatly. They can't focus on much so they focus on the same thing that controlled their lives up until the tragedy, and including now, which is work. If they are not working, they simply sleep to escape.

No one thinks about what will happen to the business if they die, which could become a reality sooner than they think.

How much money can one person spend? What good has acquiring more and more done in their life? They're never going to be happy because they're looking in all the wrong places.

What I've discovered through my illness is what really makes people happy. I certainly know, first hand, what makes people unhappy and that is putting their emphasis on acquiring things. We're often so involved in our own self satisfaction, that we can't see beyond the next precious item that we're going to buy to pacify ourselves.

We have become a me... me... me generation. We teach by example and that's how our children learn. Then we wonder what is wrong with them. We should know how important our role as a teacher is to them. They love and emulate us, all the while our health and theirs is suffering. They become motivated to acquiring things that can't satisfy their need for more.

I know what happiness is and it's not what you do for yourself, it's what you do for others. I bet you can't tell me a time when you did something good for someone else, that you don't still feel good about now.

We all feel great when we purchase a house or car, but as soon as the newness wears off, we start looking for something else to feel good about. That's not so when you help someone. You don't even have to know who they are and yet, you reap the benefits of helping others and you still feel good about it to this day.

No one needs to stroke your ego because your deed will do that for you the rest of your life. Interestingly enough, your health will improve because of it. As you do more and more for others, your health will improve exponentially. You will be able to feel it and taste it because it is a real phenomenon. You tell me when was the last time that you bought something for yourself that made you feel that good and remember that it's a feeling that lasts for a life time.

I remember giving a homeless person $20.00 around twenty years ago and I still feel good about it. Writing this book makes me feel good. I want to leave something behind that may help someone else and also to let my family know how much they mean to me.

As far as this book goes, I hope it is a phenomenal success. I hope I make enough money, not for me, but so that I can help tons of people. I fully plan on sharing with the people around me, especially the people and animals in need. I'd love to live my life practicing by the motto: "fill their needs." I hope I make the kind of money that will allow me to build one of the best veterinary hospitals ever built, that can offer people and their pets medical care that they can afford.

I would love to be a part of a hospital that won't turn anyone away because they don't have enough money to pay for the needed treatment. Even today, when people can't afford a procedure, I often tell them to pay what they can and sometimes that means they pay nothing at all. My only preface is that if they can afford to pay, to please do so because that way I am able to offer help to others in more dire straits.

I will continue to thank Richard, whom I've told you about already, because he makes it possible for me to do so much more. I love taking care of deserving people and pets free of charge, and the bonus is that my health improves each and every time.

I truly believe that the positive things I've done in my life, especially in the last five years, is why I haven't had to go through a liver transplant and why I feel as good as I do today.

Do you want better health? Do you want to be happier? If you do, then learn how to give of yourself. It doesn't have to be money. It could come down to a simple "good morning", or a parting "God bless you." It is so easy to give of yourself and there's so many ways which you can do it, but so few of us realize the simplicity of giving.

Money is not a means to happiness and we have all heard, "Money can't buy happiness." It may shock you, but I disagree with that to a point. Money in itself can't create happiness, but it can give you the means to make others happy which in turn will improve your health and the well being of those around you.

Doctors can improve your health, but only to a point. They can give you the means to make your health better, and your family can help too, but you are the only one that can really control the end results of your mission to get healthy.

I no longer worry about how long I am going to live, or about when I die. I don't entertain these thoughts. I know I will live as long as God intends for me to live, so I will let him worry about that. Dying doesn't scare me, because I've done nothing in my life that God would condemn me to hell for. So I'm not worried about eternal damnation.

Sure, I've made my mistakes and others might condemn me for them, but I've never felt that God was that narrow minded, and I know how forgiving He is. I've tried my best to do what is right, even to the point that it has been detrimental to my own health. A perfect example of that is when I do surgery on birds.

I often fix owls and hawks and I have to anaesthetize them, when I do, in order to work on them. The gas anesthetic is definitely harmful to my liver, but I'm not about to turn away from these marvelous creatures. After all, only God could have created something as magnificent and wondrous as birds. Yes, I am willing to sacrifice my life to help God's creatures. I consider myself the luckiest man alive to have the ability to fix them. I'm still consumed with the idea of helping them, just as I was as a young boy.

I want to tell you more about someone I mentioned earlier in the book and that is Sam Fox. She has been running a bird sanctuary for at least twenty or more years. Even though she is crippled and can hardly get around, she has dedicated her life to saving these beautiful creatures. No one that I know of works as hard as she does and I can't give her enough credit.

It is not a money making project because she puts every dime that is donated back into her work. She and her husband, Bob, are continually building cages and flight pens to rehabilitate birds. Their organization is called: **Wild at Heart.** [49] If you are looking to donate to a worthy cause, this is it.

You will be supporting an organization that puts these beautiful, wonderful birds back in the

---

[49] Sam and Bob Fox. *Wild at Heart.* 31840 N. 45th St. Cave Creek, Arizona 85331. (480-595-5047).

wild so we can all enjoy them. I'd like to thank both Sam and Bob for all they are doing to keep God's birds flying and in nature where they belong. This world would be a lesser place without them.

I am sure their health has improved because of their loving spirits and actions. How could God not love them? How much joy does it give you to see a big Horned Owl sitting on a branch looking back at you? Is there anything prettier than a Red Tailed Hawk or a Harris Hawk soaring through the air? Just as the song suggests, they put the wind beneath our wings and enable us to soar with them.

In case you haven't gotten the message yet, I'll repeat: that part of being healthy is letting go of your supercilious wants as well as some of your money. I'm sure you've heard many times that someone would give anything just to be healthy again and yet in the same breath, they would tell you about the latest model car or home. I guess they just don't get it.

We all need to reach out and touch some-one. When was the last time that you tried it? You'll remember, because we don't forget such times. I get to go to work and touch several people every day. Right now, I'm still riding high from the contacts I made today alone and I'm especially excited about the animals I was able to help.

I have been truly blessed with my wife and family as well as my work. I get to save lives and to touch those around me in very special ways. If I'm not fixing their pets, I'm listening to their problems. I've become a better listener and that enables me to make better diagnoses and to help animals as well as their owners. That in turn has helped me become a healthier individual.

Through everything, I've gone from only being able to work two hours a day, then six hours a day to where I can work all day. Before I was working every other day and now I can work six days a week and still be energized. I've gotten to where sleep doesn't seem that important anymore. It's like I'm afraid I'll miss out on something.

If I'm in town, I will always work because I won't cheat myself out of the joy it brings to me and the people around me. I continue to work at not letting the stress of work get to me. Time seems to be flying by. I used to pray for the day to be over because I felt so bad. I was weak and tired much of the time, but not anymore.

With the changes I've made in my perception of life, I feel so much better and enjoy not only my private life, but also my work. I love my job, the people who work with me, my clients, patients, and especially my wife and children. My life has been truly blessed.

As I reflect back on my illness, I could never wish it away because I owe my insight and lifestyle changes to it. So I will gladly go through it because time is all relative in the first place and if I am given only another year to experience what I have been experiencing, then so be it.

I could have lived a lifetime and not ever known what true happiness really was. Happiness is all around me, I merely have to open my eyes and recognize it. I would never trade that for the way I used to perceive life, or for all the money in the world. If I were to be offered such wealth, I'd turn it down if I had to sell my health and soul to get it.

If it were offered with no strings attached, I'd accept it because I would be like St. Francis and give it to the people and animals that need it most. I'd love to be a conduit to health and happiness. I suppose that you don't think people ever do that sort of thing. Well, they do and St. Francis of Assisi is a perfect example.

He was a spoiled little rich kid who wanted for nothing. His mom and dad had plenty and were willing to give him everything he desired. They gave him everything he wanted, but none of it made him happy. His father apparently even paid for his first love, but none of this satisfied him.

He started helping people just as I did for the Westmans. He found what I found, and it felt so good. To this day, I savor those feelings of long ago. He gave everything he owned to the needy people around him. When his father witnessed this, he became very angry and demanded him to stop or he would disown him. So he gave whatever he had left, including the clothes from his back, to his parents. His parents still wanted more, so he gave them back his inheritance and left their home naked and penniless. He found a cheap cover and wore it as a cloak for the rest of his life. I don't think he even had sandals to wear, but he commenced to do God's work.

After the change, he lived life to its fullest. There weren't enough hours in a day for him to do all that he wanted. He continually worked himself to the point of exhaustion. He spent all day helping people in need and trying to rebuild God's church. There were times when he would retreat into the mountains where he learned to love animals and they learned to love him back. He treasured those times that he spent alone with only his animal friends around him.

He is remembered for his love of animals, which is ironic, because he loved people even more. Animals were so attracted to him because of his gentle ways and they flocked to him so much that he became known as the Patron Saint of Animals.

I keep two statues of him in my home and have tried to pattern my life around him, but I'm sorry to say that I'm just not St. Francis, but I'd like to be. He loved God, people, and animals so much that he was able to embrace poverty and deny his own needs. He carried this cross to the point of perfection. Who amongst us is that dedicated? He was actually able to embrace pain and offer it up so others might not experience it.

He should have lived to a ripe old age, but he was just too hard on himself. Maybe it was because he experienced a great deal of guilt for leaving his parents the way he did, but they had left him no choice, by not accepting his life style changes. They had liked him better when he was a playboy and then rejected him when he accepted a life of poverty and dedication to helping his fellowman.

St. Francis impressed everyone that he met. They could tell that he was special and that he didn't care if they were poor people or the Pope himself. He treated everyone the same. He was not intimidated by power or money because he had already experienced those and had realized how shallow they were.

He appreciated money, but only so he could give it to others and they respected and loved him for his love and caring. He rebuilt the

Catholic Church from the ground up, with no money. He did more good in forty years than Popes have done through the millennium. To this date, he is one of the most influential figures of religion, no matter what your faith. He did it penniless and without help from the Catholic Church.

Wouldn't you love to possess that kind of resolution to love and happiness and to know that you made a difference? In the end isn't that what we are all about? That's the main reason I love my job so much, because I know I make a difference. It may only be to an owl or hawk, but I don't care, because I know I at least made a difference in their lives. My main goal is to make a difference in the lives of everyone I meet, man or animal.

I've had sixty-one good years, which is twenty more than St. Francis had and I can't hold a candle to what he did, but I can keep trying. I don't think it's important how long you live. It's only important how you live.

Some of us barely have a chance to live at all. When a baby dies, no one can understand why life has to be that way. I don't profess to know why either, except I do know that each tiny life makes a difference in someone's life. We can turn a tragedy such as this into an experience that can positively affect others, because of the love felt toward that tiny baby. That love can carry us through other difficulties. Maybe that is why this precious gift was sent in the first place.

Some only have a negative perception of the world and think of it as a cruel place. They think that there just can't be a God. They question how He could have done this. They say that it is God's fault. They blame God for everything wrong in their lives.

Others have a positive view of life and thank God for letting them feel such deep love, even for a short time. They see that love is something that will stay with them through all their days and that will open their hearts and minds. Sure there is tremendous pain in losing someone we love, but the love inside us prevails for a lifetime.

You can live your life in a positive or negative mode. The choice is yours. You can look at the down side and focus on it and watch your health go down with it, or you can look at the positive side and make sure something good comes from it.

We all need to realize that there is a choice to be made, no matter what the state of our health. Health is not stationary. We are either getting better or we are getting worse. How we deal with every moment in our lives will have an affect on our health and the health of those around us. The important point here is that we do have a choice. Most things don't just happen.

There are accidents and diseases passed down through genes that cause illness and death. Sometimes we have no control at all over these types of situations. I want to clearly state that some people are simply victims and that they have lived a good life and have tried their best.

But more often than not, we don't take steps to stay as healthy as possible. If someone dies at age fifty of a heart attack, maybe that choice was made a long time ago. It could be a reflection of how s/he thought, ate, exercised, and/or the amount of stress s/he was willing to put themselves through. They may not have made a conscious decision, but they made a decision.

My friend, who lost her husband, loved him dearly, but now she may subconsciously make a decision to let that ruin the rest of her life. She is paralyzed by his death and can't get on with her own life. The loss she feels is devastating and it possesses her every thought and action. It immobilizes her physical and spiritual being. She is consumed by it. How can she find her way out?

We all feel the need to mourn a loved one's death and it is healthy to do so. But, it then becomes a matter of how far we are willing to let it take us down. Some people can't deal with the loss and die within a short time. Others bury themselves in their daily tasks, experiencing little joy or happiness and the end result is often sickness and death.

Others find refuge in helping others and miraculously their lives are given new meaning and they find love and happiness that they had never experienced before. It is not that some love less than others, it is more about how we deal with the tragedies in our lives and how we find our way through them and eventually out into the sunlight.

In the end, when everything is said and done and you look back on your life, you suddenly realize that life is what you perceived it to be. It is exactly what you thought it to be, good or bad. **Your life is exactly what you make it.**

Guard your thoughts and be careful what you think and how you perceive life to be, because that is exactly what it will become for you. It will be as healthy or as unhealthy as you want to make it. It will be as dark or as bright as you perceive it to be. You can control your destiny, but if you feel like a victim, you will be! If you feel that you are not in control, you won't be! If you feel unhappy, you will be! If you perceive life as something ugly, it will become ugly!

You can change all of that by changing how you think. You can control your own destiny. You are writing your own story. It's your life, so what have you chosen for yourself? You can let the hard times destroy you or you can try to grow from them and visualize the world as a beautiful, caring place where people take care of each other.

We seem to become victims at some point in our lives. There are all kinds of injustices in the world as well. Many of these injustices involve illnesses. We all get our turn because nobody is immune to pain and suffering. It is just a matter of what illness and on what day it happens. That is the best reason I know to do whatever it is that you dream about today, because tomorrow you may not be physically able to complete the task.

In my case, it involved my liver. I didn't feel I deserved what I got. I wasn't a drinker and I didn't have a virus. I couldn't imagine. Why me? Does it really matter that I got a liver problem? I would have gotten something and it might have been even worse. At least, I'm not five years old and dying of leukemia or a brain tumor.

I'll take my cards as they were dealt to me. There is a reason why things happen, even though we can't explain them. Life could be so much worse and would be if I didn't watch out how I was thinking. I really have very little to complain about. I've had a good life and I'm looking forward to the rest of it, no matter how long or how short it is.

I still feel like the luckiest man alive, but this revelation never would have happened without my illness. I look for guidance from people like St. Francis, who loved people and animals, and Tony Snow, who loved his family. Their courage astounds me. I envy their fortitude and guts to face life head-on and without whining because it is so hard. I love their passion for their families and their fellowman.

I salute them for showing me how to approach life. They met their struggle with life head on with no regrets. They witnessed the goodness in the world and ignored the things that brought their spirits down. You fix the things you can fix. You try to save the ones that will allow you to help them.

Of course it's hard, but it is hard for everyone. We're not the victims, the young people are, who haven't had a chance at life. They're dying at very young ages and they have so much to live for. Yet they do not whine and they approach each day with as much strength as they can muster. They're the heroes. We should learn from them. They seem to have a positive attitude that goes unexplained and every now and then they beat the odds and so might you.

Let's take our precious money and help those who really need help. Let's experience how good it feels to give and see if we can make a difference. The young people of the world are our legacy. If we're not willing to help, what will be left besides misery and condemnation?

It will be the younger generation condemning us for our thoughtlessness in the way we treat the world and all its beautiful creatures. The sad part is we may outlive them because of our poor examples of how we handle our food and water supply.

Money is not the catch-all. You can throw money at a problem every day of your life. It doesn't necessarily fix anything. It may help, but it doesn't always fix it. Your love and understanding are more important, but then you would have to give of yourself. It is easier to just throw money at them.

As far as life's problems go, our children pick up our ways and when we grow old, they just set us aside and put us in an old folks' home. Money solved that problem. Not exactly the way we envisioned ending our lives. I was able to be there for my father and mother at every turn. I am proud of how they were able to die, in peace with a loving family around them.

We need to become involved with people and animals of every age. If we don't nurture the people around us, their spirits will whither and life becomes less meaningful for them. You've heard it over and over again: "Life is what you make it." Smarter people than I made that statement. We need to make the best of our own lives and leave the world a better place.

How long one's life is, is not important. How one spends those few short years means everything. I've always said that when I die that I want an inscription on my grave stone that reads: *He Cared.*

I don't know why I feel such love for animals and my fellow human beings, but I do. I figure the best explanation is that I was made in God's image and likeness and so were you. Obviously that makes us all very special. God gave us the animals of the world so we could witness their unconditional love. We need to hold them as an example of how to love each other.

Embrace the animals of the world and enjoy their love, and we need to give back their kindness, warmth and devotion. Give them longer and healthier lives by feeding them properly and spending time with them. We owe them at least that much for what they do for us.

If you have an illness that doesn't seem to have any answers, like mine, you learn how to embrace it. When you do this, it empowers you to the point where you can control it instead of it controlling you.

St. Francis did this better than anyone I know. He was able to embrace pain and offer it up for others. I've worked with this and it seems to mute the pain, or in my case the itching, and I'm learning to live with it. It just becomes a fact of life and I'm learning to ignore it.

I do have a neuroma in my foot that drives me crazy, but since I've worked on embracing the pain and offering it up to help someone else, the pain seems to diminish to the point that it's possible to co-exist with it.

It still goes back to controlling how you think. When I'm at work I experience no itching or pain, I just have happiness. There seems to be a way out as long as we're willing to look for it. You need to attack your illness from every angle you can possibly think of. Use your imagination.

The ball is in your court, where your health is concerned. Don't blame your doctor if you're not healthy. It is up to you to watch how you think and live, down to the smallest details. Your health depends on how you approach life.

1. You will be healthier if you live everyday as if it were your last.

2. Start thinking about what you're doing and how you approach life.

3. Work at eating healthier, because you are now responsible for any food additives that may cause cancer in you

or your family's diet, because you now know better.

4. A positive attitude is critical to your health. You do have a choice to be positive or to be negative. I like the results better when I'm positive.

5. There's no question that stress is a killer. I've often said that the number one killer was cancer and I didn't know what number two was. I've since realized that it has to be stress. I used to joke about stress being a killer and I'd say: "If it is, I'm dead." That's no longer a joke.

6. I believe in exercise, but for some reason none of us seem to find the happy medium. We either don't exercise or we're there trying to kill ourselves by over exercising, and some of us do kill ourselves.

My miracle happened when I could see myself being well, and now I realize that because of my illness, I have become the man I've always wanted to be. The kind of man my father would look up to.

Chapter 20

You are a slave to your mind

When I started out I was looking for the cause and treatment of my disease. I wanted some idea of what I might do to deal with a disease that had and still has no known treatment.

We are all aware of viruses, bacteria, chemicals etc. But, I kept pointing my finger elsewhere as to the cause for my disease. There were many possibilities such as: anesthetic gases, over supplementation of vitamins A and D, Hepatitus C, and diet (especially coffee) which could certainly have caused some of my liver problems. But I never dreamed that I was the bigger part of the problem. I didn't even consider such a thing, until nothing I tried worked. I have tried just about everything possible for the last five years because I have been fighting for my life.

I saw little improvement until I started changing the way I was thinking. There were many reasons why my liver was having problems, but the biggest problem was my minute to minute thinking.

Trying to figure out what was causing my medical problem seemed so illusive, but it was also so obvious. It took me those five years to realize that the biggest problem was my lack of mental control. It is not easy to put into words what I want to explain, but I will try.

We are all figments of our imagination. You become whoever you think you are. A rancher's son often becomes a rancher because he sees himself as a rancher. A doctor's son becomes a doctor because he sees himself as a doctor. But, a rancher's son could become a doctor if he visualized himself as one. Your mind is really that powerful and it can give you almost anything you want.

You affect your health the same way. If you can see yourself as being strong and healthy, usually you are. The important thing here is that you have to truly believe what you're thinking. The opposite can be just as true. If you see yourself as weak and sickly, you probably are.

The reason I bring this up is that I have learned how powerful the mind is and that we need to pay attention to what we are thinking. It turns out that we need to be on guard all the time of our thought process because we might be sinking our own ship. Our thought process can and does create addictions. Initially, we don't realize what we are doing and as time passes and we do realize it, it can be too late. We have already created an addiction that we may not be able to control. Of course, that is only true if you decide it is true. That goes right back to the power of your mind. You're only stuck if you decide you're stuck.

Addictions are important because they have everything to do with your health. Usually, we unknowingly create them and they progress to affect our health adversely. By the time we realize what has happened to our health, it is too late because we are addicted and we proceed to continue with our unhealthy practices. Remember where it all started (in your mind) and where it ended up (poor health) and why we can't stop (addiction).

Why is it so hard to lose weight, stop drinking or control our destructive behavior? It is simple. We are not in control of our mind. It is in control of us. One thing I am sure of is that it will take a lifetime of continued diligence to keep our minds in a state of helping our health instead of harming it. Our mind feeds off of our addictions. It is like the inner monster that has control of you and the monster is hoping that you will never figure it out.

It is not all bad because you can establish processes in your brain that promote health. All I know is that you are either digging yourself out of a hole or you are digging yourself into one. Life is not static. You are either improving or you are getting worse and that is why you had better stay on your toes.

I know about addiction because I am addicted to food. There are many things that I eat that will aggravate my medical condition. One of the worst is caffeine. I loved my "quad vente latte" and I could hardly get through a day without one. Obviously, it became a major addiction and I was not about to let it go in spite of the fact that it gave me chronic diarrhea.

I could live with the gastrointestinal problems but I was not going to live without my coffee. I would not face up to what coffee was doing to me until I was diagnosed with PSC and my life was truly at risk. My biggest problem was not the coffee; it was my addiction to it. This one realization made me see the bigger picture. The real problem was how much control did I have over my mind or more important how much control did it have over me.

It turns out that you must be on guard as to what you are thinking and more important, which direction your thoughts are taking you? Are they helping you or hurting you, or in other words are they nurturing or hindering your health?   In a sense I guess you might say that we do create our own state of health.

How you think has everything to do with what your addictions are and how much stress you are going through and how you deal with your day to day tasks. I can go through the same situations and have two different outcomes. It all depends on how I handle it. I can allow a situation to suck the life out of me resulting in hypertension and very possibly some form of a gastrointestinal problem, or I can choose not to go there resulting in no ill effects on my body. What we do not seem to understand is that there is a choice. I would rather choose to not be involved with a negative thought process so that I do not have to suffer consequences.

The bottom line is that you are either in control or you're not. It is not easy to accomplish. You have to work at it all the time. It takes time patrolling your brain to see where you're at. It takes days, weeks, months and even years of diligent observation. I can feel the effects of trying to do things in a positive light and I like what I am feeling. My body is also responding in the same manner. It is ever so slow but it is happening. I have a long way to go but believe me I can feel the difference. When I slide backwards I can actually physically feel it and I do not like what I feel so I switch directions. I have learned to listen to my body. You need to pay attention to how your body is responding to your thought process and it will pay great dividends in your responding health.

Dr. Harrison told me that I am the most successful "PSC" patient that he has ever treated. He is always asking me what I eat and my reply is always the same. It is very important what you eat, but it is even more important what you think. We need to realize how controlling and crippling our minds can be. Our mind can be so inventive and allow us to create beautiful things but it can also be totally destructive and lead us to a life of serious health problems.

It wasn't until I changed the way I was thinking that I had a noticeable improvement. Our brain controls (either directly or indirectly) the physiology of your body. This all sounds rather vague until you really start to think and even meditate on the subject.

I have worked at this for well over a year and I am noticeable better. I spent five years relying on my doctors to save me but they could not because they were not in my mind. I am the only one that can control it. I can choose to make changes that will improve my health by guarding against allowing it to run out of control. The doctors can buy me time but they can not change what I think and how I deal with my environment.

You may have liver problems, gastro-intestinal problems, diabetes, hypertension, cholesterol problems, etc. You may think your doctor has the answers, but you're wrong. She or he can only give you direction and a pill, but that cannot change your ever controlling mind.

Look at some of the biggest success stories. The successes came from the people's minds and then you look at their biggest failures. They as well came from what they thought.

Everyone understands greatness and how it happens but nobody seems to recognize failure and where it comes from. We are in control of how we handle illness and to a certain degree we are responsible for its cause and its cure. There is hope for me and there is hope for you if you are willing to recognize that we are responsible for ourselves. We need to use doctors for what they are good for. For me that is to pay attention to the current information that is out there and have an occasional ERCP which will buy me time so I can fix what I created.

They say the obvious is not always obvious, and this is a perfect example. You go to the doctor because you are having gastrointestinal problems such as gastric ulcers or ulcerative colitis, which can lead to vomiting, diarrhea, and/or severe abdominal pain. You end up taking medication to control the problem. If things get worse, you are in for a long battery of tests which are very costly and also put your life at risk due to the exposure to radiation. In most cases, you end up with a similar diagnosis and stronger medication but no one has really established what caused the problem or stopped the process that got you there in the first place.

If you are in my shoes, you have lots of time to think about it. I tried all kinds of medication and supplementation. I tried being "holistic", "organic", and "vegetarian." I had people bringing me all kinds of "wonder fruits." There wasn't a vitamin or supplement that I did not try. I can honestly say very little helped me and in most cases, I felt most of it hurt me more than helped me.

I lost 20 pounds and I felt like I was dying and in fact, I was. It wasn't until I quit relying on the medical profession and supplementation that I started to think things through. At that point I started to get better. It was ever so slow but I could tell there was improvement. I knew I was onto something and I was not going to let it slip away. I suppose you might refer to it as "mind control."

When I realized that I was never going to get a liver transplant, (because people with my condition rarely do) I started changing how I was thinking. I was relying on the medical profession to save me and I suddenly realized that if things were going to get better, it was going to be up to me to change things.

There is no question that Dr. Harrison helped me by dilating my bile ducts which has "bought me some time." However, he could not "fix me." I finally realized that if I was going to get well that it had more to do with me coming up with the right answers, however, I did not envision that the culprit was my mind.

My condition is associated with ulcerative colitis. There is an inseparable connection between your liver and your colon. I know this because when they did my liver biopsy, it turned my colon "inside out." Plus, if my liver condition is always associated with ulcerative colitis, it only makes sense that there is a link. It was easy to make the connection between my colon and my liver but it took a while to pull my mind into the scenario. I started thinking of cause and effect when I suddenly realized that maybe my brain is where it all started. THINK ABOUT IT!!!!

Many intestinal problems can be related to stress and where does stress begin? That's right! It starts with your brain and is brought on by how it perceives the world around it. It starts with a situation that your brain reacts to in an adverse way and that physiological reaction is resonated through your body in many different ways and none of them are good. Almost anything can cause your brain stress. Just watching television can cause you stress. There are many kinds of violence and your brain will internalize them with no problem at all and I truly believe that it ultimately affects your health. You know when things stress you. You can feel it. There is a certain tension in your body that is totally recognizable. If you feel enough stress the physiological reaction continues thus affecting your muscles and on into your inner organs. If it lasts long enough, it will dampen your defense mechanisms, and ultimately your health diminishes.

I believe stress is a bigger cause of gastrointestinal problems than diet. I can eat almost any food and it doesn't cause me to break down with cramps and diarrhea. I can break down with bloody diarrhea in a matter of minutes if I am exposed to a certain level of stress. I have also come to realize that it can happen easier as I get older because my ability to handle stress has lessened. I believe part of the problem is that your adrenal gland function has diminished with age. In a sense it is wearing out due to overload. This is not as farfetched as it seems if you look at our hectic life styles. My life has been my job and I have worked day and night. I have always said that if stress kills, I am dead. It was kind of a joke, but it is not a joke now.

At this point in my illness, I watch what I eat and I can have minor intestinal problems which I will control with Imodium, but if I am extra careful, I will not break down. If I allow myself to be stressed, I can't take enough medication. I have learned to "patrol" my mind to make sure that I am not feeling stress. If I do, I stop myself and literally tell myself that "I am not going there." If I am at work, I will walk out the back door into the fresh air and take in a few deep breaths. I stay there until I feel myself relaxing. I do everything I can to avoid stress or confrontation.

Since I have worked at this for weeks to months my condition has steadily improved. I gained back 15 pounds and I work out once or twice every day. Exercise has proven to be one of the best stress relievers there is and is found to supersede medication. I can work all day without doing myself in, but I have to stay on guard all the time. It is so easy to slip back and let the people around you, and life itself, grind you down. You should consider whatever condition you have and see how stress and your mind might have something to do with causing it.

A good example of an illness caused indirectly by your mind is diabetes. Your mind becomes addicted to food especially if it happens to be sweet. You have got to have it and nothing is going to stop you from eating it. As time passes you become more and more addicted. You stress your pancreas and its islet cells to the point of exhaustion and the next thing you know is you're diabetic.

Most GI problems are more directly caused by your mind. Your mind goes into a stress mode which causes your stomach to produce excessive gastric juices and the next thing you know is that you have an ulcer. Your colon goes through a similar process only it produces mucous and you end up with excessive mucous production and diarrhea. Over a period of time it progresses to ulcerative colitis. The main thing to remember here is that it all started in your mind, usually initiated by stress.

You can feel stress in many ways. It might not be from something negative. It can even be from excitement. I have a racehorse, who before, during and after a race, (even if she wins) can turn me inside out. You need to stay on an even keel. You must be on your guard all the time. It is difficult to stay on an even keel because your brain is never static. It reacts on a moments notice and if we are not on guard as to how it is reacting, we will suffer the consequences. It is not that hard to dampen a reaction as long as we recognize it.

I can show you how food gets me in trouble. My brain makes me think I am hungry all the time. I have a difficult time not eating. I eat healthy enough but I can't stop.

My wife, Karn, has said that a "normal" person consuming this much food should weigh in about three hundred pounds. I also eat before we go out to eat. I'll eat while she is getting ready to go eat. I also eat after we get done eating. It's not pretty. This total obsession about food has her gaining weight when she is around me and losing weight when we are not together. She is starting to think that the latter might be a good way for her to go…….just kidding.

It doesn't really matter what is around I will eat a banana, apple, pineapple, blueberries, anything I can get my hands on. I am so addicted that if I were a drug addict, I would be dead.

I have developed two fudge factors. When I feel stress I just tell myself that I am not going there. When I want something to eat which is almost all the time, I touch the Franciscan cross that I wear around my neck and tell myself I do not need it. It seems to work.

Develop any crutch that you can. They do help and we need all the help that we can get. We need to take back the control of our brains or we will perish. We all have our demons. They may be different problems but they all accomplish the same thing which is our ultimate destruction and they all start with our brain.

We need to be as vigilant as we can possibly be. Most of the time I need to check myself several times an hour. I can not afford the stress and I need to catch myself when I play into it. When I am at work, I might need to check every ten or fifteen minutes. It is the price I have to pay if I want to get well. I could stop working but then I would have to give up what I love doing. When you have two children in college, stopping work does not seem to be a great idea and besides if I learn how to handle it, it will help me get through the rest of my life.

You can feel stress anywhere. You do not have to be working. I think my brain produces stress on an hourly basis no matter what I am doing. I need to take back control and hopefully change my life forever.

If you want to know how your day is going, check the tension in your jaw. It is one of the parameters that I use to see where I am related to stress. I am amazed at how many times I find myself clinching my teeth. Ultimately I feel it in my whole face.

When I find myself clinching my teeth, I stop whatever I am doing and I try to relax my jaw and at the same time change my thought process. The best way to relax your jaw is to separate your teeth slightly and concentrate on relaxing the jaw muscles.

If I am tense enough, I will actually physically message my face and work at taking several deep breaths. It helps me immensely. Just the process of relaxing my face, seems to relax my intestinal tract which in turn seems to spare my liver. Every part of your body is interconnected and there is no way to separate one from the other.

I know it seems too simple and you might wonder how it could possibly work, but after you work with it awhile you will see that it does works. It is a way to check your stress level which has everything to do with your health. You need to stay on guard all the time because your stress level can change in a second. If it does, stop what you're thinking, relax and decide to deal with whatever you're doing in a different light.

Trying to be healthy is a decision and it involves a thought process that affects the total physiology of your body. It starts with a thought process that has an affect on your muscles, especially in your face, that proceeds to affect your inner organs. In the long run it can have far greater affects. The chronic stress placed on your body and its organs cause your immune system to fail and you end up with autoimmune disorders and very possibly cancer.

The important thing to remember is that it starts in your mind resulting in physiological reactions in your body which can be very detrimental to your health. It is cause and affect and it is very real. Mastering your mind is not easy and it is not just day to day. It is minute by minute and you have to stand guard continuously and realize how things around you are affecting you. If you don't like the way you're feeling you had better change the way you're thinking because your life depends on it.

Of all the things that I have tried in the last five years this is by far the most important and rewarding thing I have done. The results are obvious and I can not thank God enough for leading me to this space in my life. I work on keeping my mental state at a level mode. I do not want to be too excited and I do not want to get down. I work at not letting people or circumstances around me upset me. It brings a certain calmness to my life.

There is nobody that can help you stay calm like God can. Just a moment of prayer or just a thought of him can calm you right down. I often resort to prayer as a calming influence in my life and it works every time. We all experience God in different ways. You have your God and I have mine. All I know is that his presence has a very calming influence and it can only help us in our quest to be healthy. I just saw a license plate that said "God loves you" and just that thought made my day.

The bottom line is that you have to crawl before you can walk and you have to walk before you can run. I am at the point of starting to walk and I am making progress and I hope to run before it is all over. I am enjoying myself more than ever and I am glad I have made the journey. It has totally enriched my life and I would not have wanted to pass it by. I do not want to go back if I would have to give up what I have learned.

These last few pages may not mean anything to you but they mean everything to me because it is the most important realization that I have had. I know they will extend my life and I honestly believe for quite some time. If I have ever had a divine intervention this is it. I do not want to take the credit for these insightful words. I give it all to God, whoever He or She may be. I am just glad to have a Divinity in my life and I hope you are as lucky. This is in hope that God will bless all of us and yes He or She does love you.

I find my worth in my earthly father and mother who guided me to adulthood and in my Heavenly Father who will give me everlasting life and happiness with the people and animals that I have grown to love.

Remember where it all started (in your mind) and where it ended up (poor health) and why we can't stop (addiction).

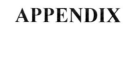

APPENDIX

A better way to feed your dog

When people think about changing their pets' diet, they seem to hyperventilate. It is just too much for them to deal with, so I tell them not to go there. It is not that difficult.

The problem is we came along and changed things dramatically from what dogs were used to eating. It did not seem like we had done anything wrong until enough time had passed; we could then see that something was really wrong.

There are too many bizarre illnesses including, but not limited to autoimmune diseases and cancer. There has been such a dramatic increase in these diseases; the only reasonable explanation is that diet has to be the problem. I believe that because I have seen the changes in pets that have occurred since I have changed the way I feed them. I have come to the conclusion: if you eat healthy that you need to feed your pet what you eat because anything is better than what is being offered pet foods. I will have to say that your diet is not necessarily the best because a lot depends on whether you eat like a vegetarian, an omnivore, or a carnivore. Your pet needs to eat like a carnivore.

All you need to do is feed like you always have and start adding in small amounts of the new diet, even if it is just a teaspoonful. The only criterion is that what you are adding has to come out of a refrigerator. It can be your refrigerator or the pet store's refrigerator, but it can't come from the shelf.

Absolutely no dry foods after you have weaned your pet off of them. It may take a week or two, but afterwards, the old routine dog food and treats should be history.

I have no problem with raw or cooked, but I do not want you to feed sterilized meat of any kind. If you honestly think your pet can be healthy eating spam, then go for it, but I know better, and so do you. Even the treats are out unless they are human grade jerky. Milk bones are basically dry dog food that has denatured protein and rancid fat. Pet jerky is not necessarily meat at all. If it was, it would have been sold as jerky for human consumption.

If possible I prefer raw over cooked because there are more viable vitamins, enzymes, co-factors and other things we can't measure in it. Just remember the more you cook food, the more you lose. Not every pet can handle raw food, especially the smaller dogs such as Yorkies.

Some cats have similar problems as well, but they both seem to handle the semi-cooked meats just fine. There are special new diets in the pet stores that these animals seem to do very well on. Deli Fresh and Pet Fresh are just two examples of such diets.

I get a very high gastrointestinal tract approval rate for the animals on these types of diets. It is so close to one hundred percent that it is not worth mentioning any of the problems because they are minor. The results have been more than spectacular. The diets seem to clear up most chronic vomiting, diarrhea, skin and weight problems. I'm not sure that you can mention a medical condition that they don't help. A change in diet has become the main treatment for most of the animals that come through my front door, sick or otherwise.

My yearly physicals involve a major discussion about diet. Not even in my wildest dreams can I see feeding dry food as a healthy practice for your pets. Canned food is only one step up from there.

Good raw and cooked diets are available and easy to come by. They might be a little more expensive, but that expense does not compare to what you will save in veterinary bills. You need to remember that most conditions your pet might get are preventable through diet. I think you would have to go a long way to find one that isn't directly or indirectly caused by food. Just remember that you are what you eat. If you eat garbage, you become garbage and the same is true for your pet.

Do not be sucked in by advertisements that tell you about all the wonderful ingredients contained in their vitamins and mineral supplements. The problem is not what is in the food; the real problem is how it is processed and handled afterwards. Basically in processing, the protein and vitamins, co-factors, and vital elements are denatured, thus eliminating them.

The food is sprayed with essential fatty acids and then the lost vitamins and essential elements of life are supposedly replaced. There is only one problem: in the process of bagging and storing the food, the elements of life are lost through oxidation. So we are back to talking about lost protein, oxidized vitamins and rancid fat. It doesn't sound like something I would want my pet to eat.

Dry food is also horribly fattening and I believe that is because the protein has become more of a carbohydrate. Everyone knows that carbohydrates are fattening and if your pets have a weight problem, do not feed them your carbs. Conversely, if they are skinny, you can feed them anything out of a refrigerator.

Finally, if you're worried about vitamins and minerals, give them a vitamin once a day that is made by a reputable company. Look for capsules that are sold in sealed brown bottles. Do not buy large quantities. AVOID OXIDATION!

People are always looking for proof that this is a better way to feed. The proof is easy because all you have to do is try it for two months. There will be obvious differences: especially in weight loss, muscle structure, improved hair coat, and their attitudes. You will get all the proof you need. The people who question the diet have not tried it.

All I can tell you is that it is worth trying. I have nothing to gain in telling you this. I am not connected to any food companies. If you have spent the time reading this book, you know where my heart is. My hope is that you your pet will have a happy and healthy life. If I have something to do with that, then that will be the only reward I need. Another point I need to make is that I can only tell you the best diet for most pets. It is up to you to find the one that works for your pet. If you feed a small amount of raw and your pet vomits or gets diarrhea, then raw probably isn't for them.

If you feed a particular kind of meat and it doesn't agree with their digestive system, then try something different. Chicken might not always work, but beef or some other meat might. Do not be deterred by a few set backs. Give some Pepto-Bismol and hold your pet off food for a day and then put him back on a bland diet and try again in a couple of days. In most cases, the animal advances quickly, however, especially with the smaller animals, it might take more time.

You will be continuously playing with the diet for the first few months, but then it will become obvious what your pet can handle. Does it not make sense that the fresher food is the healthier? I truly believe that with diet you can stem the tide of cancer, diabetes, and most pet related illnesses. I tell everyone that I can fix your animal's vomiting or diarrhea but I can not fix his cancer.

You may have to work at it a little but you will be rewarded in the end with a healthy happy pet that is likely to live a long happy life and ultimately die of old age. You know, like they used to.

Remember to start slowly and work up to a full diet. Usually it will be around four ounces per ten pounds of body weight, per day.

Usually the younger animals need more because they are still growing and the older ones need less because they are not as active. When feeding the young you want to emphasize protein and calcium. It is no different than feeding your children. There is no magic food for the young. They just get more of it.

Basically, if your pet looks good, just keep feeding the same amount. If he is losing too much weight, feed more and if he is gaining too much weight, feed him less. It does not take a veterinarian to tell you how to feed your pet.

If your veterinarian lived with you and could see what was happening to your pet's weight and see how they were handling the new diet, then the vet could be of some assistance. Since they are not there, they have to rely on what you tell him and observe how the pet looks. All I can tell you is that if your veterinarian is recommending dry food, good luck.

The pet food industry wants you to think that they have everything in their diet that your pets would ever need to keep them healthy. I say let us take a minute to think about it. Most people feed dry food mainly because it is convenient. That is the best thing you can say about dry food. We all know that dry food is continuously oxidizing and at some point the protein, essential fatty acids, vitamins and minerals are not worth much.

I can not say one good thing about dry food, other than convenience. A good example to explain this is that if you squeeze an orange, the vitamin C is only good for a few hours. What keeps the rest of the vitamins in dry food from oxidizing?

When you buy vitamins for human consumption, they are packaged in brown bottles to keep the sunlight out and they are often in gel cap form to protect them from oxidation. Even with all of that protection, it is questionable as to how much good vitamins do for people. If you feel you want to supplement with the best vitamins and minerals available, give your pet your vitamins.

Personally I have found vitamin supplementation more detrimental than helpful. With my condition, clients have brought me every supplement on the market. I have not had a single one help me. I actually did better without them and I also felt better.

There are certain vitamins and minerals that are actually toxic to your body. Vitamins A and D and E are good examples. Too many minerals can be just as toxic, such as iron and copper. These are only a few examples.

Everyone knows about mercury, but that is only one of many minerals that can be toxic to your liver. If you want to keep your pets healthy, feed them like they evolved eating. If that had not been a healthy way to eat, they would not be here today. They would have all died off through the evolutionary process.

The healthiest diet for a cat is probably a mouse, but most people won't feed that, so feed him the next best thing and that would be organ meat such as heart and liver. I have found that cats absolutely thrive on that. If you have a diabetic cat, feed him this diet and it is almost certain that he will become non-diabetic. Every single diabetic cat that I have tried it on became non-diabetic. I do not use supplements and so far it has not come back to bite me. I am not saying that vitamins and minerals are not necessary. What I am saying is that most natural diets are not likely to be lacking in them.

All you have to do is vary their diet enough so that your pets will get what Mother Nature wanted them to have. One of the more important supplements is calcium and they can get that from many natural foods, including raw bones.

When I was in Whole Foods the other day, I was surprised to see that they were selling raw shank bones. All I could do was smile because I was so glad to see that things are changing and diets are going to be so much better than they have been.

It seems that bones are a major concern for the veterinary profession. Many veterinarians do not recommend bones. There are dogs that have had trouble with bones. The problems usually consist of vomiting, diarrhea, constipation and possible obstruction or perforation of the gut. That is a formidable list and warrants our attention.

I used to be afraid of bones too, but no more. After seeing how healthy dogs keep their teeth by chewing on bones, I have decided to re-evaluate my standing on bones. First of all, I rarely see a serious bone problem. In thirty- eight years, I might have seen two dogs lose their lives from bones. If you factor in the number of deaths due to anesthesia while doing dental work, the number of deaths from bones is very small.

If the owners of the dogs that died from bones had just been a little more careful, they probably wouldn't have lost their pets. I do not care what you do in this world, there are risks involved. You need to consider the ups and downs of whatever you are doing and go with the least risky situation. I pull teeth pretty much everyday. It is not uncommon to do full mouth extractions, especially on the smaller dogs. I rarely have to even clean, let alone pull any teeth on the dogs that chew on bones.

The problem is that some people decide to give their dogs all bones or no bones. We need to find the happy medium. If you do, you are not likely to have any problems. First of all, I only recommend shank bones. They are heavy duty bones and are not likely to splinter. But if you see your dog breaking them up, throw them away. If you have small dogs, especially less than fifteen pounds, you might try lamb shanks so they can get some of the bone in their mouth. Bigger dogs can break a lamb shank so I recommend beef or buffalo shanks for them.

I want to reiterate that if they are breaking the bones up, throw them away. I do not recommend cooking bones because it makes them more brittle and that causes them to be more breakable.

When you first start giving your dog a bone, only let him chew on it for ten minutes because it will allow you to see if the bone marrow agrees with his digestive tract. Almost always it does not bother them at all, but for the first week or two, control his chewing time.

If you see vomiting or diarrhea, give him Pepto- Bismol and restrict his water for one day, as well as stop food for that day. It should clear up. But if the problem lasts longer than one day, I would advise you to go see your veterinarian.

Once you get to the point that the bones do not bother your dog, you should give him a bone weekly. Important points are: buy the appropriate sized bone for your dog, give one at least weekly, make sure they're not breaking them up, and be careful if you have multiple dogs because some will fight over bones.

You need to remember that your dog needs something to chew on that is as hard as a bone. Milk bones are a joke. Think of all the milk bones you have fed your dog and he has still lost his teeth anyway. A good bone chewer rarely loses any teeth. Chewing on bones accomplishes a lot of good things. It hardens the bone around teeth so they are less likely to loosen. It makes the gums healthier because it keeps the tarter off the teeth. The dogs end up with healthier heart valves and kidneys because bacteria are not accumulating (that is formed by the tarter). Therefore the bacteria are not floating around the blood stream that is filtered by the kidneys, or growing on the heart valves causing them to thicken, thus preventing them from close properly.

That is the big reason why many dogs die of congestive heart failure. The problems from giving your dogs bones do not compare with the problems that you will have because you did not give them bones.

The main thing you need to remember here is that if they do not use their teeth, they are going to lose them and there are multiple medical problems that come along with bad teeth.

One last point that I want to stress is that even if you have a veterinarian clean your pet's teeth under anesthetic once a year, they will still lose their teeth because you are doing nothing to help the bone around the teeth. God put that chewing instinct in them for a reason and we need to nurture it.

I want you to be careful but I do not want you to panic every time you give your dog a bone. In the same sense, I do not want you to get careless as times goes along. You might decide that you can give them any bone and you would probably get away with it, but I do not want them to have problems so stay conservative and just use shanks and throw them away if your dog starts breaking them up.

There are dogs that will not chew on bones, or they will only chew on them once and that's it. If they will chew on them at all, I would keep offering them one at least weekly. Basically you are going to take what you get and it is better than nothing. For the ones who won't chew, I say try everything that is out there including rawhide, Bully sticks, etc.

The following pages will help you as you change your pet to a healthier diet. I actually feel like a doctor now because I no longer control problems, I cure them. Trust Mother Nature when it comes to feeding your dog. Diet is everything.

Tips for feeding your dog:

Feed 4 ounces of refrigerator meat per every ten pounds your dog weighs (per day). You can feed that in one meal, or split that into two or even three meals if you choose. Don't complicate the diet. **These examples apply to dogs of normal weight, not obese dogs. These are also just a starting point and will need to be adjusted according to your dog's metabolism and activity level.**

Examples:

A 5 pound dog would get 2 ounces of raw meat per day.
A 10 pound dog would get 4 ounces of raw meat per day.
A 20 pound dog would get 8 ounces of raw meat per day.
A 40 pound dog would get 16 ounces of raw meat per day.
A 60 pound dog would get 24 ounces of raw meat per day.

Refrigerator meat recommended: buffalo, beef, venison, lamb, chicken, turkey.

Fish is fine, but you **must cook it,** because of a hydatid tapeworm cyst that can be present throughout its body.

Usually all tapeworms are killed, if the meat is frozen thoroughly, so I recommend freezing for a minimum of five days at -4°C, all raw meat and then thawing it before feeding it to your pet. That is why sushi for humans is always frozen prior to being served. Tapeworms are easily recognized in the stools and can be treated with one pill. Don't make them a bigger problem than what they are.

Refrigerator meat should make up 60 to 70% of the dog's total daily diet and the rest should be simple leftovers of healthy people food. If you don't have leftovers on some days, then don't worry about feeding more that day.

Besides the refrigerator meat, you must provide calcium for your dog. Feed cottage cheese and/or yogurt once a day. If you do not feed enough calcium, then you must supplement with human grade vitamins. I do not trust those sold for pets.

Treats: fruits, vegetables, beef, buffalo, or turkey jerky and your leftovers, if they are healthy. Beef or buffalo jerky is especially good for training purposes, but you want human grade.

Young animals (puppies and kittens) need to eat a little more calcium and a good source of protein. This would include: cottage cheese, egg whites, milk and yogurt. If they get diarrhea, try a milk substitute such as: goat or soy yogurt/milk.
Do you realize how ridiculous the following statement is? "Human food is not healthy for dogs and cats." I guess that would mean that what is in a can of dog food is healthier than what you eat!

Calcium is one of the more important minerals to supplement; especially on an all meat diet because meat contains a lot of phosphorus. Phosphorus will bind with calcium in the intestinal tract, therefore preventing it to be utilized by the body. They can get osteoporosis if you ignore the calcium level in the diet. When changing them to this new diet, start slowly by adding 1 teaspoon to 1 tablespoon to their current food, twice a day to avoid vomiting and/or diarrhea. Work up to the full amount over two weeks. If your dog has some problem adjusting, don't let this discourage you. The end results will be worth it. If it makes them sick, you may be introducing it too rapidly or you may need to try a different meat source. What works for one, doesn't always work for another.

Start people leftovers just as slowly, just like you introduce new food to a baby.

If cooked canned or dry food is so healthy, why don't the zoos and wild parks feed it to their carnivores? They always feed raw because they know how much healthier it is and that it is closest to their natural diet.

If you run into a little diarrhea right after changing your dog's diet, give the following:

½ teaspoon liquid Pepto-Bismol for a 1-9 pound dog.
1 teaspoon liquid Pepto-Bismol for a 10-19 pound dog.
2 teaspoons liquid Pepto-Bismol for a 20-39 pound dog.
1 Tablespoon liquid Pepto-Bismol for a greater than 40 pound dog.

(Words of caution, if diarrhea persists, check with your veterinarian because the diarrhea may be caused by something else.)
Feeding your dog this way is really simple, and if you look for meat sales in the grocery stores, it **can be even cheaper than dog food**. (I just bought London broil for $1.69 a pound.) If you are lucky enough to have a hunter in the family or know someone who is, wild game, especially deer and elk would be superior to all other raw meats, because they are not raised in a feed lot and filled with hormones. **If you think feeding dog food is easy, just try raw meat and people food and you'll see that it is no trouble at all.**

The problem with dog foods (dry and can):

1. Most use 4-D meats and slaughter house by-products.

2. The essential fatty acids that are in dog foods oxidize in a very short time which would make them somewhat dangerous (carcinogenic). Fatty acids are very important to your immune system. Your immune system is critical to your state of health and is what stops you from getting most cancers.

There are so many kinds of human food that you can give your dog, and only a few that might be harmful to your pet. Please stay in touch with the APCC (Animal Poison Control Center) for their updated list. The main things include: alcoholic beverages, avocado, chocolate, coffee, macadamia nuts, raisins, grapes, mushrooms, onions, and products sweetened with xylitol. However, some clients tell me that they have fed some of these, in moderation, without problems. The only toxicity problems I have actually read about involved grapes and chocolate. Personally I have not found any human food that has created any toxicity problem in animals, but I've seen a great deal of problems associated with pet foods, especially the canned foods that had melamine in them.

So far, I've found the success rate very high with very few failures. I truly believe that many of our pets' diseases are actually caused by a deficiency in their diet, especially the allergy, autoimmune complex and cancer. Fresh meat is what they need. Hyperthyroidism in cats did not exist prior to commercial pet foods. Diabetes was a rare problem in cats and it is now very common and is usually cured with an all meat diet.

If your animal(s) has a medical problem, you will see a marked improvement within two to eight weeks. What you've been doing so far hasn't worked, so now see the difference in what fresh wholesome food can do. Hypothyroidism and obesity in dogs is rampant with commercial diets and in my experience is corrected with a refrigerator diet.

I know people are worried about Salmonella and E-coli. I've never diagnosed it. I truly doubt that it is that common because dogs eat cat and dog feces like they're Hershey bars. There is a risk involved in everything we do. Feeding raw meat undoubtedly has some risks even though I haven't seen them. Feeding raw bones has a risk involving splitting a tooth. It's a problem but not compared to the problems dogs get when they don't chew them. I rarely see a sheared tooth due to raw bones. I almost never have to anesthetize and clean the teeth of a "good chewer."

The permanent cures of many medical conditions of pets when on a refrigerator diet is very surprising, but not unexpected and truly like a miracle.

A better way to feed your cat

"Dogs have owners, Cats have staff."
You don't really dictate what cats eat, they do.

A cat's diet should be almost all meat. It has actually been shown through research that cats are healthier on raw meat. Cats will dictate what they will or won't eat. Some like their meat raw, while others like it cooked just a little. Turkey is one meat most cats prefer cooked just a little, but that is still much healthier than the long cooking time used in canned foods. Most cats go nuts for raw buffalo.

As a starting point, feed 2 ounces of meat two or three times a day. It's basically 4 ounces per 10 pounds per day.

Cats also need calcium and you can provide that with milk, cottage cheese and yogurt. Since cats are finicky eaters, you may have to give them supplements to provide the calcium. The easiest way to do that is to use liquid human baby vitamin and mineral supplements. Just put a drop or two onto their meat. I do not trust vitamins made for animals.

Feed some form of calcium everyday.

Order of preference:

1. Organic raw meat (kidney, heart, and liver). It is easy to find ground: buffalo, venison, duck, lamb, turkey, or Cornish game hens. We don't recommend chicken because of it being genetically manipulated, laden with antibiotics and possibly hormones. Cooking denatures food and ruins important vitamins (B-complex) and critically important digestive enzymes.

2. However, some cats prefer their meat cooked. You can cook all the above meats. A study done at Colorado State University Medical School showed that almost all (18 out of 20) diabetic cats become non-diabetic on all meat diets.

3. Canned people food: Tuna, salmon, sardines and/or canned fish or meat. Only feed these two or three times a week because of high mercury.

4. Treats: Beef Jerky (they love it), Lox (smoked salmon), any smoked fish, canned sardines in olive oil.

5. Give raw beef or lamb bones. Unlike dogs, cats can chew on any kind of bone, except for poultry which has a tendency to splinter, so when you go to dinner, bring them home. Bones are a natural source of glucosamine, chondroitin which is very beneficial for their joints. Some people think that if you don't feed dry cat food, that their teeth will go bad, but the raw bones keep them clean, and are the best dental hygiene for them.

6. **Dry cat food – Not a Choice – Don't feed it! They are also high in cereal grains, denatured protein, lacking in essential fatty acids, and high in rancid fat.**
It is a denatured protein, high in carbohydrates (cats are carnivores and they don't utilize carbohydrates and rancid fat (associated with cancer).

Raw meat recommended: buffalo, beef, venison, lamb, turkey. (No chicken, because it has been genetically engineered, and no pork because of trichinosis).

Fish is fine, but you **must cook it,** because of a hydatid tapeworm cyst that can be present throughout their body.

Moose and elk can carry the hydatid tapeworm cyst in their lungs, so I do not recommend feeding lung, but there is no problem with the muscle meat.

All tapeworms are killed if the meat is frozen thoroughly, so I recommend freezing all raw meat and then thawing it before feeding it to your pet.   That is why sushi for humans is always frozen prior to being served.

If you've ever been to the zoo during feeding time, you've noticed the lions and tigers all eating raw meat. That's what they grew up on and they are fed this way because that keeps them the healthiest. Your cat is also healthiest on raw meat.

The biggest improvement I've seen with cats on raw meat is their weight, attitude, quality of hair coat, and their stools. Their stools don't smell or at least nothing compared to when they were on a dry/canned cat food.

Feeding your cat this way is really simple, and if you look for meat sales in the grocery stores, it **can be even cheaper than cat food.** I just bought some London broil for $1.69 a pound. If you are lucky enough to have a hunter in the family or know someone who is, wild game, especially deer and elk would be superior to all other raw meats, because they are not raised in a feed lot and filled with hormones. **It you think feeding cat food is easy, just try raw meat and you'll see that it is no trouble at all. I believe in a vitamin mineral supplement of human grade. Your better vitamin mineral supplements come from natural sources. Don't overdo them. Twice as much is not better. It's possible that three times a week with a commercial supplement might be better. It's hard to know, but I do have faith in what God has provided more than what man has provided.**

I want to emphasize that you have to feed your cats what works for them. If raw gives them diarrhea or vomiting, it means it does not work. You also are stuck with the fact that they eat what they want, not necessarily what you want. So you would not try to starve them into it because you may end up with a cat that

has a fatty liver syndrome and you have to force feed it to bring it out of it.

The bottom line is you do the best you can. Dogs are easy, but cats can be impossible!

Additional nutritional information is provided by my son, Dr. Michael Soltero, who is also my partner at Saguaro Animal Hospital. Mike is a wonderful, caring person and I can't say enough good things about him. He is especially knowledgeable when it comes to good healthy nutrition both for people and animals.

"Why Feed Your Dog as You Feed Yourself?"

By Dr. Michael Soltero

Why would you want to feed your dog as you feed yourself or what does it mean? Take for instance that the average number of dog food manufacturers is about 50, but the number of dog food labels is somewhere between 8,000 and 9,000 [1]. That said we can only picture the same food going into different colored, different named, different sized bags; but the bottom line is it's all the same food. While one company may claim their food to be different than the other the food could very possibly be identical. So if you really want to know what you're feeding your dog, you need to make it. A homemade diet is more likely to be nutritious and balanced for you individual companion as well as it is more likely to be free of by-products, chemical additives and rancidification. Rancidification is the decomposition of fats, oils and other lipids by hydrolysis or oxidation, or both. Hydrolysis will split fatty acid chains away from the glycerol backbone in glycerides. Oxidation primarily occurs with unsaturated fats by a free radical-mediated process. These chemical processes can generate highly reactive molecules in rancid foods and oils, which are responsible for producing unpleasant and noxious odors and flavors. These chemical processes may also destroy nutrients in food. Under some conditions, rancidity, and the destruction of vitamins, occurs very quickly. (2) Another clear advantage is the ability to formulate a balanced diet around a particular medical condition. So if you have an animal that will not eat a commercially formulated diet, homemade diets are good options. Making your own food for your dog can also help you avoid the possible contamination of commercial pet foods. In 2006 and 2007 Menu Foods, Inc. initiated a voluntary recall involving a large number of both dog and cat foods produced at its facilities in Emporia, Kansas, and Pennsauken, New Jersey. The products are sold by many different distributors under a number of different brand names in the United States, Canada and Mexico. Testing of the food revealed that some of the recalled pet food contained aminopterin, a product used to kill rats in some countries, but its use in the United

States is prohibited by the federal government. Further testing is required to confirm if this contaminant is responsible for causing animals consuming the recalled pet foods to become ill or die. There are also clear problems with home-cooked pet foods. One of the biggest disadvantages is that homemade diets are often not balanced nutritionally, while commercial pet foods are thoroughly tested. Through careful examination and care in what goes into your "homemade diet" this can be avoided by following the steps laid in place further in this article. It is not advised that owners make the substitutions on their own rather they should consult their veterinarian to make the proper changes for their individual companion to avoid possible imbalances. The number one mistake made with "homemade diets" is calcium deficiency which may lead to rickets or other problems. But let's not forget about the variety of freshness. Feeding a homemade diet can sometimes be cheaper than a commercial diet. I know of many kennel owners who purchase outdated frozen chicken and beef for as little as 10 cents a pound and formulate their own diets with this meat as the base. A homemade diet can also be a huge benefit in animals with food allergies or digestive disorders. (3)

Some of the more common reasons to use homemade diets:

1. They wish to use ingredients that are fresh, wild grown, organic or natural.
2. They wish to avoid additives that are present in some commercial pet foods.
3. They wish to avoid contaminants thought to be present in prepared foods.
4. They are concerned that the ingredient list is an indecipherable list of chemicals.
5. They fear an ingredient in a commercial food, such as a "by-product".
6. They wish to maintain adequate food intake in a finicky pet through exceptional palatability.
7. They desire to personally cook for their pet.
8. The pet is addicted to table foods or single grocery item.
9. They wish to feed major quantities of an ingredient not found in commercial pet foods.
10. They hope to construct a nutritional profile for dietary management of disease for which no commercial food is available.
11. They hope to restrict the allergens/causative substances during an elimination trial or for long-term feeding of animals with adverse reactions to food.
12. They wish to support a sick or terminally ill animal through home cooking and hand feeding.
13. They wish to provide food variety as a defense against malnutrition, or because of the popular idea that pets need variety.
14. They wish to lower feeding costs by using significant quantities of table food and leftovers.
15. They wish to feed a pet according to human nutritional guidelines (e.g., low fat, low cholesterol). (4)

Ingredient Selection

When thinking about making ingredient selections for your pet consider the source of the three main energy sources in food such as protein, carbohydrates and fats. Next consider the amount of trace minerals and supplementations so that you are neither deficient of, or in excess of the recommended levels. When considering protein it would be recommended that it be quality beef, buffalo, venison, chicken or fish. When considering carbohydrates, you'll want to choose an easily digestible food such as rice, pasta, potatoes or sweet potatoes. Dogs lack the enzymes to digest cellulose (the outside covering of vegetables). So it is better to put it in a juicer or food processor. This releases all the important enzymes, anti-oxidants and minerals. Also keep in mind that dogs are unable to digest the outsides of the potatoes so removal of the skin of the potato is recommended. Fat sources can include fat that is encompassed within the meat or by addition of yogurt, cottage cheese, peanut butter or cooking oils. Trace minerals and supplementation can be added via capsules, using human grade components.

Lately the big choice is raw versus cooked meat; is there a difference? First let's examine exactly what is meat? After an animal is slaughtered, blood circulation stops, and muscles exhaust their oxygen supply. Muscle can no longer use oxygen to generate ATP and turn to *anaerobic glycolysis*, a process that breaks down sugar without oxygen, to generate ATP from glycogen, a sugar stored in muscle. The breakdown of glycogen produces enough energy to contract their muscles, and also produces lactic acid. With no blood flow to carry the lactic acid away, the acid builds up in the muscle tissue. If the acid content is too high, the meat loses its water-binding ability and becomes pale and watery. If the acid is too low, the meat will be tough and dry. Lactic acid buildup also releases calcium, which causes muscle con-traction. As glycogen supplies are depleted, ATP regeneration stops, and the actin and myosis remain locked in a permanent contraction called *rigor mortis.* Freezing the carcass too soon after death keeps the proteins all bunched together, resulting in very tough meat. Aging allows enzymes in the muscle cells to break down the overlapping proteins, which makes the meat tender. (5)

Cooking makes meat safer, but if you overcook, you can destroy vitamins and enzymes necessary for digestion. Enzymes are extremely important for proper digestion. Lacking enzymes may lead to improper digestion which contributes to many illnesses especially vomiting, diarrhea, arthritis, infections and food allergies. Your immune system needs all the help it can get. Your joints need what it takes to produce cartilage and joint fluid. Improper digestion can lead to severe food allergies because the proteins are not being broken down into simple amino acids. Instead we end up with chains of amino acids that appear to be foreign proteins to our immune system and they produce antibodies against them causing allergic reactions to the food. Digestive enzymes are an especially good idea if you have food allergies. These enzymes come from fruits, vegetables, and plant enzyme supplements. All three of these can improve your digestive process and eliminate problems. Also, if you overheat fat, you actually make it dangerous. Oxidized fat is considered carcinogenic.

When meat is cooked, individual protein molecules in raw meat are wound-up in coils, which are formed and held together by bonds. When meat is heated, the bonds break and the protein molecule unwinds. Heat also shrinks the muscle fibers both in diameter and in length as water is squeezed out and the protein molecules recombine, or *coagulate*. Because the natural structure of the protein changes, this process of breaking, unwinding, and coagulating is called *denaturing.* Protein is an essential part of our (living) body and there is a difference between protein that has been cooked and protein in its raw (living) form. We should realize that our companion animals' body (which is made of some 100 trillion living cells) is composed of 15 percent protein, making protein the primary solid element in their body, and second only to water, which composes 70 percent of their body. Protein is composed of amino acids, and amino acids are made up of chains of atoms. These atoms that make up amino acids that make up protein literally become the building blocks for their body.

One of the best-known studies of raw versus cooked foods with animals was a 10-year research project conducted by Dr. Francis M. Pottenger, using 900 cats. His study was published in 1946 in the *American Journal of Orthodontics and Oral Surgery.* Dr. Pottenger fed all 900 cats the same food, with the only difference being that one group received it raw, and while the others received it cooked. (6)

The results dramatically revealed the advantages of raw foods over a cooked diet. Cats that were fed raw, living food produced healthy kittens year after year with no ill health or pre-mature deaths.

But cats fed the same food, only cooked, developed heart disease, cancer, kidney and thyroid disease, pneumonia, paralysis, loss of teeth, arthritis, birthing difficulties, diminished sexual interest, diarrhea, irritability, liver problems and osteoporosis (the same diseases common in our human cooked-food culture). The first generation of kittens from cats fed cooked food was sick and abnormal, the second generation were often born diseased or dead, and by the third generation, the mothers were sterile. [6]

Dr. Norman W. Walker, who lived to the age 118, emphasizes there is a difference between atoms that are alive and atoms that are dead. Dr. Walker says heat from cooking kills and changes the vibration of the atoms that compose amino acids that compose protein that compose our body. In a human body, Dr. Walker notes that within six minutes after death, our atoms change their vibration and are no longer in a live, organic form. So the difference between cooked and raw protein is the difference between life and death of the atoms that make up 15 percent of our body.

Dr. Walker writes: "Just as life is dynamic, magnetic, and organic, so is death static, non-magnetic, and inorganic. It takes life to beget life, and this applies to the atoms in our food. When the atoms in amino acids are live, they can function efficiently. When they are destroyed by the killing of the animal and the cooking of the food, the vital factors involving the atoms in the functions of the amino acids are lost." (7)

The concerns about eating raw meat include but are not limited to parasites such as Toxoplasmosis, Sarcocystis, Trichinella, Echinococcosis, Anisakis, Taenia, and other bradyzoites. Intestinal sarcocystosis can be prevented by thoroughly cooking or freezing meat to kill bradyzoites in the sarcocysts. Freezing at -4 and -20°C for 48 and 24 hours, respectively also rendered bradyzoites in pork noninfectious. (8) Whole carcasses of carnivores, intestines, or fecal sample possibly containing infective Echinococcus eggs can be decontaminated by deep-freezing at -70 to -80°C. Care should be taken that the effective temperature reaches all parts of the material and is maintained for at least 97 or 48 hours, respectively. The temperatures of household deep freezers are too high to inactivate eggs. Echinococcus eggs are killed within 5 minutes at -60 to -80°C and instantly at -100°C. (9) Freezing at -4°F (-20°C) for at least 5 days will kill anisakid larvae, as will blast-freezing to -31°F (-35°C).(10) Echinococcosis cysts can be killed by freezing meat at less -18C for prolonged periods.(11)

How much should you feed your dog?

There are important considerations when starting a new diet. First, how much should you feed? This can be estimated by calories in the diet based on the ideal weight of your pet. The basic formula for determining your pet's caloric needs starts with the formula for Resting Energy Requirement, 30(BWtkg) + 70. For example if your pet weighs 22 lbs, this is the same as 10 kg (achieved by dividing 22 by 2.2), so the Resting Energy Requirement for your pet would be (30 * 10 kg) + 70 or 370 kcal/day (kcal=Calories). Since we know that animals, just as people do, have different lifestyles or activity levels we must also take this into consideration by:

The Daily Energy Requirements factor listed in the following tables:

Canine Maintenance Classification	Factor for the Daily Energy Requirements
Neutered adult	1.6
Intact adult	1.8
Obese-prone	1.4
Weight Loss	1.0
Weight Gain	1.2 - 1.4
Light working canine	2
Moderate working canine	3
Heavy working canine	4 - 8

Feline Maintenance Classification	Factor for the Daily Energy Requirements
Neutered adult	1.2
Intact adult	1.4
Obese-prone	1
Weight loss	0.8
Weight gain	1.2 - 1.4

By taking the DER factor and multiplying by the RER you can obtain your pet's caloric needs on a daily basis. So using the previous example of a 10 kg dog that is a light working dog you would multiply 370 kcal/day by 2 and the total kcal/day for this dog would be 740 kcal/day. This calculation only gives us a baseline and should be monitored because just like us no one animal has the same internal metabolism to burn calories. Your pet may lose weight on this formula or gain weight on this formula because of their unique individual genetic structure. So this formula should be used as a starting point and is in no way set in stone, but it will give you a general idea of how much food your pet should be consuming on a daily basis.

You need to start the diet slowly; try one thing at a time and give it a day or two before making any additions or changes. You need to see how it agrees with their digestive system. If it creates a problem such as vomiting and diarrhea then don't use it. If you gave too much, try giving less. If it seems to agree with them, add another ingredient and repeat the process. Over a two to three week period you can have them on a full homemade diet. You can be continuously adding new things to the diet as long as you know they're healthy. If they develop vomiting or diarrhea, stop their food and restrict water for 24 hours. You can give your dog liquid Pepto-Bismol, two to three times a day. You will usually only need to use it the first day.

Your dog's weight in pounds	Amount of Liquid Pepto-Bismol
1-9	½ teaspoon
10-19	1 teaspoon
20-39	2 teaspoons
Greater than 40 pounds	1 tablespoon

Only repeat if you have more diarrhea. If severe diarrhea occurs you may add Imodium to your treatment. Use the same dosage as you do for Pepto-Bismol, and you can use both of them together so if one doesn't work, try the other. The most important thing to do is to stop food and limit water for a 24 hour period. After the 24 hour period, they can drink all the water they want and you can feed mashed potatoes or hard boiled egg whites or both. If everything is going well, you can reintroduce the regular food on the third or fourth day. (12)

Vitamin and mineral content of the diets need to be accurately calculated and signs monitored. There can be severe consequences with not only deficiencies but also excess.

To calculate the content of each ingredient, multiply the amount found in the ingredient by the amount of that specific ingredient being fed.

Required Mineral	Daily Allowance	Signs of Deficiency or Excess (15)
Calcium	0.75 g	Skeletal abnormalities nutritional secondary hyperparathyroidism
Phosphorus	0.75 g	Reduced weight gain; poor appetite
Magnesium	150 mg	Reduced weight gain; irritability
Sodium	100 mg	Increased heart rate and water intake
Potassium	1 g	Poor growth in puppies
Chlorine	150 mg	Reduced weight gain
Iron	7.5 mg	Oxidative reactions leading to tissue and gastrointestinal reactions
Copper	1.5 mg	Anemia
Zinc	15 mg	Vomiting; poor weight gain
Manganese	1.2 mg	None reported
Selenium	90 ug	Anorexia; muscular degeneration
Iodine	220 ug	Excessive tearing; salivation; nasal discharge; enlarged thyroid glands
Required Vitamin	Daily Allowance	Signs of Deficiency or Excess (15)
Vitamin K	0.41 mg	None reported
Vitamin B1	0.56 mg	Failure to grow; weight loss
Riboflavin	1.3 mg	Weight loss; muscular weakness
Vitamin B6	0.4 mg	Impairment of motor control and balance muscle weakness
Niacin	4 mg	Bloody feces; convulsions
Pantothenic Acid	4 mg	Erratic food intake; reduced antibody production; gastrointestinal symptoms
Vitamin B12	9 ug	Appetite loss; anemia
Folic Acid	68 ug	Weight loss; decreased hemoglobin
Choline	425 mg	Decreased body weight; fatty liver

Example Diet 1 and Mineral Content (16)

	allotted	W.Rice	PB	venison	suplmn	Meal Total
Calcium	0.75 g	0.211	0.0132	0.00935	0.48	0.71 g
Phosphorus	0.75 g	4.37	0.1014	0.171	0.00	4.64 g
Magnesium	150 mg	1.8	50.8	17.85	480.00	550.4 mg
Sodium	100 mg	70.5	65	63.75	0.00	199.25 mg
Potassium	1 g	4.3	0.24	0.281	0.00	4.82 g
Iron	7.5 mg	19.53	0.6	2.47	0.00	22.60 mg
Copper	1.5 mg	5.04	0.2	0.085	0.00	5.33 mg
Zinc	15 mg	59.9	0.8	3.57	0.00	64.27 mg
Manganese	1.2 mg	13.2	0	0	0.00	13.20 mg
Selenium	90 ug	28.35	2.4	8.5	0.00	39.25 ug
Vitamin K	0.41mg	0.0189	0.0002	0.00102	0.00	0.02 mg
Riboflavin	1.3 mg	2.52	0	0.255	0.00	2.78 mg
Vitamin B6	0.4 mg	3.78	0.2	0.425	0.00	4.41 mg
Niacin	4 mg	68.04	4.4	4.85	0.00	77.29 mg
Pantothenic	4 mg	10.71	0	0.595	0.00	11.31 mg
Vitamin B12	9 ug	0	0	1.62	0.00	1.62 ug
Choline	425 mg	353	20.4	74.7	0.00	448.10 mg

Example Diet 2 Mineral Content (16)

	allotted	potato	hamburger	suplmnt	Meal Total
Calcium	0.75 g	**0.156**	**0.055**	**0.48**	0.69 g
Phosphorus	0.75 g	**0.74**	**0.595**	**0**	1.34 g
Magnesium	150 mg	**299**	62.5	480	841.50 mg
Sodium	100 mg	**78**	22.3	0	301.00 mg
Potassium	1 g	**5.5**	1.02	0	6.52 g
Iron	7.5 mg	**10.4**	7.25	0	17.65 mg
Copper	1.5 mg	**1.3**	0.25	0	1.55 mg
Zinc	15 mg	**3.9**	16.5	0	20.40 mg
Manganese	1.2 mg	**2.6**	**0**	0	2.60 mg
Selenium	90 ug	**3.9**	54	0	57.90 mg
Vitamin K	0.41 mg	**0.025**	**0.0325**	**0**	0.06 mg
Riboflavin	1.3 mg	**0**	0.5	0	0.50 mg
Vitamin B6	0.4 mg	**3.9**	1	0	4.90 mg
Niacin	4 mg	**14.3**	**15.75**	0	30.05 mg
Pantothenic	4 mg	**3.9**	**2**	0	5.90 mg
Vitamin B12	9 ug	**0**	7	0	7.00 ug
Choline	425 mg	**157**	2.24	0	159.24 mg

Example Diet 3 and Mineral Content (16)

	alloted	Sw pot	Grn. bn	Raw beef	chkn	yogurt	Meal Total
Calcium	0.75 g	0.41	0.02	0.0135	0.012	0.3	0.75 g
Phosphorus	0.75 g	0.48	0.02	0.154	0.22	0.23	1.11 g
Magnesium	150 mg	241	13.75	16.2	60.8	29.40	331.15 mg
Sodium	100 mg	65.6	3.3	59.4	71.5	113.00	312.80mg
Potassium	1 g	0.39	0.115	0.266	0.28	0.38	1.43 g
Iron	7.5 mg	5.5	0.55	1.89	0.77	0.10	8.81 mg
Copper	1.5 mg	2.2	0.05	0.1	0	0.00	2.35 mg
Zinc	15 mg	3.3	0.15	4.05	0.88	1.40	9.78 mg
Manganese	1.2 mg	7.7	0.1	0	0	0.0	7.80 mg
Selenium	90 ug	6.6	0.35	14.19	19.6	5.40	46.14ug
Vitamin K	0.41mg	0	0.0079	0.001	0.0002	0.00	0.01 mg
Riboflavin	1.3	1.1	0.05	0.18	0.11	0.30	1.74mg
Vitamin B6	0.4 mg	2.2	0.05	0.27	0.55	0.10	3.17mg
Niacin	4 mg	6.6	0.4	4.15	12.3	0.20	23.65 mg
Pantotheni	4 mg	5.5	0.05	0.45	0.88	1.00	7.88 mg
Vitamin 12	9 ug	0	0	2.01	0.44	0.90	3.35 mg
Choline	425mg	0	8.4	55.4	80.7	37.20	181.70mg

How Much? The following chart displays "recommended requirements: for *normal neutered healthy dogs* according to weight.

Weight (Lbs)	Total Calories	Total Protein (gm)	Total Fat (gm)	Total Carbs (gm)
5	222.1	9.3	7.0	30.3
10	330.2	13.9	10.4	45.2
15	439.3	18.5	13.9	60.1
20	548.4	23.1	17.3	75.0
25	657.5	27.7	20.8	90.0
30	766.5	32.3	24.2	104.9
35	875.6	36.9	27.7	119.8
40	984.7	41.5	31.1	134.8
45	1093.8	46.1	34.5	149.7
50	1202.9	50.6	38.0	164.6
55	1312.0	55.2	41.4	179.5
60	1421.1	59.8	44.9	194.5
65	1530.2	64.4	48.3	209.4
70	1639.3	69.0	51.8	224.3
75	1748.4	73.6	55.2	239.2
80	1857.5	78.2	58.7	254.2
85	1966.5	82.8	62.1	269.1
90	2075.6	87.4	65.5	284.0
95	2184.7	92.0	69.0	299.0
100	2293.8	96.6	72.4	313.9

Multiply the above figures from the prior chart by the following numbers to obtain requirements more specific for your dog.

Intact adult	1.13
Obese-prone	0.87
Weight Loss	0.63
Light working canine	1.25
Moderate working canine	1.88
Heavy working canine	2.5-5

Sample Menu:

Food	Fat	Prot	Carb	Total Cals
Ground Beef 85%, raw (3.5 oz)	15	19	0	211
Ground Beef 85% browned (3.5 oz)	10	18	0	162
Chicken Skinless, raw (3.5 oz)	3	21	0	111
Chicken Skin on, raw (3.5 oz)	9	21	0	165
Chicken Skin on, stewed (3.5 oz)	5	20	0	125
Ground Venison, raw (3.5 oz)	7	22	0	151
Potato, raw (1/2 medium size)	0	2	18	80
Sweet Potato (1/2 medium size)	0	2	20	88
Green Beans (1 cup)	0	2	7	36
White Rice, cook (1 cup)	0	4	53	228
Wild Rice, cooked (1cup)	1	7	35	177

Diet Example 1 (60 pound dog)

Food	Amount	Fat	Protein	Carbs
Wild Rice	6.3 cups	0	44.1	220.5
Peanut Butter	2.2 Tblsp.	18.7	7.7	7.7
Venison	3 oz. raw	6	18.7	0
	Totals	24.7	70.5	228.2
1417.1	Calories	222	282	913

Diet Example 2 (60 pound dog)

Food	Amount	Fat	Protein	Carbs
Swt Potato	5.7 medium	0	22	220
Gr. Beans	½ cup canned	0	1	3.5
Beef	Raw, 4.55 oz	13.5	16	0
Chicken (skinless)	Raw, 4.55 oz	3.3	23.1	0
Yogurt	1 cup	8	9	11
	Totals	24.8	71.1	234/5
1445.6	Calories	223.2	284.4	938

Diet Example 3 (60 pound dog)

Food	Amount	Fat	Protein	Carbs
Potatoes	6 ½ med.	0	26	234
Gr. Beef Browned	8.75 lb.	25	45	0
	Totals	25	71	234
1445	Calories	225	284	936

What else can you do to improve the health of your companion?

Recommended Supplements:

1.   Goat Yogurt - Probiotics are very important to maintaining the healthy bacteria in their intestinal tract. It is a good source of calcium, protein, phosphorus, riboflavin and potassium. Small dogs: one tablespoon per day; medium dog-one-half cup per day; large dog- one cup per day.

2.   Garlic - Raw garlic is better than cooked. Raw garlic has anti-fungal antibiotic and anti-viral effects which are lost when you cook it. Garlic also has the properties of being anti-inflammatory, anti-cancer, lowers cholesterol, and protects the heart. Minced fresh garlic - small dog-one-fourth teaspoon; medium dog-one-half teaspoon; large dog one teaspoon. Especially appetizing to your dog with pasta, rice and potatoes [13].

3.   Olive Oil - This is one of the best anti-aging foods available. It is also one of the most beneficial fats your dog can consume. Dosages-small

dog- 1 teaspoon; medium dog-two teaspoons; large dog-one tablespoon. Especially good when mixed with pasta, garlic and salmon.

4.   Essential Fatty Acids - (MOST IMPORTANT FOOD ADDITIVES). Omega-3 and Omega-6 oils have been shown to have beneficial effects in many species including but not limited to humans, dogs, cats and birds.   Omega-3's have an anti-inflammatory effect whereas Omega-6's have a pro-inflammatory effect (13). The ratio of the two that you want for optimal health effects range from 5:1 to 10:1. As a dosage this corresponds to Omega-3 at around 440 mg/kg body weight is required to maximize plasma levels of DHA.   Bauer et al. A ration of omega-6 to omega-3 fatty acids between 5:1 and 10:1 produces the least amount of pro-inflammatory compounds and the largest amount of less inflammatory eicosanoids. High ratios of omega-6: omega-3 (such as 50:1) will produce more inflame-mation. (14) Essential fatty acids are important to every cell in your body. They   especially   enhance   your immune   system.   They   reduce   the

incidence of heart disease. They prevent hypertension. They are especially good for arthritis and skin problems. Proper Handling: Buy in a gel capsule in a dark bottle and keep refrigerated. Improperly Handling: Exposed to air, sunlight, or heat they will oxidize and can become mildly carcinogenic.

a. Flaxseed Oil
b. Fish Oil
c. Primrose Oil
d. Borage Oil

Three of the above four normally come in one gel capsule. This is a good way to get a broad range of essential fatty acids. I still recommend that you take all four, so one will be by itself. I especially like the idea of buying fresh flax seed and grinding it in a coffee grinder. Only grind enough for one week and refrigerate. Give small dogs one-half teaspoon and you can go up to a whole tablespoon for large dogs. Put it in all their main meals. It is exceptionally good as a source of flax seed oil and the fiber is extremely soothing to the intestinal tract. If your dog has a problem with loose stools, you can't find a better supplement. Dosage for gel caps: Small dogs (0-10 pounds) one gel capsule per day: medium dogs (11-25 pounds) one gel capsule twice a day; large dogs (25 pounds, or greater) two gel capsules twice a day ([12]).

References:

1. Hammond, D. FeedingDogs and Cats. Lecture Apr 10, 2008.

2. Wikipedia, The Free Encyclopedia. Rancidification. Available at: en.wikipedia.org/wiki/Rancidification. Accessed Arp 10, 2008.

3. Bodewes, J. Homemade Diets for Dogs. Veterinary Services Department, Drs, Foster 7 Smith, Inc). Available   at: www.peteducation.com/article_print.cfm?articleid=672. Accessed Apr 10, 2008.

4. Hand, M; Thatcher, C; Remillard, R; Roudebush, P. Small Animal Clinical Nutrition. Mark Morris Institute. 2000.

5. Goodsell, D.   What is meat?   Available at www.exploratorium.edu/cooking/meat/INT-what-is-meat.html. Accessed Apr 10, 2008.

6.   Schmid, R. Francis M. Pottenger, MD and "The Hazards of a Health Fetish". Available at: www.realmilk.com/schmid_healthfetish.html. Accessed April 10, 2008.

7.   Dye, M. Protein and Propaganda. Available at: www.alphaomegafood.com/protein-truth.htm. Accessed Apr 10, 2008.

8.   Fayer, R. Sarocystis spp. In Human Infections. Clin Microbiol Rev. Oct 2004; p 894-902.

9.   Eckert, J; Deplazes. Biological, Epidemiological, and Clincal Aspects of Echinococcosis a Zoonosis of Increasing Concern. Clin Microbiol Rev. Jan 2004; p 107-135.

10.   Weir, E. Public Health, Sushi, nematodes and allergies. Can Med Assoc Journ. Feb 1, 2005; 172 (3).

11.   Kemp, C. Echinococcosis (Hydatid disease). Available   at: www.3.baylor.edu/~Charles_Kemp/echinococcosis.htm. Accessed Jan 23, 2008.

12.   Soltero, R, Stoffels, C. It's Like   Miracle.   Arctic Tern Publishing, 2007.

13.   Schoen, A; Wynn, S. Complementary and Alternative Veterinary Medicine, Principles and Practice. Mosby, Inc. 1998.

14.   Vaughn, D; Reinhart, G. "Evaluation of Effects of Dietary n-6 to n-3 Fatty Acid Ratios on Leukotriene B Synthesis in Dog Skin and Neutrophils". Veterinary Dermatology 1994; 5(4): 163-173.

15.   Feuer, D. Your Dogs' Nutritional Needs, Science-Based guide for Pet Owners. National Academy of Sciences, 2006.

16.   Nutrition Data, Available at: www.nutritiondata.com. Accessed   Apr10,2008.

"My acknowledgements of life, love and family that have enabled me to write this book."

by Dr. Rick Soltero

When I hear the song that I could sing of your love forever, I think of my parents. It embodies the total sum of their lives. They loved their children above all else and I am sure that it is true of most parents. Their total day was spent trying to make sure we were taken care of and guiding us the best way they knew how.

None of us have a mapped out plan on how to raise children but my parents did their best because they had pretty good teachers in my grandmothers and grandfathers. We had the best nick names for them: On my mom's side, we called her parents Nonny and Pa. and on my dad's side, we called them Gramma Sally and Babba. They were totally respectful, dedicated, loving and very religious people. They all lived and died for their family. This is why it is easy to see how my parents turned out. I give them all the credit for any act of goodness or kindness that I have ever performed. It is because of these people that I can fix an eagle and just as important, soar like an eagle. Every ounce of greatness that I possess in my body and soul I owe to my family. I give my mom and dad the most credit. They are me and I am them. I do not ever have to miss them because I am them. I am totally consumed by their presence. I do not like to admit it because I love my mother so much but I owe my dad the most because he allowed me to be such a big part of his life.

I was able to accompany my dad to just about anywhere he went. My memories are especially full of the times he spent with his patients and his visits to the hospitals. If you ever really want to know how good a doctor is watch how the nurses react around him. My dad's words were gospel when he spoke to the nurses and it was so easy to identify their love and respect for him. They all seemed so relaxed and happy around him and it made me so proud because he was my dad. It was definitely a mutual respect. I was actually in pre-medicine in college before I realized that people even questioned a doctor's opinion. I do not remember my dad ever being wrong. I do remember when my dad was on his death bed, he talked about how he had given a boy a penicillin shot and the boy had an anaphylactic reaction and died on the way to the hospital. It was when penicillin first came out and no one knew exactly what to expect. It was the new wonder drug and the side effects were not totally clear at the time. The responsibility of his action weighed on him heavily and weighed on his soul even on the day he died. His love for his family and his patients consumed him. The difference between now and then is that it was a seven day a week job. It also took its toll because it was a twenty-four hour a day job. I hardly remember him being home at night because he was delivering a baby, taking out an appendix, fixing a broken bone, etc. He lived in a day when he had to be all doctors to everyone and I am proud to say that he was good at it and everyone knew it. He had the softest blue eyes, kindest smile, gentlest hands and a caring demeanor that was second to none and he lived and slowly died over his profession. If it had been up to me, I would have wished him a more gentle life. God knows he deserved one.

All I know is that my dad's work was not in vain and I am here to make sure of that. He could not have a son who loves him more and that was the case for his mother and father. He went to daily Mass and Communion with his mother and father. After church they would go to his parents' home and have breakfast. He would always change into a freshly laundered shirt that Gamma Sally had waiting for him. Even at the time of his death he told me that he was awakened by his deceased mother who was stroking his head. He said that she told him that it wouldn't be long now and he died a few days later. It was on a day that he felt good and there were very few drugs involved. I will never forget because my wife, Karn, and I had spent over four hours with him. He told us the most wonderful stories. He talked about things that he had never shared with us before and I felt so fortunate to be there just to listen to what he had to say. He held Karn's hand the whole time. He always thought the world of Karn. He loved Karn so much, just as I do, but that is nothing new because everyone loves Karn. Just before we left his side, he said, "Do you see them?" He implied that there were people walking everywhere. I did not know how to reply so I said nothing. He was totally awake and not drugged.   I did feel that he was implying a spiritual realm but he was also talking about obvious movement. No one expected him to die that night but within a few hours after we left he passed on. I can only assume that they were all there to take him home.   In case you do not believe in God, I suggest that you take a much closer look because I would not want to miss you in your life after death. It will be a much grander place that is not so full of trial and tribulation. I hope and pray that all your efforts are rewarded with peace and tranquility: the two things that we seem to lack the most in our lives here on earth.

The luckiest thing that has happened to me is that I got to watch my dad die with dignity. He showed me how to live and just as important he showed me how to die. I used to believe in assisted euthanasia but no longer. I spent as much time as possible with him while he was dying. I could not believe how well he handled all the pain. He always displayed that wonderful smile and that gentle touch that consumes my soul even today.

If you do not believe in life after death then you couldn't have been in the room when my father died. It was something I wish I could share with you but you would have had to experience it to understand what I mean. I only hope and wish I can do as much for my children. I know this, I am going to try and I am betting I can do it because the fruit doesn't fall far from the tree. I am my Father's child.

This is what it all comes down to. I am a piece of the family puzzle. I am talking about both my immediate family and my distant family. This includes my brothers, sisters, aunts, uncles, and cousins. We are all connected to one big beautiful family picture. It is the summation of all the puzzle pieces that creates our greatness. I truly love each and every one of them. They are who complete me. I truly feel their presence in my life. I am who I am because of them. We are the summation of all the parts. We are truly all a part of the jigsaw puzzle that completes the picture for each and every one of us. That is why I say in the end, your family is all that matters. I am so lucky to be a part of all the caring and loving that has passed through time. It is like I know what is in the heart of each and every one of the members of my family tree because it has been instilled in all of us since birth. In my family it extends all the way back to God because He is where it all started and each and everyone of us know this.

If you were going to write an acknowledgement, who would you acknowledge? For me that is easy. I would start with My Maker and progress down my family tree. My special thanks go to my immediate family because they had the most to do with molding me, but my heart and soul belong to my Fathers: both of them. The nice part is they are so much a part of me that all I have to do is stop and realize that I am one with both. Can you imagine how comforting it is to know that they are right there with me every second of the day? I really don't make a distinction between my father and my Heavenly Father. We are all so intertwined that after a while it is hard to make a distinction of one over the other. The way I look at it, eventually we will all be a part of this symphony of Love. If we work at it, we all become an extension of our

Heavenly Father and then it is no longer important to make us separate entities from God. I guess you might say we are "All for One and One for All." I just know my family is in His presence and I look forward to my chance to share in this peaceful tranquility but in the mean time I will do what I can to heal the animals of the world and comfort my fellow man. My family will always be in my foremost thoughts. I hope and pray that I have been able to continue the love and devotion that my family tree has shown the world so that it can be passed on to future generations. The world needs people who care about each other and the medical profession has always been at the head of the line when it comes to caring; I am so proud to say that my family has been a part of it.

I dedicate all I have done and will do to my family. I thank God for giving me the ability and know how to touch a body and a soul in such a way that it makes a difference to a person's or an animal's life. It is one of the greatest privileges that a man can possess.

There is something that I don't think most people understand about life. It is not so important what we have done in our lives because we have all made mistakes, some bigger than others. What we need to know is that God is full of forgiveness and all it takes is a simple request. It goes like this: "Please forgive me." You will be forgiven as long as your request is sincere, it will be granted. Focus more on the good things that you have accomplished and in case you feel lacking in this category, you will have plenty of time to change it. It is not so important what we have done, it is more important what we are about to do. I truly believe that this is what God and mankind will focus on. So make plans for grand and glorious things in your life because you are capable. I say go for the gusto and see what you can accomplish. You have the ability and you are deserving. Start creating wonderful memories for yourself and your family. As you grow older you find that memories are important and seem to sustain you in your later years. There are many times in my life that I wish I would have done it different. If I focus on that I become immobile and depressed. I have learned not to focus on the past but to try to create a productive and rewarding future. This gives me boundless energy and has done more to improve my health then anything else I have tried including exercise and diet. This seems to create an unquenchable thirst for doing more. I have only been able to sleep about two hours tonight because I can not stop thinking of what I want to say. Even now I can not seem to stop even though I realize it's time to put the period at the end of the sentence. May God Bless You All and May you all find what you are striving for now and forever. My GRAMMA SALLY was our family patriarch and a full blooded Irishwoman so I thought that it would be appropriate to finish with an Irish blessing: "May the road rise up to meet you and may the sun always be at your back." Her prayers and a life of giving to her family and the people around her were a big part of our family puzzle that helps complete our family's destiny. The important thing for people to realize is that they all have a piece of that puzzle that completes the picture. I guess what I am trying to say is that we all have a stake in this life and the life hereafter. I will continue to do what I know what to do and I hope I make a difference.

"You are only limited by your imagination"

by Rick Soltero

My faith in myself was pretty much zero. How could I possibly find my way? I know what I want to be but everyone doubts my ability but not as much as I do. I have never really excelled at anything so what makes me think I can now. I want it so bad I can taste it. If only there was a way to become a veterinarian.

My GPA for my first two years of college was a 1.3. I had pretty much hit rock bottom. I remember spending most of my time feeling sorry for myself and I cried a little too. I was so upset that the best I could do was sleep, eat and work out. I couldn't see my way clear. I didn't know what to do so I spent my summer vacation at the Westmans in Decker, Montana. I loved that family and just wanted to be with them. I felt at home with them and I just wanted to be some place that I felt safe. The country was always a place where I could excel and feel totally at home.

It was just as I thought. It was wonderful and I loved being around the horses and cattle. I remembered how much I missed calving and branding season. I remembered how I used to sit on the hay stack and dream about being a rancher. I also remembered the time I decided to be a veterinarian. That summer rekindled the fire inside of me that made me want to be around animals for the rest of my life.

By the end of the summer I knew what I had to do and nobody was going to stop me especially not myself. I had enrolled at Montana State University in Bozeman, Montana. I stayed at one of their dorms and prepared for what was ahead. I planned out my strategy and made up my mind that nothing was going to deter me. My strategy was simple. I was going to eat, sleep and study. I would not cut any classes. I would review my work daily. I would not get behind. I wouldn't party and my sole consideration was to learn.

I could not believe how well I was doing. I actually enjoyed what I was doing and I did not miss the usual partying that goes on in college. I was so prepared for my tests that when I took one I knew that I had the answers. I began to thrive. I couldn't get enough. I loved it all. I had received a D and an F in two previous chemistry classes but now I was going to get an A. I will never forget my first report card. I received a 4 point. I could not believe it. I skipped all the way to the dorm. It's hard to explain what you feel especially after having done so poorly. One of my proudest achievements was when my Histology teacher pulled me aside and told me that in his 20 years of teaching that I was the first one that had ever received a 100% on my practical exam.

I never let up. I was totally consumed by the memories of passed failures and I was never going to go there again. I fulfilled all my requirements for veterinary school and I applied to Washington State University at Pullman, Washington. That was in a day when everyone had to go through an interview in order to be accepted into veterinary school. I will never forget the day because I was interviewed by Dr. Richard Ott. He told me that he had never seen anyone go from a 1.3 to a 4.0. My mother's maiden name was Ott so I asked him if that helped. He just laughed and continued with the interview.

I heard from Washington State Veterinary School about a month later and it was official I had been accepted. Obviously I was more than delighted and I have never looked back. My life has been even more rewarding than I thought it would be. My life as a veterinarian has been more fruitful than I expected and I wouldn't change it for anything. My only regret has been that I wish I could have spent more time with my family. I remind the veterinarians who work with me to spend more time with their families so they do not have the same regret.

The main reason I wrote this was in hopes that someone might read it and realize that determination and dedication are more important than being smart. I've decided that we are all as smart as we think we are. I used to think I was stupid so therefore I acted stupid. There came a day when I realized that stupidity is a perception and if I could change my perception of being stupid to smart that things would change. It took awhile but it ever so slowly happened. My two favorite sayings are: "If you don't like the way you're feeling, change the way you're thinking" and "You are only limited by your imagination."

I can still remember my friends and the people around me telling me how I would never make it. I especially remember Father Pat, a priest friend of the family, telling me I would never be a veterinarian because I was not smart enough. I can only tell you this. I wanted it so bad I never really heard what they had to say. I truly believe that you can do anything you want to do or become the person you always wanted to be. It takes guts and determination but it is truly within your reach. So what's stopping you?

Dedicated for life!

by Dr. Rick Soltero

I found out today that the Pathologist at Mayo Hospital found precancerous cells in my bile duct scrapings from my last ERCP that was performed last week by Dr. Winn Harrison. It should have come as a surprise to me, but it did not. I have known that my wheels were coming off for the last couple of weeks.

It started with a dizzy and light headed feeling which progressed to generalized weakness. When I called Dr. Harrison, he was nice enough to get me in the next day to perform the ERCP. He has always been so nice to me and it gives such a feeling of comfort to know that I have a doctor who honestly cares about me. He comes from the same mold as my father and grandfather. They seem to be few and far between these days.

At this point, I know the real battle begins because I am confronted with chemotherapy, radiation, and a lot more tests. I am not likely going to be doing much at work and that distresses me because it has always been my saving grace. When I am involved with so many positive things, it keeps my mind off of my health problems. I do not want to focus on the negative side of life. I would like to keep repairing and mending the animals of the world because I can see how much good I am doing them and how much it helps their people companions.

I do not take this job lightly because I know how important these creatures of God mean to you. It has been such a privilege to be blessed with the direction and the ability to be a Doctor of Veterinary Medicine. My family and my job have been my saving grace in life. I give all the credit to God, my Creator, and my parents for helping me find the way. I was so fortunate to have parents that I could emulate, love and respect. They also gave me the room I needed to explore and examine the ways of the world so I could develop into a useful and self reliant member of society.

You are probably wondering why I named this book: *It's Like A Miracle.* There have been many things that have happened around me and to me that have consolidated life and the after life for me. It has been a revelation that would have never occurred if I had not gone through my illness. I am now totally satisfied with life and am looking forward to my afterlife. In the mean time, I will do everything in my power to make each and everyday something special because it is special. Everyday that you do not realize this, you lose a special part of your life. If you participate in this day to day extravaganza, your life becomes filled with laughter and love, which translates into health and happiness.

I started a little too late. I did not get my realization until I was already sick. My dad always said that I was a late bloomer and that is okay, because it is better late than never. Early or late does not really matter because it is the realization that matters. All of a sudden you feel satisfied and your worries seem to pass. Your fear of death leaves you. My life has become a comfort for me and I look forward to each and every day. I can hardly wait to confront the next day. Every person that I spend time with has become very special to me. If possible I will lift their burden and try to show them a better way. Work is no longer a drudge for me. There are times when I feel myself drifting backwards, but I will do everything I can to stop this and put myself back into a positive mode so that I will enjoy the rest of the day. I can not tell you how much I look forward to the next surgery that I get to perform. It is such a gift to have hands like my father's and to be able to use them in such a gifted way.

This is why I like the song "The Ride" so much because it is the daily ride and how you handle it that determines health and happiness. Your destination is determined by what you do right now!

I want to tell you more about two songs that I love: "The Ride" and "Just Might Make Me Believe." They are both by a group called Sugarland. I love to listen to them and it is difficult to get them out of my mind. I keep playing them over and over again. They give me a glimpse of what my life has been all about; in a sense, a shortened 'mini' version of an intriguing, but difficult journey.

The first song is "JUST MIGHT MAKE ME BELIEVE." It was written by Kristen Hall, sung by Jennifer Nettles, and starts off with these words: "I got miles of trouble spreadin' far and wide. Bills on the table gettin' higher and higher. They just keep on comin'. There ain't no end in sight. I'm just holding on tight." Boy can I relate to this song! All I could think was: "THIS IS MY LIFE."

It describes my whole working life in a nut shell. Initially I found the song rather depressing. It bubbled up thoughts of how depressing my younger life was when I was full of thoughts of how stupid I was and questions about how I was possibly going to make it through life. I never saw myself as being very successful at anything.

At some point I decided to become a veterinarian. The only positive feedback I received concerning that decision was from my father. He called me his "late bloomer" and encouraged me in everyway because he knew I could do it and he was willing to help me in anyway which included financing my education. He always had hope and faith in me which was more than I had in myself.

As I progressed through the jungle of my mind my thoughts were much more negative than positive. It was amazing to most who knew me that I succeeded in somehow becoming a veterinarian. I never gave myself credit for being that smart. I would always tell people that I made it because I wanted to be a veterinarian that bad and there was no amount of energy that I would not expend to get there. I ate, slept, and studied every minute of the day for six long years of my life.

As I proceeded through life, my thoughts turned to raising a family and taking care of my business. This was no easy task because I lived in a day when you worked seven days a week. On top of that, you had to take all the "after hours" emergencies so I worked day and night. It seems that I spent the bigger part of my free time sleeping and worrying about how I was going to pay my bills.

In hind sight I should have spent much more time with my children being a father rather than their provider. It is all a matter of priorities and mine were not where they should have been. I know I wanted to be a good father, but somehow I was blind in the way to accomplish that and work consumed me. I know it was a big mistake, but I could not find a way around it. I only hope that my children can learn from my mistakes.

As life progressed, I moved on to worrying about my children's education because I did not want them to experience the feeling of self doubt the way I had. I wanted them to have a good education and I never wanted them to doubt their abilities. More important I wanted them to want it as bad as I wanted it for them.

If all of that was not enough, along came my liver problem. It turns out that my liver threw me for a loop because I had no idea how to deal with it. It had control of me. At least with all the proceeding problems, I had some control and some idea of how to get through them.

Chronic Sclerosing Cholangitis was a whole new beast, especially since there was no cure. It is a progressive disease that you can do little or nothing about. All I knew was the roof was coming down on all of us and there was nothing I could do about it. At this point, the words from the song: "Just might make me believe" *'I'm just holding on tight',* meant a lot to me.

As the song continues, my demeanor changes and the sun begins to rise and the world seems a better place, especially when Jennifer sings, *"If you look in my eyes and tell me we'll be all right. If you promise never to leave. You just might make me believe."*

When I heard those words things changed. Instead of a sunset I could see a sunrise. Who wouldn't want to hear those words? It was a time in my life where I desperately needed to hear such words.

It brought me back to my father's death and reminded me of how I felt then. In that instance, I could feel the strength that my father bolsters up in me. It all came about as I was trying to save my father's memory after he died. My father's death was a very depressing experience and I did not want to lose any memories I had of him. I would spend time just trying to see his warm smile, his soft blue eyes, and feel the warmth of his hands. I would look at his pictures because I did not want to forget what he looked like. I would go to his grave just to try to feel his presence, but it did not work. I found it to be a cold and lonely experience.

All through this experience there was something gnawing and nagging at me. It made me very uncomfortable until I realized what it was. It turned out to be the presence of my father. The very thing I was looking for was always with me and that he had become a part of me. I would always feel his presence and be able to feel his love. Just the thought of him enables me to make the right choices. I suddenly realized he had never left me and he never will. For some reason when I heard those words, *"If you look into my eyes and tell me we'll be all right"* in an instant I could see my father's eyes and I just knew that he would be with me the rest of my life.

I just hope my family has the same realization about me. I must say I loved feeling the warmth of his hands. He had such wonderful hands that could heal any wound and give people the comfort they needed in dealing with any medical crisis; for a son, they brought "warmth" and "security."

The only part of the song that I have a problem with is where she sings, *"I used to believe in us when times got tough but lately I'm afraid that even love is not enough."* I have always believed that love is enough. It is my driving force. It is the main reason I get out of bed in the morning. I have always said that I have been lucky in love. Karn's love and the love of my children is all I care about. I basically have and will do anything for them and I hope they know that everything will be all right. I can only say that I will be there as long as they want me there. Death does not separate family and friends. It only pulls them closer together. Time does not pull loved ones apart it only pushes them closer together. My thoughts of my father are not diminished with time. They truly intensify.

As the song continues, I find that I can relate to it even more, especially when she sings, *"It's just day to day tryin' to make ends meet. What I'd give for an address out on easy street. I need a deep margarita to help me unwind. Leave my troubles behind".* Well all I can say is I think I found that address on easy street. There are no more bills, no more taxes, no more possessions, no more sickness to battle. Yes, I have moved over to God's house and my only hope is that I did my job of loving you and caring for you the way you would have liked.

Jennifer's (Sugarland) other song that means a great deal to me is called "The Ride." As I listen to this song, it makes me think that this is the way people should approach life. It seems they spend their whole life looking forward to their destination and in the process they are missing "The Ride". I know I haven't. I look forward to it. I have learned that the destination is just a fleeting moment in time. It's something you enjoy for a day, a week or maybe longer but it doesn't last. "The Ride" never stops until the day you die and even then I'm sure that it continues on the other side.

I just love this song and it just keeps going through my mind. It is basically a song about the journey of life. It flows out like water falling over a waterfall. *"It doesn't matter where we go. There's something new to see. It's not the destination that holds the thrill for me. It's the Ride, Oh it's the Ride. It takes a lot of tears to find love. The kind of love you can be proud of. I don't care where we're going and I don't care where we've been. It's not about who's right or wrong, who loses or who wins. It's the Ride. Oh' it's the Ride."*

I feel like I have had a great ride. There are things we all would have done differently and they might have affected the destination, but I like where I've been and I especially like where I'm heading so I'm going to just worry about "The Ride."

I have found the kind of love that I'm proud of. It's all about family and friends that completes me. My final destination is on the other side and I don't spend much time worrying about it either. I have faith in God and you know what I always say, "If I'm going to Hell then God help the rest of you." I have found the kind of love I'm proud of and in the end I do trust in God and what ever He has in store for me. Just know I love you all and may God be as kind with you as He is with me.